T0329627

Human Rights or Global Capitalism

PENNSYLVANIA STUDIES IN HUMAN RIGHTS

Burt B. Lockwood, Jr., Series Editor

A complete list of books in the series is available from the publisher

Human Rights or Global Capitalism

The Limits of Privatization

Manfred Nowak

PENN

UNIVERSITY OF PENNSYLVANIA PRESS

PHILADELPHIA

Published by

University of Pennsylvania Press

Philadelphia, Pennsylvania 19104-4112

www.upenn.edu/pennpress

Printed in the United States of America

on acid-free paper

10 9 8 7 6 5 4 3 2 1

Library of Congress Cataloging-in-Publication Data

ISBN 978-0-8122-4875-3

Contents

Introduction

When the Communist regimes in Eastern Europe collapsed in 1989 leading to the end of the Cold War, the time seemed ripe for a new international social order built upon pluralist democracy, the rule of law, and universal human rights. The Vienna World Conference on Human Rights in 1993 solemnly proclaimed the universality, indivisibility, and interdependence of all human rights. But this window of opportunity for creating a more equal and more secure world order remained open only for a short while. Rather than celebrating the victory of democracy over autocracy and political freedom over totalitarian rule, the West seemed only concerned about celebrating the victory of capitalism over communism. The neoliberal ideology of deregulation, privatization, and minimizing the role of the state, which had dominated politics in the United Kingdom and the United States under the conservative governments of Margaret Thatcher and Ronald Reagan during the 1980s, reinforced by the Washington Consensus of 1989 as a global policy to be promoted by the World Bank and the International Monetary Fund, was vigorously forced upon the newly emerging transitional societies in Central and Eastern Europe as well as on economically weak and politically fragile states in Africa, Asia, and Latin America. Twenty-five years later, we see the results of globalization driven by neoliberal market forces: growing inequality, poverty, and global economic, food, financial, social, and ecological crises. In addition, we witness increasing threats to our global human security resulting from transnational organized crime and terrorism, a proliferation of weapons and armed conflicts, fragile states and global climate change.

Much has been written about the pros and cons of the neoliberal economic theory and its application in times of globalization, including through privatization. But there are only a few studies that look at these phenomena from a human rights perspective. Of these, most deal with the relationship between business and human rights, corporate social responsibility of transnational corporations, obligations of the home and host states to protect human beings against abuses by non-state actors, including the corporate sector, as well as ways and means of holding transnational corporations directly accountable under international and domestic human rights law.

The present study on the relationship between privatization and human rights is not primarily concerned about the consequences of privatization and outsourcing of traditional public functions to the corporate sector, including accountability for human rights abuses committed by non-state actors. It rather looks at the permissibility of privatization under international human rights law and the limits imposed on future privatization measures by human rights standards, both in the field of economic, social, and cultural rights and in the field of civil and political rights. The analysis of a selected number of human rights addresses the question of the limits to future privatization policies deriving from the context of these specific rights.

The present study challenges a widely held belief among human rights scholars that human rights are "neutral" toward privatization. While it is true that human rights may be fulfilled in different economic systems, effective implementation of international human rights obligations requires states and the international community to develop, maintain, and progressively improve a certain level of public infrastructure in order to enable all human beings to effectively enjoy and exercise all human rights. Political rights and freedoms require states to establish the necessary democratic infrastructure in order to enable citizens to participate in political decision-making processes by means of free and fair elections, organizing political parties, and expressing their political opinions in independent media and public gatherings. Similarly, economic, social, and cultural rights demand that states create the conditions to empower people to lift themselves out of poverty through equal access to free educational facilities, affordable health care, housing, food, water, social insurance, and other services which ensure social security and an adequate standard of living. Finally, civil rights, the rule of law, and the right to an effective remedy require states to establish and maintain a system of administration of justice which provides everyone with equal access to justice and protection against violence and other threats to their personal security by professional law enforcement structures. Not all these infrastructures and services have necessarily to be provided by public state bodies. On the other hand, far-reaching privatization of these structures and services will make it very difficult, if not impossible, for states to live up to their domestic and international human rights obligations. The aim of the present study is to define, on the basis of a thorough analysis of international human rights law in light of its historical genesis, those core governmental functions which cannot be outsourced to the corporate sector because such privatization would entail a violation of the respective human rights obligations of states.

The research question underlying this book is a purely legal one, namely whether international human rights law provides limits to privatization in certain fields, such as education, health care, and social or personal security. The economic and social facts described and analyzed in Chapter 3 relating to the extent of privatization in these areas in selected countries, such as the phenomenon of privatized prisons in the United States, UK, Australia, New Zealand, Canada, Germany, and Austria; the privatization of water in Chile, UK, Bolivia, Argentina, and South Africa; or the role of U.S.- and UK-based private military and security companies in armed conflicts in Iraq, Angola, or Sierra Leone, are purely illustrative to show to the reader that my research question is not merely hypothetical. Far-reaching measures of privatization, often under the pressure of the international financial institutions, bilateral and multilateral development agencies, or the European Union, constitute an essential element of neoliberal economic policies, underlined by the Washington Consensus and structural adjustment policies. As a lawyer, I am not entering into an economic debate about the pros and cons of Keynesian economic policies versus those developed by the Chicago school of economics. I am fully aware that neoliberal economic policies in times of globalization have led to rapid economic growth, which, for instance in China, has enabled millions of human beings to lift themselves out of poverty, and which has provided millions of people in Africa, Asia, and Latin America with access to clean drinking water. I am also not arguing out of principle against privatization. In many fields (industry; banks; means of transport, including railways, airlines, airports, and roads; means of communication, including postal and telecommunication services), privatization has led to more efficiency and has had no direct positive or negative impact on the enjoyment of human rights. The book only analyzes some fields of privatization that have a direct impact on human rights, namely the rights to education, health, social security, water, personal liberty, security, dignity, and integrity. In discussing these rights, I selected a few country-specific situations and practices on the basis of relevant domestic jurisprudence, literature, and practice of international human rights monitoring bodies in order to show possible consequences of privatization on the enjoyment of these civil, political, economic, social, and cultural rights. These empirical case studies as well as the jurisprudence and literature on which they are based are highly selective and by no means claim to provide an exhaustive picture and debate on those issues. They simply serve the purpose of illustrating possible scenarios and problems in relation to the respective human rights. At the end of each chapter, I attempt to assess whether and at which stage practices of privatization may amount to a violation of the rights chosen for my analysis.

Similarly, the short survey of the history of human rights in Chapter 2 is certainly not exhaustive and puts a certain emphasis on the development of economic, social, and cultural rights and on the synthesis between the Western and Socialist concepts of human rights in the United Nations during the first decades following World War II. These three decades, called the Trente Glorieuses in France, represent a period of economic growth that was strongly influenced by the economic policies of John Maynard Keynes and led to the rise of the advanced social welfare state. In other words, the synthesis between the Western and Socialist concepts of human rights was achieved during a historical period based on the "Keynesian consensus." This leads me to the conclusion that international human rights law, as codified in the International Bill of Human Rights and many other universal and regional human rights treaties, is based on the model of the advanced social welfare state and requires all states parties to these treaties to take measures aimed at the progressive realization of the goals of the advanced social welfare state. In reality, the economic policies of neoliberalism, which have gradually replaced the Keynesian consensus since the late 1970s, led in the opposite direction, namely the progressive dismantling of the social welfare state. This explains the somewhat provocative and generalizing title of the book, *Human Rights or Global Capitalism: The Limits of Privatization*. The research question addressed in the book is, however, much narrower and deals with only one aspect of neoliberal economic policies in times of globalization, namely the trend toward privatization and its limits from a human rights perspective.

PART I

Historical Observations

History of Human Rights—A Dialectic View

Every attempt to describe the history of human rights is a fascinating journey through some of the most inspiring ideas of philosophers and their impact on political reality, usually in the course of revolutionary changes. Human rights declarations and bills of rights were drafted and promulgated by states and international organizations in reaction to experiences of injustice, discrimination, repression, violence, and barbarity, often explained in the preambles that put them into a particular historical context. Although the values underlying human rights can be found in most religions, cultures, and philosophies, the very idea of human rights as legal claims of human beings against those who have the power, on the one hand, to violate such rights, and on the other hand, to respect, protect, and fulfill such rights, only developed during the age of Enlightenment. Like any other legal rights, human rights empower rights-holders, put legal obligations on duty-bearers, and provide for certain remedies to hold the duty-bearers accountable in case of noncompliance. Human rights can be considered as the most fundamental of all legal rights in the sense that they respond to the most basic needs and aspirations of human beings, which are often described as being "inherent" and "inalienable." The answer to the question which needs and aspirations of human beings are so fundamental that they ought to be codified as human rights, of course differs among cultures, religions, and political systems around the globe. But the history of human rights originating during the age of Enlightenment in Europe and gradually having developed toward a globally recognized value system enshrined in a growing number of UN human rights treaties with universal recognition by governments and a global civil society reveals a surprisingly broad consensus on these fundamental values. Most important, the recognition of economic, social, and cultural rights by the United Nations as being equal to civil and political rights was not simply the result of political pressure by the former Communist states during the time of the Cold War. It rather reflects the deep conviction of the international community after two world wars and the Great Depression that states have a historic obligation both to respect individual freedoms and to ensure social justice by pursuing the economic model of the social welfare state. This entails certain core functions of states and thus also limits to the privatization of human rights.

Origins of the Western Concept of Civil and Political Rights

During the age of Enlightenment, struggling to liberate the individual from the divine order of the Middle Ages in Europe and the power of absolute dynasties, feudalism, and the Catholic Church, life, liberty, equality, security, property, and participation in democratic government seem to have been the most important values that inspired revolutionary changes. They were based in the rationalistic doctrine of natural law and in theories of the social contract developed by philosophers such as John Locke, Thomas Paine, Jean-Jacques Rousseau, and Samuel Pufendorf. In his *Second Treatise of Government*, published in 1690 and inspired by the revolutionary movement in Great Britain that had led to the English Bill of Rights of 1689, John Locke had asserted: "The great and chief end, therefore, of men uniting into commonwealths, and putting themselves under government, is the preservation of their property—that is, their lives, liberties and estates."[1] This statement was based on his belief that in the state of nature, all men were free, equal, and independent, but the enjoyment of these natural rights was "constantly exposed to the invasion of others, . . . very unsafe, very unsecure."[2] These ideas were directly reflected in the American Declaration of Independence of 1776:

> We hold these truths to be self-evident, that all men are created equal; that they are endowed by their Creator with certain inalienable rights; that among these are Life, Liberty and the pursuit of Happiness.—That, to secure these rights, Governments are instituted among Men, deriving their just powers from the consent of the governed,—That whenever any Form of Government becomes

destructive of these ends, it is the Right of the People to alter or to abolish it, and to institute a new Government, laying its foundation on such principles, and organizing its powers in such form, as to them shall seem most likely to effect their Safety and Happiness.

The former British colonies, which later formed the United States of America, were eager to defend their newly won independence by defining and protecting the civil and political rights of their inhabitants in the first comprehensive written Bills of Rights, most notably the Virginia Bill of Rights of 1776. A similar, though far less comprehensive Bill of Rights is contained in the first ten amendments (1791) to the U.S. Constitution.

The same ideas had inspired the French Revolution, this time not against colonial rule, but against the oppressive rule of the old regime of the Bourbons. The first six articles of the famous French Declaration of the Rights of Man and of the Citizen of 1789, which was incorporated into most French constitutions until the present, read as follows:

1. Men are born and remain free and equal in rights; social distinctions may be based only upon general usefulness.
2. The aim of every political association is the preservation of the natural and inalienable rights of man; these rights are liberty, property, security and resistance to oppression.
3. The source of all sovereignty resides essentially in the nation; no group, no individual may exercise authority not emanating expressly therefrom.
4. Liberty consists of the power to do whatever is not injurious to others; thus the enjoyment of the natural rights of every man has for its limits only those that assure other members of society the enjoyment of those same rights; such limits may be determined only by law.
5. The law has the right to forbid only actions that are injurious to society. Whatever is not forbidden by law may not be prevented, and no one may be constrained to do what it does not prescribe.
6. Law is the expression of the general will; all citizens have the right to concur personally, or through their representatives, in its formation; it must be the same for all, whether it protects or punishes.

Apart from reflecting, almost literally, the ideas of Jean-Jacques Rousseau, including his concept of the "volonté générale," published in 1762 in his

Du contrat social,[3] these six articles encompass in a very compact way all essential elements of what later used to be called the Western concept of human rights: rooted in the doctrine of natural law and the social contract; liberalism and democracy as the two philosophical ideas behind the concept of civil (liberal) rights of men and political (democratic) rights of citizens;[4] liberal freedom as the right of all human beings to do whatever is not injurious to others (Article 4) and political freedom as the right of citizens to participate in the democratic decision making of the people or the nation (Articles 2 and 6); the interdependence of human rights, democracy, and the rule of law (Article 5), as later expressed, for instance, in the Statute of the Council of Europe 1949; and the protection of human rights as the essential function of democratic governments and sovereign states. The latter idea, namely that internal sovereignty of states means more than simply exercising effective power and control over people and territory, as often asserted by states and scholars of general international law, and that sovereignty also implies governmental obligations to protect human rights of their populations, was taken up by the General Assembly of the United Nations when defining the concept of the Responsibility to Protect (R2P) in 2005.[5] States are only sovereign and, therefore, protected by the principle of nonintervention, as long as they are able and willing to protect their own people against the worst forms of gross and systematic violations of human rights, including genocide, ethnic cleansing, crimes against humanity, and war crimes. If governments are themselves responsible for such crimes or are either unwilling or unable to protect their people against such crimes by third parties, they gradually lose their internal and external sovereignty toward the international community. The United Nations, represented by the Security Council, takes over the responsibility to protect populations against such crimes, first by assisting governments in their efforts to protect human rights, and, as a measure of last resort, by taking coercive measures under Chapter VII of the UN Charter, including authorization of military intervention, as in the case of Libya in 2011.[6]

Origins of the Socialist Concept of Economic, Social, and Cultural Rights

The Western concept of civil and political rights, as proclaimed in the revolutionary bills of rights of the late eighteenth century and further developed in the constitutions of many other states during the nineteenth century, such as the Belgian Constitution of 1831 and the German Paulskirchenverfassung of 1848, did not mean, of course, that these lofty principles were immediately put into effect. In particular, the proclamation of the right to equality stood in stark contrast to the reality of those times. The word "man" was understood in its literal meaning in bourgeois societies of the eighteenth and nineteenth centuries, excluding not only women and children, but also all men who were not considered "free" in the bourgeois sense, above all slaves, workers, and peasants. It is thus no surprise that the bourgeois concept of civil and political rights, most notably the right to property, came under heavy attack by socialist philosophers and by communist revolutions in the early twentieth century. In his essay *On the Jewish Question*, written in 1843, Karl Marx developed a fundamental criticism of the very concept of civil and political rights, as contained in the French Declaration:[7]

> The *droits de l'homme*, the rights of man, are as such distinct from the *droits du citoyen*, the rights of the citizen. Who is *homme* as distinct from *citoyen*? None other than the *member of civil society*. Why is the member of civil society called "man," simply man; why are his rights called the *rights of man*? How is this fact to be explained? From the relationship between the political state and civil society, from the nature of political emancipation. Above all, we note the fact that the so-called *rights of man*, the *droits de l'homme* as distinct from the *droits du citoyen*, are nothing but the rights of a *member of civil society*, i.e., the rights of egoistic man, of man separated from other men and from the community.

Marx continues by analyzing the concepts underlying the French Declaration, namely liberty, property, equality, and security. Most important, he notes:

> The practical application of man's right to liberty is man's right to *private property*. What constitutes man's right to property? *Article 16* (Constitution of 1793): "The right to *property* is that which every citizen has of enjoying and of disposing *at his discretion* of his goods and income, of the fruits of his labour and industry." The right of

man to private property is, therefore, the right to enjoy one's property and to dispose of it at one's discretion (*à son gré*), without regard to other men, independently of society, the right of self-interest. It makes every man see in other men not the *realization* of his own freedom, but the *barrier* to it. But, above all, it proclaims the right of man.[8]

With respect to the principle of equality, Marx's criticism is similar:[9] "*Égalité*, used here in its nonpolitical sense, is nothing but the equality of the *liberté* described above, namely: each man is to the same extent regarded as such a self-sufficient monad."

On the basis of these writings, the socialist concept of human rights developed as an antithesis to the Western concept, both in philosophy and reality. On the one hand, some of the key features of the bourgeois concept of human rights, namely the individualistic and "egoistic" concept of civil rights, above all the right to property, were criticized as being incompatible with a socialist perception of human rights. It is interesting to note that the right to property, despite being one of the pillars of the Western concept of human rights, was excluded from the International Covenant on Civil and Political Rights (CCPR) because of the strong opposition by Communist states during the time of the Cold War.[10] Even today, almost thirty years after the fall of the Iron Curtain and in a time dominated by neoliberal thinking, the right to property has not yet been included in the core UN human rights treaties.

Second, the principle of equality was further developed from a purely liberal concept of equality of free men before the law to a concept that should benefit all human beings, irrespective of class, race, gender, and other distinguishing criteria, and which should be applied to all areas of life, including political, social, and economic equality, that is, real equality of opportunities. In his well-known essay *Anti-Dühring*, Friedrich Engels envisaged in 1878 that the working class would pick up the promises of the bourgeoisie and implement the principle of equality in real life, in society and the economic sphere.[11] In order to implement equality in real life, it was necessary to first address the most obvious forms of inequality, discrimination, and domination of human beings over other human beings, above all slavery and the exploitation of the working class during the age of industrialization. The desire to create equal rights and opportunities for all people is the driving force behind the gradual development of economic, social, and cultural rights, the very essence of the socialist concept of human rights and the modern welfare state.

The origins of real equality and economic, social, and cultural rights go back to the French Revolution. The first Declaration of the Rights of Women was drafted by Olympe de Gouges in 1791 in reaction to the French Declaration of 1789, which only applied to men. She was, however, convicted and executed for her counter-revolutionary activities under the terror regime of Robespierre in 1793. It is rather paradoxical that the Jacobins had in the same year adopted their own Declaration of the Rights of Man and of the Citizen of 1793, which clearly had put equality of human beings above the liberal concept of 1789. The Jacobin Declaration was spearheaded by the French agitator Gracchus Babeuf and his Society of Equals. Babeuf also perished on the scaffold, after conspiring in 1795 to lead a nascent urban proletariat against the establishment of a bourgeois regime.[12] The declaration of 1793 never became effective, but it is interesting as it contains a number of elements that clearly distinguish it from the bourgeois concept of the 1789 declaration. According to Article 1, the "aim of society is the common welfare. Government is instituted in order to guarantee to man the enjoyment of his natural and imprescriptible rights." According to Article 2, these rights are "equality, liberty, security and property." Article 18 proclaimed that "Every man can contract his services and his time, but he cannot sell himself nor be sold: his person is not an alienable property. The law knows of no such thing as the status of servant; there can exist only a contract for services and compensation between the man who works and the one who employs him." Similarly, Article 19 imposes certain restrictions on the right to property: "No one can be deprived of the least portion of his property without his consent, unless a legally established public necessity requires it, and upon condition of a just and prior compensation." In the same vein, Article 20 established that "No tax can be imposed except for the general advantage. All citizens have the right to participate in the establishment of taxes, to watch over the employment of them, and to cause an account of them to be rendered." This principle known as "no taxation without representation" also played an important role in the course of the American Revolution. Finally, Articles 21 to 23 contain the first core of rights, which later came to be called economic, social, and cultural rights:

21. Public relief is a sacred debt. Society owes maintenance to unfortunate citizens, either procuring work for them or in providing the means of existence for those who are unable to labor.

22. Education is needed by all. Society ought to favor with all its power the advancement of the public reason and to put education at the door of every citizen.

23. The social guarantee consists in the action of all to secure to each the enjoyment and the maintenance of his rights: this guarantee rests upon the national sovereignty.

Babeuf and other early socialist thinkers, including Michel Buonarroti, had already at that time concluded that as long as the working class was excluded from political participation, they would "have to fight an uphill battle to gain equal economic and social rights."[13] Such early socialist visions of political rights and social welfare were fostered by the rapid industrialization of England and France during the first half of the nineteenth century. The Chartist Movement in England adopted in 1837 a People's Charter calling for a "Law for Equally Representing the People of Great Britain and Ireland" that would guarantee universal suffrage and abolish all property qualifications for the right to vote.[14] Although it still took quite a while until universal suffrage was achieved in England and other countries, a number of Reform Bills and antipoverty laws, enacted in England in the 1830s, widened male suffrage, prohibited some of the worst forms of child labor, and introduced the first social benefits for the poor.

Similar developments in France, spearheaded by socialist thinkers, such as Pierre-Joseph Proudhon[15] and Louis Blanc, led to the inclusion of certain economic and social rights in the French Constitution of 1848, including the prohibition of slavery and the death penalty, limitations of the right to property in the general interest and expropriation only with adequate compensation, as well as the right to free primary education aimed at the full development of the physical, moral, and intellectual faculties of human beings, the right to work as the right of every member of society to live by labor, and the right of orphans, vulnerable groups, and the elderly to be supported by the state. At the same time, the 1848 German Paulskirchenverfassung contained a comprehensive bill of rights, including prohibition of servitude and capital punishment, limits on the right to property in the general interest and expropriation only with adequate compensation, as well as the right to free primary education. Further economic, social, and cultural rights were, however, not yet included in the German Constitution of 1848. Nevertheless, Germany became well known as a European state that introduced far-reaching social welfare and social security legislation and implemented economic and social rights during the second half of the nineteenth century. Although the German Constitution of 1871 did not contain any bill of rights, the authoritarian government under Otto von Bismarck extended social rights in 1883 in order to "politically neutralize a radical working class."[16] Other countries, including the Nordic states that later became models of the European welfare state, soon followed to establish social insurance and social security legislation.[17]

The most radical expression of the socialist concept of human rights is the Russian Declaration of Rights of the Working and Exploited People, drafted by Vladimir I. Lenin, approved by the Third All-Russia Congress of Soviets on 25 January 1918, and subsequently forming the basis of the Soviet Constitution. But it does not contain a catalogue of economic, social, and cultural rights, as its title might suggest. Article II simply states:

> Its fundamental aim being to abolish all exploitation of man by man, to completely eliminate the division of society into classes, to mercilessly crush the resistance of the exploiters, to establish a socialist organization of society and to achieve the victory of socialism in all countries, the Constituent Assembly further resolves:
> 1. Private ownership of land is hereby abolished. . . .
> 2. . . . the complete conversion of the factories, mines, railways, and other means of production and transport into the property of the workers' and peasants' state
> 3. The conversion of all banks into the property of the workers' and peasants' state.

In other words, rather than establishing specific economic, social, and cultural rights, as later Socialist constitutions, starting with Josef Stalin's constitution of 1936, did, Lenin's declaration only aimed at abolishing the bourgeois right of private property by expropriating all private lands, banks, factories, mines, railways, and other means of production. In addition, Article II(4) introduced "universal labour conscription," that is, the general obligation to work rather than a human right to work.

But economic, social, and cultural rights were developed after World War I in other constitutions, most notably the 1919 Weimar Verfassung of Germany. It contains one of the most comprehensive bills of rights, with more than 50 articles (109 to 165). The fourth section is dedicated to the right to education and guarantees free and compulsory primary education for at least eight years as well as free secondary education up to age eighteen. The fifth section pertains to the economic sphere, which shall be organized in accordance with the principles of justice aimed at securing human dignity (Article 151). Private property includes obligations toward society and can be expropriated in the general interest with adequate compensation (Article 153). Private companies may be nationalized for the common good (Article 154). The rights to work, freedom of association, and trade unions, the right to healthy working conditions, and a comprehensive social security system and other social rights shall be protected (Articles 157 to 165).

On the international level, these economic and social rights were also further developed by the International Labour Organization (ILO), created by the Treaty of Versailles in 1919. The Preamble to the ILO Constitution starts from the observation that "universal and lasting peace can be established only if it is based on social justice; And whereas conditions of labor exist involving such injustice, hardship and privation to large numbers of people as to produce unrest so great that the peace and harmony of the world are imperiled." In other words, social injustice was seen by the drafters of the Treaty of Versailles as one of the main conditions endangering international peace. Therefore, the ILO was established with the aim of improving working conditions, preventing unemployment, reducing working hours, providing for equal and fair remuneration, social security and insurance, freedom of association, and the right to vocational and technical education. It is interesting to note that the international protection of economic, social, and cultural rights preceded the international protection of civil and political rights, as the League of Nations, which was also established by the Treaty of Versailles, had no general mandate to protect human rights.

The best-known catalogue of economic, social, and cultural rights before World War II was Chapter X (Articles 118 to 133) on Fundamental Rights and Duties of Citizens of the Stalin Constitution of the Soviet Union of 1936. It starts with the right to work, which included the abolition of unemployment, followed by the rights to rest and leisure, the reduction of the working day to seven hours, the right to social insurance and free medical services, the right to education, including compulsory and free primary education as well as free higher education, equal rights of women in all spheres of economic, state, cultural, social, and political life, and equality of rights of citizens, irrespective of their nationality or race. The second part of this bill of rights contains certain civil and political rights under the specific conditions of a socialist society, including right of asylum of foreign citizens persecuted for defending the interests of the working people, and duties toward the fatherland, including to "safeguard and strengthen public, socialist property as the sacred and inviolable foundation of the Soviet system" (Article 131).

The Universal Declaration of Human Rights as a First Synthesis

The United Nations Organization was created in 1945 in reaction to World War II and the atrocities committed during the Nazi Holocaust. For the first time in history, the human being was put at the center of international relations, and human rights became one of the three main aims and objectives of the world organization, in addition to security and development.[18] Already in January 1941, U.S. president Franklin Delano Roosevelt had delivered his famous Four Freedoms speech, in which he had defined the four most important human rights as freedom of speech and freedom of worship, both contained in the First Amendment to the U.S. Constitution, as well as freedom from want and freedom from fear "everywhere in the world." While "freedom from fear" refers to the liberal concept of civil and political rights, the concept of "freedom from want" is based on the experience of President Roosevelt with the world economic crisis and his New Deal legislation, which had led to the enactment of some economic, social, and cultural rights even in the United States. At the same time, the concepts of "freedom from fear" and "freedom from want" link the human rights goal to the other two main objectives of the UN: international peace and security on the one hand, and development and poverty reduction on the other.[19] In the Atlantic Charter of 12 August 1941, President Roosevelt and British Prime Minister Winston Churchill confirmed their desire that after destroying the Nazi tyranny, they would establish peace in which all nations should refrain from using force and in which human beings could live in all countries of the world in freedom from fear and want. Yet the Dumbarton Oaks proposals for a Charter of the future United Nations, agreed upon in the fall of 1944 by the governments of China, the Soviet Union, the UK, and the United States, only contained one general reference to "promote respect for human rights and fundamental freedoms," which, according to John Humphrey, the first director of the UN Division of Human Rights, "hardly met the expectations of a public opinion aroused by the atrocities of the war."[20]

Compared to this short reference and taking into account the preoccupation of the four allied powers with matters of military security, rather than human rights, it is surprising that the final text of the UN Charter, adopted on 26 June 1945 in San Francisco, contains quite strong language on human rights: "promoting and encouraging respect for human rights and fundamental freedoms for all without distinction as to race, sex, language, or religion" is prominently mentioned in Article 1 as one of the main purposes of the United Nations, and various tasks in implementing this goal have been entrusted to the General Assembly, the Economic and Social Council (ECOSOC), and the Trusteeship Council. Most important, ECOSOC was requested in Article 68 to set up a Commission on Human Rights. This relatively strong language, above all if compared to the Covenant of the League of Nations established in reaction to World War I, is generally attributed to the lobbying of civil society and a group of Latin American states.[21] In February 1943, the American Law Institute produced a draft of an International Bill of Human Rights, which later played an important role in the drafting of the Universal Declaration.[22] In early 1945, twenty-one American countries meeting at the Inter-American Conference on War and Peace in Mexico City agreed that they wanted to see a bill of human rights as part of the UN Charter, and three of them (Chile, Cuba, and Panama) submitted the draft of the American Law Institute as a formal proposal to the San Francisco conference with strong support of various civil society groups invited by the U.S. government to attend the San Francisco conference.[23] None of the four major powers was willing to adopt such a far-reaching proposal. But during the last session, U.S. secretary of state Edward Stettinius gave in at least to some minimum demands of the lobbyists and then persuaded the other great powers to accept a few amendments with explicit human rights language. "How this was achieved has never been explained," wrote John Humphrey in 1984: "Perhaps, in the rush of last-minute decisions, not much thought was given to the revolutionary character of what was happening."[24]

Although the text of the UN Charter contains seven references to human rights, this term has nowhere been defined. It was generally understood that the task of defining human rights and drafting an International Bill of Human Rights had been entrusted to the Commission on Human Rights, which was soon established by ECOSOC. It consisted of the following 18 states representing all world regions: Australia, Belgium, Byelorussian Soviet Socialist Republic, Chile, China, Egypt, France, India, Iran, Lebanon, Panama, Philippine Republic, Ukrainian Soviet Socialist Republic, United Kingdom, United States of America, Union of Soviet Socialist Republics, Uruguay, and Yugoslavia. The individual members representing their respective countries included well-known personalities, such as Eleanor Roosevelt (United States) in the chair, Peng Chung Chang (China), Vladimir Koretsky, Alexandre Bogomolov, and Alexej Pavlov (USSR), Charles Malik (Lebanon), René Cassin (France), Hansa Mehta (India), Geoffrey Wilson (UK), Hernán Santa Cruz (Chile), William Hodgson (Australia), and Vladislav Ribnikar (Yugoslavia). They were assisted by the newly created Division of Human Rights, headed by John Humphrey (Canada). The Latin Americans further pursued their goal of quickly adopting a binding International Convention on Human Rights, and the British also submitted their own draft of a binding convention.[25] Australia strongly argued for the establishment of an International Court of Human Rights, but the Commission soon agreed that it would first draft a nonbinding declaration, and only later work on a binding treaty and measures of implementation. In retrospect, it is still surprising that it took these 18 states and these personalities with their completely different views about human rights less than two years to agree on the text of a Universal Declaration of Human Rights (UDHR), which turned out as a compromise between the two dominating concepts of human rights.

There is plenty of literature on the drafting history of the Universal Declaration, which I do not wish to repeat here. My emphasis will, therefore, be put on the inclusion of economic, social, and cultural rights in Articles 22 to 27 and on the question how this could be achieved against the opposition of Western states that used to argue, and partly still argue today, that economic, social, and cultural rights are no real human rights and can only be realized in a Communist society. Is it true, as is often suggested, that inclusion of these "socialist" rights were only pushed by the Soviet Union and its allies? Or is Johannes Morsink correct to assert:[26] "This is one of the misconceptions this history clears up, for it is not the Communists but the Latin American socialists—and John Humphrey as their conduit—to whom we owe the presence of these rights in the Declaration"? Ashild Samnoy argues in the same direction, but even more strongly:[27] "The inclusion of social and economic rights in the UDHR was a novelty at that time. It has been argued that this was a result of pressure from Eastern

Europe and, in particular, the USSR, but this is a myth which may, in part, be a result of later political developments." In the same vein, Asbjørn Eide and Wenche Barth Eide state:[28] "During the subsequent Cold War, it became part of the rhetoric of some Western states that economic and social rights had been included at the insistence of the Socialist countries. Historical evidence shows that this is completely wrong."

When the Commission on Human Rights held its first session in January and February 1947, John Humphrey had just been appointed as director of the UN Division of Human Rights by his French friend Henry Laugier, assistant Secretary-General of the UN in charge of social affairs.[29] In the fall of 1946, the General Assembly had rejected a motion of Panama simply to adopt a draft bill of human rights, which it had already unsuccessfully sponsored at the San Francisco Conference, and had decided that the Commission should draft such a bill. During its first session, held in January and February 1947 at Lake Success, New York, the Commission decided to establish a drafting committee consisting of the chair (Mrs. Roosevelt), the vice-chair (Mr. Chang), and the rapporteur (Mr. Malik), who should, with the assistance of the Secretariat, submit a preliminary draft to its second session. This decision was challenged by the Soviet Union in the ECOSOC on the ground that the drafting committee did not contain any European country.[30] The conflict was solved by Mrs. Roosevelt by announcing that she would appoint a new drafting committee consisting of eight states: Australia, Chile, China, France, Lebanon, the United States, the UK, and the Soviet Union. ECOSOC approved this compromise and at the same time instructed the Secretariat to prepare a "documented outline" of the international bill of rights. This meant, in fact, that John Humphrey was entrusted with preparing a first draft, as before already suggested by Eleanor Roosevelt. Humphrey was very favorable to including economic, social, and cultural rights. When Jan Stancyck, principal director in the UN Department of Social Affairs and former minister of labor in the Polish government in exile, suggested to him to include economic, social, and cultural rights, Humphrey recalled:[31] "A socialist of the old school, he wanted to be sure that economic and social rights would be included. He need not have worried; I had already decided to include them. Human rights without economic and social rights have little meaning for most people, particularly on empty bellies." Humphrey even went so far as to claim a certain ownership in this regard:[32] "It is by no means certain that economic and social rights would have been included in the final text if I had not included them in mine."

According to Humphrey, his draft "attempted to combine humanitarian liberalism with social democracy."[33] He admitted that he had practically no experience in drafting documents and that he based his draft on various texts prepared by private individuals, including Hersch Lauterpacht, and nongovernmental organizations, most notably the draft prepared by the American Law Institute, which already had included economic and social rights.[34] The Drafting Committee of eight met in June 1947 under Eleanor Roosevelt as chair. It decided to establish a temporary working group consisting of René Cassin, Charles Malik, and Geoffrey Wilson, who had submitted the British draft convention. They asked Cassin to prepare a draft based on those articles of the Secretariat Outline that he considered appropriate for a declaration, which he did over the weekend.[35] Whereas Cassin and the French government tried to create the myth that Cassin was the true "father" of the declaration, Humphrey, on the other hand, seems to have exaggerated his own influence by downplaying the role of Cassin.[36] But they both strongly believed in the need to include economic and social rights in a truly Universal Declaration of Human Rights, which is also reflected in Cassin's draft.[37] The main opposition came from Australia and the UK, whereas Hernán Santa Cruz (Chile), whom Humphrey described as "left of the center,"[38] argued most strongly in favor:[39] "If the drafting committee did not introduce economic and social rights in to the Declaration, it would not appear to the world to be acting realistically."

In the following months, the draft was subjected to detailed discussions, changes, and regroupings by the Sub-Commission on the Prevention of Discrimination and Protection of Minorities; the second session of the Commission held in December 1947 in Geneva;[40] the second session of the drafting committee in May 1948, which was devoted primarily to the discussion of a binding convention; and the third session of the Commission in May and June 1948.[41] Finally, it was discussed by ECOSOC during the summer and by the Third Committee of the General Assembly under the chair of Charles Malik during the fall of 1948 before being adopted by the Plenary General Assembly on 10 December 1948 in Paris, with a vote of 48 states in favor, none against, and 8 abstentions.[42]

A detailed analysis of the drafting history of Articles 22 to 27 of the Universal Declaration,[43] which contain all essential economic, social, and cultural rights to social security, to work, to just and favorable conditions of work, to the formation and joining of trade unions, to rest and leisure, to an adequate standard of living, including food, clothing, housing, and medical care, as well as protection of motherhood and childhood, to education, and to participation in the cultural life of the community, shows that these articles are a joint product of many personalities, NGOs, and states from all world regions. Although the Soviet Union, and in particular Ambassador Bogomolov,[44] played an important role in making sure that these rights were adequately reflected in the Universal Declaration, one should definitely not exaggerate the role of Communist states, which often seemed more concerned with preventing any strong document encroaching on state sovereignty than with pushing for the adoption of the Socialist concept of human rights as part of international law. This is also underlined by the fact that all Communist states finally abstained when the Declaration was adopted in the General Assembly. Their explanations of the vote did not claim that economic, social, and cultural rights should have been given more prominence, but were more concerned with the sovereign rights of states and the protection of minorities.[45] As Johannes Morsink rightly observed, "the Latin American socialist tradition" played an important role in drafting the rights to food, housing, and medical care.[46] The Chilean expert Hernán Santa Cruz often played a more decisive role than his counterparts from Communist states. The right to clothing was added to the right to an adequate standard of living by the Philippine delegation, but China (which was at that time not yet represented by the PRC) and the Soviet Union also added various aspects to the overall social right to an adequate standard of living in Article 25.

Most important, at that time, most Western states were still under the influence of the world economic crisis and its devastating impact on the working class leading to social unrest and political turmoil during the prewar period. Furthermore, the West and the East were still united in their fight against National Socialism and fascism. This means that the United States and most European countries were more inclined toward ideas of social democracy and a modern welfare state based on the protection and fulfillment of economic, social, and cultural rights than in the years of the Cold War and the rise of neoliberal economic theories. Another input came from experts of the ILO who were closely involved in the drafting of the right to work and other economic rights. Even the United States had accepted that civil and political rights need to be balanced by the concept of "freedom from want." How could Eleanor Roosevelt be strongly against the inclusion of economic, social, and cultural rights, when others paid tribute to the New Deal legislation and the Four Freedoms speech of her late husband? When Australia and the UK strongly objected to Latin American insistence on including certain economic and social rights, Roosevelt, assisted by Charles Malik, repeatedly managed to find a compromise.[47] In conclusion, I would argue that the Universal Declaration of Human Rights in fact does constitute a first synthesis between two antagonistic human rights concepts, despite the fact that the ideological debates in the Commission and the General Assembly did not necessarily follow the political division between East and West. As the Weimar Constitution in Germany and many Latin American constitutions enacted in the prewar period show, economic, social, and cultural rights were not necessarily linked to a Communist economic and political system, but had already been widely accepted by social democrats in free market economies, above all in Europe and Latin America.

Two United Nations Human Rights Covenants as Expression of Cold War Politics

In retrospect, it was an excellent strategy of Eleanor Roosevelt, Charles Malik, John Humphrey, and others to press for the early adoption of the UDHR because the window of opportunity, which had been opened by the Holocaust and the joint desire of the Allies to strongly react to fascism, had been rapidly closing. In accordance with its original three-step approach of drafting first a declaration, and thereafter a binding convention and measures of implementation, the Commission started in 1949 to work on a convention. But the memories of the horrors of World War II started to fade, the Cold War was intensifying not least due to the Eisenhower administration in the United States and the Korean crisis, and the question of the self-determination of the colonial peoples in Africa and Asia became a highly controversial and sensitive topic.[48] In 1950, the newly created Council of Europe, which represented Western European democracies, adopted the European Convention on Human Rights, which provided for interstate and individual petitions before an independent Commission and, in last instance, even before a European Court of Human Rights. But the European Convention only contained civil and political rights. This was the model the West wanted to apply in the United Nations too, although the General Assembly had still emphasized the interdependence of all categories of human rights when calling on the Commission in 1950 to adopt a single UN Convention on Human Rights.[49]

Most Western countries were in favor of adopting a binding convention with an effective international monitoring system, but strongly believed that civil and political rights were only "negative" rights against state interference that did not require any positive state measures. Economic, social, and cultural rights, on the other hand, would require positive measures of implementation and, therefore, merely represent programmatic goals to be achieved in the distant future, depending on the economic resources available. As a consequence, they were regarded as not immediately binding and not being capable to be enforced by means of individual petitions before an international court. Even John Humphrey, who had claimed a certain ownership for having included economic, social, and cultural rights in his first draft of the UDHR,[50] was deeply convinced that most of these rights were "nonjusticiable program rights, the implementation of which can only be achieved progressively,"[51] as he even still maintained in 1984 in his book on the "great adventure" of human rights in the United Nations. He expressed this opinion by recalling a conversation he had with René Cassin in 1951 in Paris in preparation for a highly controversial session of the General Assembly. Cassin had been "insisting that the complaints system, which had been devised for the implementation of civil and political rights, also be made applicable to economic, social and cultural rights." Humphrey even claims that he had convinced Cassin in this conversation that "this was impossible" because of the nonjusticiable nature of these "program rights" and that, as a "compromise," he would try to convince the Americans to extend the state reporting system to both sets of rights.

The Soviet position was fairly ambiguous. On the one hand, Socialist states claimed ownership of economic, social, and cultural rights and insisted, therefore, on the equality and interdependence of all rights. But throughout the drafting history of the Covenants, they seemed to be more concerned about state sovereignty than pushing for the adoption of economic, social, and cultural rights with strong state obligations. In their opinion, human rights were a matter for states to achieve on the domestic level in accordance with their respective national political and economic systems. Human rights were objective goals for state policy, but not subjective legal claims that the individual could enforce by means of an individual petition against the state, neither on the domestic nor on the international level. For this reason, the Socialist states were in fact against any meaningful system of international monitoring and supervision.[52] The goal of subjecting all human rights on an equal basis to a system of individual complaints

before an international court of human rights, similar to the European
Court of Human Rights, was, therefore, a vision of a few committed individuals, such as Cassin and Santa Cruz, believing deeply in social democracy and the empowerment of the poor. But it was not a vision to be
achieved during the time of the Cold War.

In order to pursue their goal of submitting civil and political rights to a
system of complaints and at the same time sidelining economic, social, and
cultural rights, Eleanor Roosevelt suggested in 1951 to split the International Bill of Rights into two instruments, which should be approved and
opened for signature at the same time. John Humphrey "still preferred one
instrument divided into two parts, but the American suggestion, which was
the one adopted, had at least the merit of treating the two categories
equally."[53] But the American suggestion provoked a "largely ideological
controversy and decision" which "split the United Nations down the middle."[54] Chile, Egypt, Pakistan, and Yugoslavia had moved in the Third Committee to reaffirm the decision taken in 1950. But the Americans strongly
lobbied for splitting the Covenant and managed to defeat this joint motion
of like-minded states from different world regions by a small majority.
Chile reopened this controversial question in the plenary and moved again
to draft one single Covenant with both kinds of rights. "After a bitter debate,
the Chilean amendment was defeated by a roll call vote of 29 to 25 with 4
abstentions."[55] This was a decisive turn in the history of the International
Bill of Rights, since from now on the Commission on Human Rights and
the Third Committee of the General Assembly drafted a "Western" and a
"Socialist" Covenant with two different types of state obligations and two
different sets of international monitoring procedures in mind. The Commission finished its drafting work in 1954,[56] but it took the Third Committee until 1966 to finalize the text of the two Covenants and the First
Optional Protocol (OP) to the Covenant on Civil and Political Rights which
contains an individual complaints procedure. On 16 December 1966, both
Covenants were adopted by the General Assembly unanimously, while the
first OP was adopted by 66 votes to 2 (Niger and Togo), with 38 abstentions, including all Socialist states, Greece, Spain, Japan, India, Saudi Arabia, Senegal, and Tanzania.

Without going into detail, it is fair to say that most ideological debates
between Western, Socialist, and Southern states focused less on the precise
formulation of the substantive rights included in both Covenants than on
the questions, whether or not certain rights, such as the right of peoples to

self-determination,[57] minority rights,[58] or the right to property,[59] should be included in the Covenants, as well as whether and how states' compliance should be monitored by an international supervisory body.[60] Although the General Assembly in 1950 had still called on the Human Rights Commission "to proceed with the consideration of provisions, to be inserted in the draft Covenant or in separate protocols, for the receipt and examination of petitions from individuals and organizations with respect to alleged violations of the Covenant,"[61] the Commission was not able to include the right to individual petition in its 1954 draft of either of the two Covenants. At that time, agreement had only been reached to provide for a state reporting procedure in both Covenants and for a mandatory interstate complaints system relating only to the CCPR with the possibility of the states involved to bring the matter before the International Court of Justice.[62] Originally, the Socialist states considered all measures of international supervision, even the state reporting procedure, as a violation of national sovereignty and of the "domestic jurisdiction" clause in Article 2(7) of the UN Charter.[63] But they later agreed to the state reporting procedure for both Covenants, and in the General Assembly also to an optional interstate communication procedure in Article 41 CCPR, albeit only after all judicial or quasi-judicial decision-making elements had been eliminated by a joint proposal submitted in 1966 by nine African and Asian states.[64] Neither in the Human Rights Commission nor in the General Assembly did any state propose to include the right to individual or interstate communication in the Covenant on Economic, Social and Cultural Rights (CESCR) after the controversial decision of splitting the Covenants had been adopted in 1951.

But in 1966, the Netherlands, Jamaica, Nigeria, Pakistan, Iran, and other states from all world regions with the exception of the Socialist states proposed in the Third Committee to facilitate an optional right of communication on the part of individuals and groups to be added in Article 41 bis of the CCPR, in addition to the interstate communication procedure, modeled after the European Convention on Human Rights and the recently adopted UN Convention on the Elimination of Racial Discrimination (CERD).[65] After extensive consultations, a joint proposal was submitted by the following ten states: Canada, Colombia, Costa Rica, Ghana, Jamaica, the Netherlands, Nigeria, Pakistan, the Philippines, and Uruguay.[66] But since the Socialist states strongly objected to the inclusion of the right to individual petition in the text of the Covenant, which would even threaten its chances of ratification, Lebanon proposed to transfer it to a separate

Optional Protocol (OP), and this proposal was adopted by the scant majority of 41 states in favor, including all Socialist states, 39 against, including most Western states, with 16 abstentions. Since the Socialist states seemed to have supported the idea of a separate OP only for the purpose of filibustering, Nigeria quickly submitted a proposal for a text of an OP, which was further elaborated by a draft supported by the following nine states: Canada, Chile, Costa Rica, Ghana, Jamaica, Lebanon, the Netherlands, Nigeria, and the Philippines.[67] Since most states wished to speedily adopt the OP together with the two Covenants in 1966, the Third Committee had only limited time to discuss it. Since the Socialist states had been voting in favor of transferring the individual petition system to a separate OP, they could not have voted against the OP and finally only abstained, while most Western, Latin American, and quite a few African and Asian states voted in favor. The only states voting against were Niger and Togo.

The result of these highly ideological debates in the United Nations can only be described as the lowest common denominator between two antagonistic concepts. From the synthesis of the late 1940s, as expressed in the UDHR, only the fact remained that both Covenants were adopted simultaneously and contain a few similar provisions, most notably the right of peoples to self-determination in Article 1 and equality between men and women in Article 3. But the perceived differences between both sets of human rights are much more serious and are, in principle, maintained until today despite much lip service to the equality, indivisibility, and interdependence of all human rights. The most important differences between the two Covenants are the following:

- State obligations. In Article 2(1) CCPR, states parties undertake "to respect and to ensure to all individuals" the rights contained therein. The corresponding provision in Article 2(1) CESCR is, however, much weaker and expresses the idea of mere "program rights," as John Humphrey used to call economic, social, and cultural rights: "Each State Party to the present Covenant undertakes to take steps, individually and through international assistance and co-operation, especially economic and technical, to the maximum of its available resources, with a view to achieving progressively the full realization of the rights recognized in the present Covenant."
- International monitoring bodies. Articles 28 to 39 CCPR provide for the establishment of the Human Rights Committee, a supervisory

body consisting of 18 independent experts elected by states parties, similar to the Racial Discrimination Committee which had been created in accordance with Articles 8 to 11 CERD, adopted in 1965. In contrast, the international monitoring of states' compliance with their obligations under the CESCR was left to the ECOSOC, one of the main political bodies of the United Nations, consisting of state representatives. After the entry into force of the CESCR in 1976, ECOSOC started to examine state reports submitted in accordance with Article 16 CESCR. Since this was not working properly, ECOSOC finally in 1985 established the Committee on Economic, Social and Cultural Rights, consisting of 18 independent experts, similar to the other treaty monitoring bodies. This was an important step in the direction of treating all human rights equally.

- International monitoring procedures. States parties to both Covenants are obliged to submit periodic reports to the respective monitoring bodies. But only Articles 41 and 42 CCPR provide for an interstate complaints procedure, and only a separate First OP to the CCPR for an individual complaints procedure. Both monitoring procedures are optional and fairly weak. Instead of speaking of complaints or petitions, the CCPR and OP only talk about "communications." The final decisions of the Human Rights Committee are legally nonbinding and are called "final views" to underline that they should not resemble judgments. The entire procedure is written and does not envisage oral hearings or fact finding on the spot. A similar complaints procedure in relation to economic, social, and cultural rights was only introduced in 2008 with the adoption, after many years of difficult negotiations, of the OP to the CESCR.

The history of human rights in the UN until the end of the Cold War illustrates a half-hearted synthesis between the "first and second generations" of human rights or the Western and Socialist concepts of human rights. This has to do with the policy of the Soviet Union and its allies, which were more concerned about the erosion of state sovereignty by the advancement of human rights than with advocacy for economic, social, and cultural rights. The United States, on the other hand, never accepted economic, social, and cultural rights as equal to civil and political rights and bears primary responsibility for the separation of the two Covenants and the ensuing "two class" system of human rights protection, which puts more emphasis on the differences between the two categories of human rights than on the similarities between them. Such a "two class system" was also adopted in the Council of Europe with the European Convention on Human Rights of 1950 as the flagship and the European Social Charter of 1961 as the "little sister." Genuine concern for economic, social, and cultural rights was shown primarily by countries ruled by social democratic and other left-wing parties in Western Europe, Latin America, Africa, and Asia, as well as by independent experts, such as some members of the newly created UN Committee on Economic, Social and Cultural Rights.

The Fall of the Iron Curtain: A Window of Opportunity for a New Synthesis?

In 1989, the Socialist system in the Soviet Union and its allies in Central and Eastern Europe collapsed. This meant that the main opponents to an international social and political order for the full realization of human rights, as envisaged in Article 28 UDHR, had disappeared. Indeed, in this climate of new cooperation between Eastern and Western Europe, French president François Mitterand and the last Soviet president Mikhail Gorbachev spoke of a "common European house," based on the common European values of pluralist democracy, rule of law, and human rights. In the Charter of Paris for a New Europe, adopted by the Conference on Security and Cooperation in Europe (CSCE) in November 1990, the Cold War was officially declared over and the CSCE formally opened "a new era of democracy, peace and unity" with joint commitments toward human rights, democracy, and the rule of law and first attempts at institutionalizing the CSCE, which led in 1994 to its replacement by the Organization for Security and Cooperation in Europe (OSCE).

In this particular situation, the UN called for a second World Conference on Human Rights, to be held in Vienna in 1993, twenty-five years after the first World Conference in Teheran 1968. But the window of opportunity, created by the enthusiasm after the fall of the Berlin Wall and the reunification of Germany, was quickly closing due to a number of events. Most important, the countries of the global South felt threatened by the power of the united North. Much of the money traditionally spent by means of development cooperation toward the South was, all of a sudden, diverted to support the transitional economies of Central and Eastern

Europe. Second, countries in Africa and other regions of the global South that had ideological ties with the Soviet Union during the Cold War, such as Cuba, Angola, Iraq, or Vietnam, suddenly felt alienated by their former allies and somewhat lost in the newly emerging international order. Third, the ideological vacuum created by the end of Communism in Central and Eastern Europe created fears among the people that were quickly exploited by nationalist propaganda of former Communists, such as Slobodan Milošević in the former Yugoslavia or Vladimir Mečiar in the Slovak Republic, followed later by Vladimir Putin in the Russian Federation. This rapid rise of nationalism led to ethnic and religious conflicts in many countries of Central and Eastern Europe, culminating in genocide in Bosnia and Herzegovina, exactly half a century after the Holocaust. Fourth, and most important, the West had celebrated the fall of the Iron Curtain more as the victory of capitalism over communism than as the gradual replacement of totalitarian and authoritarian regimes by a system of governance based upon democracy, the rule of law, and human rights. Inspired by neoliberal policies in times of rapid globalization, including by the structural adjustment policies of the World Bank, the creation of the World Trade Organization (WTO), and the promotion of bilateral investment treaties (BITs), global capitalism quickly spread into all world regions. Many people and governments in the global South associated the aggressive promotion of global capitalism by the countries of the North with the spread of human rights and increasingly criticized Western "human rights colonialism" and imperialism. Partly, this was underlined by the policies of some countries and development agencies to link development cooperation to civil and political rights by means of negative conditionality and the concept of "human development" as applied by the UN Development Programme (UNDP). In any case, many Asian and African politicians started to argue that human rights were a purely Western concept and that they had to protect the traditional values of African and Asian societies against this human rights colonialism. They increasingly put the universality of human rights into question and asserted instead so-called Asian values, human duties, and cultural relativism. The conflict between "universalists" and "cultural relativists" quickly dominated the negotiations of a final outcome document before and during the Vienna World Conference.

Despite this growing North-South conflict, the drafters of the Vienna Declaration and Programme of Action (VDPA) were able to reach a compromise and this outcome document was adopted unanimously by 171 states. Inspired by a global desire to create a better world and strongly influenced by a global civil society human rights movement that in Vienna had called for "All Human Rights for All,"[68] the VDPA contains a wealth of important principles and visionary ideas, which have been the basis of the UN global human rights agenda, spearheaded by the newly created UN High Commissioner for Human Rights. Most important, §4 underlines that the "promotion and protection of human rights is a legitimate concern of the international community," which means that governments were no longer justified to invoke the domestic jurisdiction principle of Article 2(7) UN Charter when being criticized for human rights violations. In the last resort, gross and systematic violations of human rights may even lead to collective measures taken by the UN Security Council, as was later affirmed by the General Assembly when adopting the doctrine of the Responsibility to Protect (R2P) in the outcome document of the 2005 summit. The conflict between the "universalists" and the "cultural relativists" was solved by the following carefully drafted §5 of the VDPA:

> All human rights are universal, indivisible and interdependent and interrelated. The international community must treat human rights globally in a fair and equal manner, on the same footing, and with the same emphasis. While the significance of national and regional particularities and various historical, cultural and religious backgrounds must be borne in mind, it is the duty of States, regardless of their political, economic and cultural systems, to promote and protect all human rights and fundamental freedoms.

This provision combines the principles of universality with equality and interdependence of all human rights. In other words, the North was successful in maintaining the universality of human rights, while at the same time acknowledging a certain degree of cultural relativism. On the other hand, the South was successful in achieving the recognition of the equality, indivisibility, and interdependence of all human rights, that is, civil, political, economic, social, and cultural rights. This means, in effect, that the VDPA overruled the differences between the so-called first and second generations of human rights, as expressed in the different types of state obligations in Articles 2 of both Covenants. Rather than maintaining the ideological positions of the Cold War that civil and political rights were purely negative rights creating immediate binding effects of non-interference by states subject to judicial review, while economic, social, and cultural rights were purely positive rights creating only programmatic and nonjusticiable obligations of states to take steps to the maximum of their available resources with a view to "achieving progressively the full realization" of these rights, the new philosophy of the equality and interdependence of all rights aimed at a synthesis between the Western (Northern) and the Eastern (Southern) concept of human rights. As a consequence, human rights theory developed three types of state obligations, which were originally designed in the context of economic, social, and cultural rights and later applied to all human rights.

The *obligation to respect* represents the negative duty of states not to unduly interfere with the exercise of human rights. The rights to life, personal integrity, and personal liberty, for example, require that law enforcement officials shall not arbitrarily kill, beat, and detain people; freedom of expression and assembly prohibit prior censorship and arbitrary denials of public gatherings; the right to education obliges states not to unduly interfere with the rights of parents to educate their children in accordance with their own religious convictions; the right to housing prohibits arbitrary evictions; and the right to health prevents states from arbitrarily denying access to primary and emergency healthcare facilities.

The *obligation to fulfill*, on the other hand, constitutes the positive duty of states to take the necessary legislative, administrative, judicial, political, and practical measures to ensure that human beings can in fact enjoy and exercise their human rights. The rights to life, personal integrity, and personal liberty, first of all require enactment of legislation to reduce arbitrary killings and child mortality, to criminalize torture and ill-treatment, to regulate the admissibility of police custody and pretrial detention, and so forth. Freedom of expression, assembly, and association oblige states to enact legislation that regulates media freedom, the precise conditions under which street demonstrations can be organized, as well as the legal requirements to form and join political parties, trade unions, sport clubs, and other civil society organizations. The rights to fair trial, health, and education require legislation in which the state defines how it organizes its judiciary, health, and education system, and how it ensures equal access of all human beings to justice and to primary, secondary, and higher education, as well as to primary and other health care facilities. In addition to legislative measures, the state must train the police in accordance with the requirements of human rights, it must construct court buildings, schools, and hospitals, recruit and train judges, teachers, and doctors, and carry out many other practical measures in order to ensure that human beings can effectively enjoy and exercise their various civil, political, economic, social, and cultural rights.

The *obligation to protect* requires positive legislative, administrative, judicial, and other measures aimed at protecting human beings against abuses of their human rights by third parties. In most countries, more people are killed by private criminals and reckless car drivers than by the police. Not every private killing is a human rights violation for which the state can be held accountable. But the state has an obligation to enact criminal laws in order to deter violent crime, to recruit and train a sufficient number of law enforcement officers for the purpose of preventing crime, investigating crime, bringing the perpetrators of such crimes to justice, and to uphold public order and safety and to regulate street traffic in a manner that reduces the risk of accidents as far as possible. Freedom from fear and the right to personal security is a very important human right that significantly contributes to our quality of life, but which requires intensive positive measures by the state, ensuring a high degree of social peace and justice as well as trust in the administration of justice and law enforcement. To cite another example: many more women and children are beaten up by their husbands and parents than by the police. The right to personal integrity, therefore, in addition to the prohibition of torture and ill-treatment by the police, also requires states to prohibit and prevent, as far as possible, domestic violence, corporal punishment in the schools and homes, harmful traditional practices such as female genital mutilation, and so on. The right to education includes free and compulsory primary education, which also encompasses the obligation of states to protect children against their own parents who might prefer their daughter to work in the household rather than going to school. Most economic rights, such as the right to work and equal pay for equal work, the right to decent, safe, and healthy working conditions, the prohibition of child labor and forced labor, protect workers and employees against being exploited by powerful employers and corporations. This obligation to protect shall be achieved by respective labor laws and labor courts, trade union freedoms, collective bargaining, and other means to be provided by positive state legislation and implementation measures.

In other words: all human rights create respective state obligations to respect, protect, and fulfill. While the obligation to respect simply means that states shall refrain from certain harmful practices, the obligations to fulfill and protect always require positive measures which are subject to the principle of due diligence.[69] Positive obligations, which usually require substantial financial and personnel resources, can never be 100 percent fulfilled. They are always subject to the test of reasonableness. States are only required to take those positive measures that can reasonably be expected from them by taking all relevant circumstances and conditions into account, including possible violations of other human rights. The state, for example, cannot reasonably be expected to fully protect its inhabitants against violent crime by providing every citizen with a private bodyguard and, thereby, violating the right to privacy. But when violent crime is significantly increasing in certain areas, the state has an obligation in relation to the human rights to life, personal integrity, liberty, and security, to analyze the reasons and to take adequate measures, including more police presence, in order to protect the people and reduce the crime rate. Of course, it may take some time until these measures will bear fruit, and the aim of reducing the crime rate can only be "achieved progressively." In other words, the formulation "to take steps . . . to the maximum of its available resources, with a view to achieving progressively the full realization of the rights recognized in the present Covenant" in Article 2(1) CESCR is not specific to economic, social, and cultural rights, but to the nature of positive obligations to protect and fulfill human rights. The difference in the wording of the respective state obligations in the two Covenants does not result from the different nature of the two sets of rights but from the wrong assumption during the time of the Cold War that civil and political rights entail only negative duties of noninterference, while economic, social, and cultural rights entail only positive obligations. The synthesis between both categories of human rights achieved in the VDPA, including their equal value, interdependence, and indivisibility, require us to interpret the respective state obligations in both Covenants in this new light, taking into account that human rights treaties are "living instruments." The recognition of the equality of all rights also should have put to rest the ideological debate about the alleged "nonjusticiability" of economic, social, and cultural rights. Nevertheless, due to sustained resistance by certain Western states, it took almost twenty years until the Optional Protocol to the CESCR, which introduces the individual complaints system for the "second generation of human rights," was finally adopted in 2008 and entered into force in 2013. Similarly, only few Western states have fully lived up to their responsibility under the VDPA to treat economic, social, and cultural rights on an equal level with civil and political rights in their respective domestic and constitutional systems. In the same vein, many Asian states continue to speak about "Asian values" that are allegedly difficult to reconcile with "Western human rights standards" and, thereby, deny the universality of human rights.

From Standard-Setting to Implementation and Mainstreaming of Human Rights

The fall of the Iron Curtain not only led to a new synthesis between the Western and the Socialist human rights concepts. It also opened a window of opportunity to move from mere standard-setting to the implementation of human rights and their realization on the ground.[70] The three main goals and objectives of the United Nations, namely international peace and security, development, and human rights, moved much closer to each other, and human rights started to be mainstreamed into all UN policy areas. With the newly created concept of human development, UNDP and other multilateral and bilateral development agencies accepted the full realization of human rights (freedom from want) as the ultimate goal of development and increasingly applied a human rights based approach (HRBA) to their development and poverty reduction strategies, programs, and projects. We no longer consider a state or a society as "highly developed" merely on the basis of economic indicators (economic growth, GDP per capita, and so on). "Highly developed" in fact describes today a society where as many people as possible are enabled to live a life in freedom from fear and want and are able to enjoy all human rights. This means, of course, also that development programs and strategies aim at assisting the respective partner countries in their efforts to implement international human rights standards, be it in the field of education, health, housing, elections, the media, or administration of justice.

A similar development has taken place in the direction of the concept of human security,[71] that is, enabling human beings to live in freedom from fear. With the end of the Cold War, the Security Council of the United Nations was for the first time in the history of the world organization able to fulfill its function of providing collective security to people suffering from all forms of violence. This means, first of all, armed conflicts and aggression, as in the case of the Iraqi occupation of Kuwait in 1990.[72] But the Security Council increasingly also took action under Chapter VII of the UN Charter, from economic and "smart" sanctions under Article 41 up to the authorization of military force under Article 42, in the case of humanitarian disasters, such as in Somalia in 1992,[73] as well as gross and systematic violations of human rights, such as in Libya in 2011.[74] Unfortunately, many other examples, such as the genocide in Rwanda in 1994, ethnic cleansing in Bosnia and Herzegovina between 1992 and 1995, or crimes against humanity and war crimes committed in Syria since 2011, show that the implementation of the concept of human security is far from perfect and the Security Council remains blocked in far too many cases by the veto power of its five permanent members. In order to avoid further genocides and human rights crimes in the twenty-first century, Secretary-General Kofi Annan, therefore, aimed at a fundamental reform of the United Nations, including the composition of the Security Council. Although this ambitious goal failed at the UN Summit of 2005, he succeeded at least in introducing the concept of the Responsibility to Protect (R2P),[75] and in establishing the Peace-Building Commission. As from the early 1990s, human rights were also incorporated into increasingly complex peace-keeping and peace-building operations, starting in El Salvador in 1991,[76] and followed in Cambodia in 1992,[77] Haiti in 1993,[78] and Guatemala in 1994.[79] This trend culminated in a highly complex quasi-protectorate in Bosnia and Herzegovina in 1995,[80] and UN transitional administrations established in Kosovo (after a NATO-led humanitarian intervention without Security Council authorization in 1999)[81] and in East Timor. With respect to East Timor, a former Portuguese colony occupied by Indonesia, the UN first organized a referendum in July 1999[82] that resulted in a clear vote in favor of independence from Indonesia, then authorized a military intervention to stop violence committed by pro-Indonesian militias,[83] and finally created a UN Transitional Administration (UNTAET) in October 1999,[84] which in 2002 led to the independence of Timor-Leste, supported by a further UN mission.[85]

Other major developments in the implementation of human rights achieved in the aftermath of the fall of the Iron Curtain include the creation of the UN High Commissioner for Human Rights as the UN office with primary responsibility for implementing the comprehensive human rights program of the VDPA, mainstreaming human rights into all policy areas of the United Nations, and operating field presences in an increasing number of countries in all world regions. In 2006, the former UN Commission on

Human Rights was replaced by the Human Rights Council as a subsidiary body of the General Assembly,[86] meeting almost permanently in Geneva as the main political body of the world organization dealing with a broad range of human rights issues, including human rights emergencies, establishing in addition to its country-specific and thematic special rapporteurs and other special procedures also high level human rights fact-finding commissions, such as presently in Syria, and conducting a Universal Periodic Review of the human rights performance of all 193 member states of the United Nations.

The domestic human rights architecture was strengthened by the creation of national human rights institutions in accordance with the Paris Principles adopted by the UN General Assembly in December 1993.[87] More than half of all states have set up under their constitutions or in their domestic legal systems independent national human rights commissions, advisory committees, human rights institutes, or ombuds-institutions with the explicit mandate of promoting and protecting human rights, coordinating their activities with international human rights monitoring bodies, and acting as a sort of clearinghouse between governments, civil society, and international organizations.

The establishment of ad hoc International Criminal Tribunals for the former Yugoslavia in 1993[88] and for Rwanda in 1994[89] paved the way for the creation of a permanent International Criminal Court (ICC) in The Hague on the basis of a multilateral treaty (the Rome Statute), which was adopted after long and difficult negotiations in 1998 and entered into force in 2002. The ICC is not only competent to bring perpetrators of war crimes and the crime of aggression (crimes against the peace) to justice, but also perpetrators of genocide[90] and other gross and systematic violations of human rights (crimes against humanity). Since the establishment of the ad hoc tribunals, similar hybrid courts (in Sierra Leone and Cambodia), and the ICC, some of the key figures responsible for these worst of crimes crimes have been brought to justice, including former Yugoslav president Slobodan Milošević; the political and military leaders of the Bosnian Serbs responsible for the genocide in Srebrenica, Radovan Karadžić and Ratko Mladić; former prime minister of Rwanda, Jean Kambanda; former president of Liberia, Charles Taylor; former president of Côte d'Ivoire, Laurent Gbagbo; and many leaders of paramilitary groups and commanders of concentration camps.

The Cold War Conference on Security and Cooperation in Europe (CSCE) established in 1975 by the Helsinki Final Act was in 1994 replaced by the Organization for Security and Cooperation in Europe (OSCE) with permanent structures, based on a comprehensive security concept with human rights as a major component. With its silent diplomacy (e.g., by the High Commissioner for National Minorities), election monitoring (by the Office for Democratic Institutions and Human Rights), and long-term field missions in postconflict situations, such as Bosnia and Kosovo, the OSCE played an important role in strengthening human rights and democracy in Central and Eastern Europe as well as Central Asia during the 1990s. The oldest European organization, the Council of Europe, experienced during the 1990s a rapid enlargement toward Central and Eastern Europe, which increased its membership from twenty-three Western European states in 1989 to presently forty-seven states, covering all European states, including the Russian Federation, Georgia, Armenia, Azerbaijan, and Turkey, with Belarus the only exception. As a precondition for being admitted to the Council of Europe, all new member states had to ratify the European Convention on Human Rights (ECHR) and the European Convention for the Prevention of Torture (ECPT), thereby accepting the compulsory jurisdiction of the European Court of Human Rights to decide on interstate and individual complaints, the competence of the Committee for the Prevention of Torture (CPT) to carry out preventive visits to all places of detention, and the obligation to abolish the death penalty. Apart from Belarus, Europe is the first world region where the death penalty has been successfully eradicated.

The end of the Cold War also led to the recognition of the right of individual petition under all core UN human rights treaties (including the CESCR in 2008 and the Convention on the Rights of the Child [CRC] in 2011); the creation of a full-time European Court of Human Rights, replacing the former Commission and Court in 1998, with the power to directly hear and decide on individual complaints alleging a violation of the European Convention on Human Rights (ECHR) by any of the roughly 800 million inhabitants of 47 European states; presently, the Strasbourg Court hands down more than 1,000 judgments and tens of thousands of other decisions per year, most of them relating to the Russian Federation, Turkey, Ukraine, and other Central and Eastern European states; the creation of an African Court on Human and Peoples' Rights in Arusha (Tanzania) by an Optional Protocol to the African Charter of Human and Peoples' Rights of 1998, which entered into force in 2004; during the 1990s, the African Commission on Human and Peoples' Rights in Banjul (Gambia) has started to hand down far-reaching decisions on individual complaints in highly complex cases; after the landmark judgment in *Velásquez Rodríguez v. Honduras* in 1988, the Inter-American Court of Human Rights in San José (Costa Rica) has developed a remarkable jurisprudence on gross and systematic human rights violations, including summary executions, torture, and enforced disappearances, on indigenous peoples' rights and other highly political issues.

In recent years, we witness also the creation of subregional systems for the protection of human rights: even in regions that are usually not well known for their interest in human rights, some cautious developments can be observed. The Association of Southeast Asian Nations (ASEAN) in 2007 adopted an ASEAN Charter underlying the principles of democracy, good governance, the rule of law, and human rights, and in 2010 established an Intergovernmental Commission on Human Rights consisting of experts from the ten member states. In 2004, the League of Arab States adopted an Arab Charter of Human Rights, which entered into force in 2008 and has been monitored since 2011 by an Arab Human Rights Committee consisting of seven experts. In 2014, the League of Arab States even decided to establish an Arab Court of Human Rights. The Economic Community of West African States (ECOWAS) empowered its community court in 2005 by means of an Additional Protocol to the ECOWAS Court with contentious jurisdiction on allegations of human rights violations and an individual complaints procedure.

Despite these impressive achievements in the protection and implementation of human rights since the end of the Cold War, we observe a huge and, to some extent further growing, gap between the high aspirations of the international human rights movement and the sobering reality on the ground. Certain historical events, such as the terrorist attacks on the World Trade Center in New York and the Pentagon in Washington on 11 September 2001 and the ensuing global "war on terror" launched by U.S. president George W. Bush, undermining the pillars of international humanitarian and human rights law, or the global financial and economic crisis of 2008, seemed to have a devastating long-term effect on the universal human rights program. Very promising civil society actions and revolutions at the beginning of the second decade of the twenty-first century, such as the Arab Spring in Tunisia, Egypt, Libya, Bahrain, Yemen, Syria, and other Arab countries, and the global Occupy movement which had spread from Wall Street to all world regions, have lost much of their revolutionary energy in the wake of military repression in Egypt, Syria, and other Arab countries, and the stabilization of global financial markets by taxpayers' money without any serious attempt to learn the lessons from these global crises and fundamentally reform the global economic, trade, and financial system. In countries under the direct influence of the Russian Federation, such as Georgia, Ukraine, Belarus, and Moldova, President Vladimir Putin seems even to be determined to destroy the common European house built on the ashes of Communism and the Cold War by his predecessors and to revive another "Soviet Union" under Russian hegemony. Looking back in retrospect twenty-seven years after the collapse of Communism in Europe, it seems that the window of opportunity of 1989 to establish a "social and international order in which the rights and freedoms set forth in this Declaration can be fully realized," as envisaged in Article 28 UDHR, has not been used. In the following, we will analyze some of the reasons for this failure of the international community as well as the prospects of opening another window of opportunity in the future.

Chapter 2

Did the West Comply with the Vienna Compromise?

Equality, Indivisibility, and Interdependence of All Human Rights

In order to persuade the countries of the Global South to accept the universality of human rights, the Global North (which in the 1990s also included the Russian Federation) solemnly declared at the Vienna World Conference on Human Rights in 1993 that all human rights are indivisible, interdependent, and interrelated and that the "international community must treat human rights globally in a fair and equal manner, on the same footing, and with the same emphasis."[1] Equality of all human rights means that economic, social, and cultural rights shall be legally recognized, respected, protected, and fulfilled in the same manner as civil and political rights. The United States, which under the Clinton administration fully accepted the Vienna compromise, however, never made any serious attempt to ratify the CESCR or to accept economic, social, and cultural rights as part of its domestic legal order.[2] Similarly, China has so far failed to ratify the CCPR despite the Vienna compromise. But most other states, including all European states, ratified both Covenants simultaneously, thereby taking seriously the request of the General Assembly of 1951 to treat both Covenants (called the International Bill of Human Rights) as one unit. While the Socialist concept of human rights was based on the assumption that the rights to work, social security, health, education, and other economic, social, and cultural rights could only be fulfilled in a Socialist planned economy, this assumption is not reflected in the text of the CESCR. The *travaux préparatoires* of the UDHR and the CESCR show that the formulation of economic, social, and cultural rights was less influenced by representatives of the Soviet Union and its allies than by social democratic thinking in Western Europe and Latin America.

The right to work in Article 6 CESCR, to take just one example, does not require the state to assign to every citizen a workplace in a state-owned enterprise according to the requirements of a planned economy, but guarantees the "right of everyone to the opportunity to gain his living by work which he freely choses or accepts." This formulation and the corresponding state obligations in Article 6(2) that aimed "to achieve the full realization of this right" clearly show that the right to work can very well be achieved in a market economy. The right to education in Article 13 CESCR, which even includes the right to free and compulsory primary education for all children, does not exclude private schools. On the contrary, Article 13(3) explicitly recognizes the liberty of the parents to choose for their children schools "other than those established by the public authorities," and "to ensure the religious and moral education of their children in conformity with their own convictions." In Article 13(1), states parties agree that education shall be directed to the full development of the human personality and the sense of its dignity, shall strengthen the respect for human rights and fundamental freedoms, and shall enable all persons "to participate effectively in a free society." This is not the language used in Communist constitutions. It is carefully chosen language that puts a heavy burden on governments to establish and finance a public school system at the levels of primary, secondary, higher, and fundamental education and at the same time leaves enough room for individuals and bodies to establish and direct private educational institutions. Article 11 guarantees the "right of everyone to an adequate standard of living . . . and to the continuous improvement of living conditions," and Article 12 guarantees the "right of everyone to the enjoyment of the highest attainable standard of physical and mental health," including the "creation of conditions which would assure to all medical service and medical attention in the event of sickness." Taken together with the general obligation under Article 2(1) CESCR to take steps "with a view to achieving progressively the full realization of the rights recognized in the present Covenant," which can be interpreted also as a prohibition of deliberate retrogressive measures,[3] it becomes clear that the Covenant is based on the model of an advanced welfare state,[4] and that all states parties have an obligation to take steps to develop in this direction. In addition to enabling human beings to enjoy economic, social, and cultural rights, the model of the advanced welfare state also sets limits to growing inequality of income and wealth.

As discussed above, the principle of the equality, indivisibility, and interdependence of all human rights means that civil and political rights are no longer interpreted as merely negative rights against state interference, but as rights that equally require states to take the necessary legislative, administrative, judicial, political, and other positive measures, in accordance with the principles of due diligence and progressive realization, to fulfill these rights and to protect their inhabitants against violations by private parties. These positive obligations to construct a sufficient number of public court buildings and recruit a sufficient number of judges in order to provide everyone with the right of equal access to justice and a fair, public, and speedy trial, including free legal assistance in criminal proceedings in accordance with Article 14(3)(d) CCPR, or to hire and train a sufficient number of law enforcement officials to fulfill the rights to life, personal integrity, personal liberty and security, freedom of movement, privacy, and other human rights contained in the CCPR require a similar political and budgetary commitment of governments to take steps to develop in the direction of an advanced welfare state as the respective obligations under the CESCR. With the fall of the Iron Curtain in 1989 and the formal declaration of the end of the Cold War in the Paris Charter of 1990, for the first time in history a situation had emerged in which a new social and international order based upon universally recognized human rights could have been established, as envisaged in Article 28 UDHR. The effective realization of this vision at this particular moment in history seems to have depended primarily on the political will of the rich industrial nations of the Global North. This begs the question whether and to which extent the West has lived up to this high expectation.

The Rise of Neoliberalism

Despite a certain progress during the 1990s, as illustrated above, we have to conclude a quarter century after the end of the Cold War that the West has not lived up to this expectation and, thereby, has missed an important window of opportunity.[5] Rather than pursuing an agenda of human rights to be realized in an advanced welfare state, the West opted to pursue an agenda of neoliberalism and even pretended that neoliberalism and human rights pursued the same goals.[6] With the assistance of the international financial institutions, Western states imposed this ideological agenda on the former Communist countries in transition and on the Global South. These countries, in turn, reacted strongly against this new form of "human rights neocolonialism" by putting the very achievement of the universality of human rights into question. But mixing up neoliberalism and human rights created a dangerous myth that seriously undermined the credibility of human rights. In reality, the international financial institutions pursued their neoliberal economic policies as articulated in the so-called Washington Consensus of 1989, and rejected all attempts to integrate human rights considerations as "political."

The policies of neoliberalism have been developed since the 1960s in reaction to both Communist planned economy and social market economy, which under the influence of the economic theories of John Maynard Keynes had dominated the Western economies in the post-World War II period until the 1970s.[7] Keynes had developed his economic theory of state interventionism, countercyclical policies, and social security measures in reaction to the economic and financial crisis of the late 1920s and 1930s, the Great Depression, which was interpreted as having been caused primarily by unfettered capitalism.[8] His opponents, led by the Chicago school of economics around Friedrich von Hayek and Milton Friedman, were called "neoliberals" because their policy of privatization, deregulation, and minimizing the role of the state was based on nineteenth-century economic and political liberalism.[9] In his book *Capitalism and Freedom*, Milton Friedman does not use the term "neoliberalism" himself. But since the term "liberalism," in his eyes, had been corrupted by modern "welfare-liberals,"[10] and since he did not wish to be called "conservative,"[11] he preferred to use the term "liberalism" in its original nineteenth-century sense: "Partly because of my reluctance to surrender the term to the proponents of measures that would destroy liberty, partly because I cannot find a better alternative, I shall resolve these difficulties by using the word liberalism in its original sense—as the doctrines pertaining to a free man."[12] In 1947, the Austrian economist Friedrich von Hayek, who was at that time teaching at the London School of Economics,[13] founded the Mont Pelerin Society, named after a Swiss village where the first meeting of neoliberal intellectuals took place. There he met Milton Friedman, and in 1950 he accepted a professorship in Chicago, which became the center of a macroeconomic theory that rejected Keynesianism in favor of free market policies and little government intervention, apart from strict monetarism.[14]

In 1955, a group of Chilean students, later known as the "Chicago Boys" were invited to the University of Chicago to pursue postgraduate studies in macroeconomics. After their return to Chile during the 1960s, they were spreading the neoliberal philosophy of Hayek and Friedman in a country with a long democratic tradition that was sharply divided between conservatives and a broad and powerful left-wing movement, which tried to find a third way between capitalism and communism, a kind of "Marxism with a human face." When General Augusto Pinochet, in a military coup supported by the United States, overthrew the democratically elected Socialist government of Salvador Allende in 1973, the "Chicago Boys" got their chance to implement radical economic reforms, including extensive privatization and deregulation in the labor, social security, health, and education sectors. Among other reforms, Chile became well known as the first country that fully privatized its pension scheme, with catastrophic consequences for the poor.[15] When the Chilean example was used later by the World Bank as a model for other countries, it became a negative symbol of neoliberalism in the anti-globalization movement.

Privatization as a deliberate policy of neoliberalism became best known in the United Kingdom under the Conservative government of Margaret Thatcher during the 1980s. Under her government, and against the strong opposition of the powerful British trade unions, many traditional British state institutions, including British Telecom, Sealink ferries, British Gas, British Petroleum, British Aerospace, British Airways, British Steel, the Rover Group (formerly British Leyland), Rolls-Royce, and the regional water authorities were sold to the private sector. Under her successor, John Major, British Rail was privatized in 1993,[16] and in 1992 Wolds Prison opened as the first privately managed prison in Europe. The conservative government of Ronald Reagan in the United States had been the closest neoliberal ally of the Thatcher government. Although there were considerably fewer state-run institutions to be privatized in the United States, neoliberalism has had a strong impact on deregulation and privatization in the United States since the 1980s too. For instance, in 1984 the Corrections Corporation of America (CCA) was the first private company to take over the operation of a public jail in Tennessee. Since then, the trend toward privately operated correctional facilities has continued as a prison business with huge profits, as has the trend toward private military and security companies. Under the influence of "Thatcherism" and "Reaganomics," neoliberalism, privatization, and deregulation rapidly became a global phenomenon.

The Washington Consensus

In 1989, British economist John Williamson coined the term "Washington Consensus" in a background paper for a conference that the Institute for International Economics had convened in the very year of the collapse of Communism in Europe, in order to examine the extent to which the old ideas of development economics that had governed Latin American economic policy since the 1950s were being swept aside by neoliberal policies.[17] The ten reforms he listed in his background paper were the following: fiscal discipline, reordering public expenditure priorities, tax reform, liberalizing interest rates, a competitive exchange rate, trade liberalization, liberalization of inward foreign direct investment, privatization, deregulation, and property rights.[18] He labeled these ten points the Washington Consensus because he "thought more or less everyone in Washington would agree (they) were needed more or less everywhere in Latin America."[19] The Washington Consensus became known as the set of views about effective development strategies applied by the Washington-based institutions, above all the International Monetary Fund (IMF), the World Bank, and the U.S. Treasury. It focuses primarily on privatization, deregulation, and macrostability, that is, price stability. But it also includes some forms of liberalization not yet included in the original definition, such as capital market liberalization. As Narcís Serra, Shari Spiegel, and Joseph Stiglitz wrote in their introduction to *The Washington Consensus Reconsidered*, which sharply criticizes these policies and which aimed at achieving a new "Barcelona Consensus" on the kinds of economic policies that would best promote development of the poorest countries of the world, "the Washington Consensus has come to be associated with 'market fundamentalism,' the view that markets solve most, if not all, economic problems by themselves."[20]

The Washington Consensus formed the basis for the neoliberal development agenda of the international financial institutions, including comprehensive structural adjustment policies, during the 1990s and, despite growing criticism, in principle also thereafter. As is comprehensively documented by many economic and other studies,[21] the structural adjustment policies have forced the poor countries to carry out deep cuts into their health, education, or social security budgets, which led to growing poverty and inequality,[22] above all in sub-Saharan Africa and Latin America. The neoliberal policies of privatization went far beyond state-owned industries and affected many sectors which were traditionally considered "inherent government functions" or "core state functions," including public utilities, such as gas, electricity, mail and telecommunication, public broadcasting, public rail, buses, airlines and other means of public transport,[23] public schools,[24] public health systems,[25] public pension funds[26] and other social security networks, public water management,[27] law enforcement bodies, prisons,[28] the military,[29] and even the judiciary. While these neoliberal policies may also have led to economic growth and, thereby, contributed to poverty reduction in certain countries, there can be no doubt that they also contributed to corruption, most notably in Africa, Latin America, the Russian Federation, and other former Communist countries, and to austerity policies and the global crises of the last twenty years, including global water, food, prison, humanitarian, financial, and general economic crises. In the context of the present study, the focus will be put on the effects of these neoliberal policies on the protection and enjoyment of human rights and on the implementation of the respective obligations of states under international and regional human rights treaties. There is a wealth of literature on neoliberalism and privatization from the perspective of economic, political, and other social sciences, including law, but only relatively little literature and jurisprudence on privatization from a human rights perspective. This seems surprising in view of the fact that the rise of universal human rights law and the rise of neoliberalism in the age of globalization can be considered as the two main political developments in the second half of the twentieth century.[30] When privatization is addressed from a human rights perspective, the relevant literature and case law usually focus on the effects of privatization on human rights, most notably emphasizing that the state cannot avoid its responsibility under international human rights law by merely privatizing certain functions and services,[31] but the question to which extent international human rights law would constitute a barrier to excessive privatization projects has been rarely addressed. This might have to do with a generally held view often repeated as a kind of mantra, that international human rights law is "neutral" in relation to privatization.[32] The following analysis will also put this hypothesis under scrutiny.

Is Human Rights Law "Neutral" Toward Privatization?

Under international law, states are the primary duty-bearers responsible for the respect, fulfillment, and protection of human rights. Other entities, including intergovernmental organizations and transnational corporations, may have certain direct obligations under international human rights law, but can only to a very limited extent be held directly responsible for human rights violations.[33] When the UN was founded after World War II and recognized human rights as one of its main aims and objectives, it was clear that states would bear the main responsibility for both respecting and ensuring the enjoyment of human rights. The idea of John Locke and other philosophers of the Enlightenment that the protection of human rights constitutes the main legitimacy of governments, which was first put in practice on the domestic level during the French and American revolutions, was accepted by the international community in the aftermath of World War II and the Holocaust, but this time with a much broader human rights agenda that took into account the shortcomings of purely Western human rights thinking during the age of industrialization. The UN envisaged a new world order in which states undertook to ensure freedom from fear and freedom from want for all human beings. The role of the UN and other intergovernmental organizations was to assist states in their endeavors, to monitor them and only in exceptional circumstances to intervene in domestic policies. But the main burden of ensuring that human beings can effectively enjoy human rights rests upon states and individual governments. This vision was codified in the International Bill of Human Rights and many other universal and regional human rights treaties.

When the two Covenants were drafted during the 1950s and 1960s, the idea of the advanced welfare state was the dominant goal to be achieved, irrespective of the ideological differences between Socialist and Western states. The Socialist states aimed at realizing this goal through a planned economy, whereas in the West the macroeconomic theory of Keynes, based on state intervention to ensure a social market economy, dominated the political and economic agenda. This explains the fact that both Covenants were, after a long and controversial drafting history, finally adopted by consensus in 1966. At that time, neoliberal economic philosophy was still in its infancy. Despite the rise of neoliberal economic theories and practice during the 1970s and 1980s, the compromise of 1966 was reaffirmed and even strengthened in the Vienna Consensus after the collapse of Communism by explicitly recognizing the universality, equality, indivisibility, and interdependence of all human rights. It is, therefore, legitimate to scrutinize the legality and legitimacy of neoliberal policies, above all far-reaching privatization measures, in relation to the universally recognized and legally binding normative framework of international human rights law.

What does it mean that international human rights law is "neutral" vis-à-vis privatization? Felipe Gómez and others refer in this respect to the well-known General Comment No. 3 of the Committee on Economic, Social and Cultural Rights on the nature of states parties obligations under Article 2(1) of the CESCR.[34] However, this authoritative interpretation of the words "to take steps, individually and through international assistance and cooperation, especially economic and technical, to the maximum of its available resources, with a view to achieving progressively the full realization of the rights recognized in the present Covenant by all appropriate means, including particularly the adoption of legislative measures" in Article 2(1) does not contain any reference to privatization. Section 8 of the GenC reads as follows:

> The Committee notes that the undertaking "to take steps . . . by all appropriate means including particularly the adoption of legislative measures" neither requires nor precludes any particular form of government or economic system being used as a vehicle for the steps in question, provided only that it is democratic and that all human rights are thereby respected. Thus, in terms of political and economic systems the Covenant is neutral and its principles cannot accurately be described as being predicated exclusively on the need for, or the desirability of a, socialist or a capitalist system, or a mixed, centrally planned, or laissez-faire economy, or upon any other particular approach. In this regard, the Committee reaffirms that the rights recognized in the Covenant are susceptible of realization within the context of a wide variety of economic and political systems, provided only that the interdependence and indivisibility of the two sets of human rights, as affirmed *inter alia* in the preamble to the Covenant, is recognized and reflected in the system in question. The Committee also notes the relevance in this regard of other human rights and in particular the right to development.

This GenC was adopted in 1990 and, therefore, still carefully reflects the spirit of the Cold War and the credo that economic, social, and cultural rights could be realized in both socialist and capitalist economic systems. The term "neutral" is only used in order to stress this equality between the two most prevalent economic systems in the world. After all, the Soviet Union was still in existence in 1990, and nobody could predict in which direction the Central and Eastern European countries would develop economically. The Committee further referred to a mixed, centrally planned or "laissez-faire" economy. But it also stressed as a precondition for compliance of states with their obligations in Article 2(1) CESCR that the form of government is democratic and that all human rights are thereby respected, referring in this respect also to the interdependence and indivisibility of human rights, that is, to the fact that economic, social, and cultural rights should not be realized to the detriment of civil and political rights. Furthermore, the right to development, which aims at "economic, social, cultural and political development, in which all human rights and fundamental freedoms can be fully realized,"[35] should be taken into account. Since Article 2(1) CESCR speaks of the duty of "progressive realization," the Committee further stressed that "any deliberate retrogressive measures in that regard would require the most careful consideration and would need to be fully justified by reference to the totality of the rights provided for in the Covenant and in the context of the full use of the maximum available resources."[36]

A careful analysis of GenC 3, in my opinion, does not support the hypothesis that the Covenant is "neutral" on privatization. Privatization is not a particular type of economic system. It is a measure deliberately taken by governments in a socialist, a capitalist, a mixed, or any other economic system in order to transfer ownership from the public to the private sector or to contract out certain services to the private sector, which were before provided by the public sector.[37] Privatization aims at changing the existing situation, usually because governments believe that certain services can be more effectively or at least more cheaply provided by the private as compared to the public sector. Many forms of privatization have no or only very limited impact on the enjoyment of human rights. When steel or coal industries, banks, or airlines are privatized, this has, at first sight, no direct impact on human rights. Nevertheless, the right to work or conditions of work may be affected if the respective private owners immediately start a major restructuring by which many workers are dismissed, holidays and wages are reduced, and working conditions are made less safe and healthy. In order to prevent these detrimental effects, governments have an obligation, already during the privatization process, to ensure that the minimum standards of the right to work and rights in work in accordance with Articles 6 and 7 CESCR are upheld. If such preventive measures are not taken, even these forms of privatization may be considered as deliberate retrogressive measures prohibited under Article 2(1) CESCR.

If privatization measures are taken, however, in an area that directly touches upon the enjoyment of economic, social, and cultural rights, such as the rights to health, education, and social security, the risk of violating the respective rights is much more evident. In this case, such privatization measures must be assessed in relation to the obligation of states to take steps with a view to "achieving progressively the full realization" of the respective rights. In other words, international human rights constitute a normative framework which is not static but which aims at the progressive realization of human rights. As explained above, the duty of progressive realization applies not only to economic, social, and cultural rights, but to all positive obligations of states deriving from international human rights law, that is, also to civil and political rights. The ultimate aim of this dynamic system of international human rights development is defined in Article 28 UDHR as "a social and international order in which the rights and freedoms set forth in this Declaration can be fully realized." Similar wording can be found in other instruments, including the Declaration on the Right to Development.

Just to give one example in the context of civil and political rights: the right to life in Article 6 CCPR clearly aims at the gradual abolition of capital punishment.[38] The drafters of the Covenant were aware that this is a long-term goal, as many states at that time were not yet at a stage of development in which they were able or willing to abolish the death penalty immediately. In *Judge v. Canada*, the Human Rights Committee adopted a dynamic approach and decided that states which had already abolished the death penalty were legally prevented from reintroducing it since this would constitute a clearly retrogressive measure.[39] They are also prevented from extraditing or expelling persons to another state where they would face a serious risk of being sentenced to death or executed. The trend toward abolition of capital punishment can also be seen in the adoption of various protocols to the CCPR, ECHR, and ACHR as well as in the adoption of biannual resolutions by the UN General Assembly calling all states to gradually abolish the death penalty and at least to introduce a moratorium. In fact, a growing number of states have responded to this trend and have, de jure or at least de facto, abolished capital punishment.[40]

On a more general note, the Human Rights Committee in 1997 adopted General Comment 26 on issues relating to the continuity of obligations to the International Covenant on Civil and Political Rights,[41] where it held that the Covenant, being part of the International Bill of Rights, "does not have a temporary character typical of treaties where a right of denunciation is deemed to be admitted."[42] It justified this opinion by the fact that the rights enshrined in the Covenant belong to the people living on the territory of the state party. Once the people are accorded the protection of the rights under the Covenant, "such protection devolves with territory and continues to belong to them, notwithstanding change in Government of the state party, including dismemberment in more than one state or state succession or any subsequent action of the state party designed to divest them of the rights guaranteed by the Covenant."[43]

Since the Human Rights Committee referred to the International Bill of Rights, we must assume that the same principle also applies to the CESCR. As the Committee on Economic, Social and Cultural Rights has stressed in GenC 3, deliberate retrogressive measures can only be justified in truly exceptional circumstances, for example, when a poor country gives absolute priority to the realization of one right, such as primary education, and therefore, for a limited time, reduces budgetary means appropriated to another human right. All states parties to the Covenants, whatever their respective level of development and their state of compliance with human rights at the time the Covenants entered into force for them, have a binding legal obligation to take steps, to the maximum of their available resources, to further improve the level of enjoyment of human rights for all human beings subject to their jurisdiction. One can certainly not exclude that privatization of public services, in the particular circumstances prevailing in a country at a certain time, might lead to a further enhancement of human rights. But one can certainly also not assume that privatization, as a general rule, would lead to a better realization of human rights. Unfortunately, the history of privatization during the last thirty years, in both highly developed and less developed countries, illustrates too many examples where privatization has led to growing inequality and significant deteriorations in the enjoyment of human rights, as will be further discussed below.

In order to live up to their legal obligation to progressively improve the enjoyment of human rights, states would have to carry out a thorough human rights assessment before they start a privatization process, in particular in areas that directly affect human rights.[44] Privatization would only be acceptable under international human rights law if states, after having conducted such a human rights assessment, could prove a high probability that the respective privatization process will lead to the further progressive realization of human rights, not only for a few rich people, but for the population as a whole, and for the poor, excluded, discriminated, and disadvantaged segments of society in particular. In any case, states would have to ensure that the minimum core content of every human right concerned will be respected and fulfilled.[45] They would also have to guarantee that victims of human rights violations enjoy at least to the same degree their procedural right to a remedy and reparation in case their substantive rights have been violated.[46] One of the big achievements of human rights is the recognition of the right of victims to an effective, above all judicial, remedy against the state if they allege that governmental authorities have violated their human rights by a certain action or omission. Should the respective court or other governmental monitoring body find a violation of any human right, the victims also have a right to be granted reparation, including restitution, compensation, rehabilitation, and other forms of satisfaction, for the harm suffered.[47]

In the case of privatization, the respective state duty regularly shifts from an obligation to respect to an obligation to protect, which usually is more difficult for victims to contest. To take an example: if the state privatizes all public elementary schools in a certain district, and the private operators introduce school fees, this would clearly amount to a violation of Article 13(2)(a) CESCR. But in order to hold the government accountable for this human rights violation, the parents would have to prove that the state violated its obligation to protect by applying the test of the due diligence principle. This means that they would have to prove that the government had not taken all necessary measures that could reasonably be expected from public authorities in the particular circumstances of the case to force the private school operator to refrain from collecting school fees. If public elementary schools would, on the other hand, require parents to pay school fees, they could directly invoke this violation of the respective obligation to respect before domestic courts and, if need be, before international human rights monitoring bodies. Even though international monitoring bodies have repeatedly stressed that states cannot avoid their human rights obligations toward individuals by simply contracting out public services to private contractors or selling public assets to private companies,[48] the fact remains that, owing to the special remedies available for victims to hold government authorities accountable for human rights violations, it is usually more difficult to hold transnational corporations and other private actors accountable under domestic and international law.[49]

Taking all these arguments together, it seems difficult to maintain the hypothesis that international human rights law is "neutral" vis-à-vis privatization. International human rights law, as it was created in reaction to the Holocaust and the systematic human rights violations during World War II, and later codified in a growing number of international and regional human rights treaties, is a dynamic legally binding normative framework aimed at the progressive realization and improvement of the enjoyment of all human rights by all human beings on our planet. Under present international law, states are the primary duty-bearers and other entities, including intergovernmental organizations and transnational corporations, can, if at all, only indirectly be held accountable for violations and nonfulfillment of human rights. Privatizing governmental functions that are essential for the enjoyment and progressive improvement of human rights, therefore, in principle constitutes a violation of the respective state obligations to respect, protect, and fulfill human rights, unless the state can prove, after having conducted a thorough human rights impact assessment, that the respective private service provider respects, protects, and fulfills the human rights concerned at least to the same extent as the public service provider, and can also be held accountable for human rights violations at least in the same manner as the government. In the following, a more detailed analysis of some of the rights most often affected by privatization processes will be conducted with a view to establish the limits of privatization on the basis of the respective state obligations, taking into account some of the practical experiences with privatization during the last thirty years.

PART II

Privatization and Selected Human Rights

Chapter 3

Right to Education

Scope and Content of the Right to Education

The right to education is one of the most important rights, as its effective enjoyment is a precondition for the enjoyment of most other human rights, such as the rights to work and social security, freedom of expression and information, or the right to participate actively in the political, economic, social, and cultural ways of life.[1] Katarina Tomaševski, the first Special Rapporteur on the Right to Education, called it a "multiplier right," as it enhances the enjoyment of other rights, "while depriving people of the enjoyment of many rights and freedoms where the right to education is denied or violated."[2] In its General Comment No. 13, the Committee on Economic, Social and Cultural Rights called it an "empowerment right," as "education is the primary vehicle by which economically and socially marginalized adults and children can lift themselves out of poverty and obtain the means to participate fully in their communities."[3] As the most prominent cultural right, the right to education is included in most instruments dealing with economic, social, and cultural rights, above all Articles 13 and 14 CESCR, but it is also laid down in certain instruments on civil and political rights, such as Article 2 of the 1st Additional Protocol (AP) to the ECHR. This illustrates that the right to education has both socialist roots, above all the obligation of states to provide free public education for all children, and liberal roots, namely the right of parents, religious bodies, and other private entities to establish and direct private schools. Since the right to education is primarily directed at children, it plays also a prominent role in Articles 28 and 29 CRC. UNESCO, the UN specialized agency dealing with education, science, and culture, had a major impact on developing, defining, and implementing the right to education, most notably by adopting the UNESCO Convention against Discrimination in Education of 1960.[4] As an "empowerment right," the right to education figures also prominently in the Millennium Development Goals 2000, which aimed at full realization of universal primary education by the year 2015. Similarly, when adopting its Agenda 2030 with a total of 17 sustainable development goals (SDGs), the UN General Assembly in September 2015 agreed in its SDG 4 to "ensure inclusive and equitable quality education and promote lifelong learning opportunities for all."[5] The following analysis of the respective state obligations and possible barriers to privatization of educational institutions will focus on Articles 13 and 14 CESCR and Articles 28 and 29 CRC, which are modeled upon the CESCR.

In her preliminary report as Special Rapporteur on the Right to Education of 1999, Katarina Tomaševski had proposed the 4-A Scheme of availability, accessibility, acceptability, and adaptability as the four essential features that primary schools should exhibit.[6] This analytical tool of state obligations has also been adopted by the CESCR Committee,[7] extended to other economic, social, and cultural rights,[8] and is today also widely accepted in the relevant literature. Availability means that states have to ensure that there are a sufficient number of educational institutions (buildings) with safe drinking water, sanitation facilities, trained teachers, teaching materials, and so forth. Accessibility requires states to ensure that everyone has equal access, without discrimination on any ground, to educational institutions and programs, including physical and economic accessibility. In order to facilitate economic accessibility, Articles 13(2) CESCR and 28(1) CRC require that primary education shall be "compulsory and available free to all," and that states shall take steps to ensure the progressive introduction of free secondary and higher education. If states parties to the CESCR, at the time of becoming a party, have not been able to secure compulsory primary education, free of charge, they are obliged under Article 14 "to work out and adopt a detailed plan of action for the progressive implementation, within a reasonable number of years, to be fixed in the plan, of the principle of compulsory education free of charge for all."[9] Since achieving free and compulsory education might require for poor countries international assistance and cooperation, as envisaged in Articles 2(1) CESCR and 28(3) CRC, the goals of achieving universal primary education by 2015 and eliminating gender disparity in primary and secondary education preferably by 2005, and at all levels by 2015, figure prominently in the

Millennium Development Goals solemnly adopted by the Heads of State and Government of UN member states in 2000. Acceptability relates to the form and substance of education, including the quality of curricula and teaching methods, taking into account cultural differences and the right of parents to ensure the religious and moral education of their children in conformity with their own convictions.[10] Adaptability means that education shall be flexible so it can adapt to the needs of changing societies and communities and respond to needs of students within their diverse social and cultural settings.

Irrespective of the need for cultural differences, adaptability, and flexibility of school curricula, it is interesting to note that Article 13(1) defines the substance and aim of education in a fairly detailed manner. States agree that "education shall be directed to the full development of the human personality and the sense of its dignity, and shall strengthen the respect for human rights and fundamental freedoms. They further agree that education shall enable all persons to participate effectively in a free society, promote understanding, tolerance and friendship among all nations and all racial, ethnic or religious groups, and further the activities of the United Nations for the maintenance of peace." Article 29 CRC adds to these goals that education of the child shall be directed to the "development of the child's personality, talents and mental and physical abilities to their fullest potential," to the "development of respect for the child's parents, his or her own cultural identity, language, and values, for the national values of the country in which the child is living, the country from which he or she may originate, and for civilizations different from his or her own," and the "development of respect for the natural environment."

In its General Comment 3 of 1990, the Committee on Economic, Social and Cultural Rights introduced the idea of minimum core obligations to ensure the satisfaction of, at the very least, minimum essential levels of each right. With respect to the right to education, the Committee defined this core as follows:[11] "to ensure the right of access to public educational institutions and programs on a nondiscriminatory basis; to ensure that education conforms to the objectives set out in Article 13(1); to provide primary education for all in accordance with Article 13(2)(a); to adopt and implement a national education strategy which includes provision for secondary, higher and fundamental education; and to ensure free choice of education without interference from the state or third parties, subject to conformity with 'minimum educational standards'" (Art. 13(3) and (4)).

In view of these detailed provisions and minimum core obligations laid down in international human rights law, the question arises to what extent states may privatize the public education system. On the one hand, Articles 13(4) CESCR and 29(2) CRC explicitly recognize the "liberty of individuals and bodies to establish and direct educational institutions." This human right to run private schools, which we do not find in the formulation of other human rights, has to be read in connection with the liberty of parents under Articles 13(3) CESCR, 18(4) CCPR and 2 1st AP to the ECHR, to choose for their children schools, other than those established by the public authorities, to "ensure the religious and moral education of their children in conformity with their own convictions."[12] While Article 13(3) CESCR acknowledges the existence of private schools, para. 4 was added during the negotiations in the Third Committee of the General Assembly as an explicit right to found and run private schools.[13] The drafters of these provisions had, therefore, primarily private schools in mind which were to be established by religious communities, not necessarily private schools run for profit. Nevertheless, the Committee on Economic, Social and Cultural Rights stressed that this provision "includes the right to establish and direct all types of educational institutions, including nurseries, universities and institutions for adult education."[14] This certainly also includes private schools run for profit. But the Committee added that, given "the principles of non-discrimination, equal opportunity and effective participation in society for all, the State has an obligation to ensure that the liberty set out in article 13(4) does not lead to extreme disparities of educational opportunity for some groups in society."[15]

Privatization in the Field of Education

Under the influence of neoliberalism, public education was also affected by recent moves toward greater privatization, above all in the United States and in the Global South, driven by structural adjustment policies of the World Bank and the IMF. In his famous book *Capitalism and Freedom*, Milton Friedman already advocated in 1962 far-reaching privatization of public schools:[16]

> Governments could require a minimum level of schooling financed
> by giving parents vouchers redeemable for a specified maximum

sum per child per year if spent on 'approved' educational services. Parents would then be free to spend this sum and any additional sum they themselves provided on purchasing educational services from an 'approved' institution of their own choice. The educational services could be rendered by private enterprises operated for profit, or by non-profit institutions. The role of the government would be limited to insuring that the schools met certain minimum standards, such as the inclusion of a minimum common content in their programs, much as it now inspects restaurants to insure that they maintain minimum sanitary standards.

In the United States, which is not a party to the CESCR or to the CRC and, therefore, not legally bound by the detailed provisions on the human right to education, this idea was taken up to a certain extent by establishing charter schools, by private management of public schools by so-called educational management organizations (EMOs), and by voucher programs.[17] Charter schools are publicly funded schools allowed to operate free from many of the rules governing traditional public schools. They are usually established on the initiative of private individuals or groups, headed by private boards, and a significant number are managed by EMOs, usually for-profit entities. Under voucher plans, the government provides a set amount of public funding per student to help cover tuition at private or out-of-district public schools. Research shows that overwhelmingly, students obtaining vouchers enroll in sectarian schools, which is a reflection of the religious character of most private schools in the United States and can also be explained by the low subsidies provided under these plans, which generally are only sufficient to cover tuition at religious schools.[18] Even in the United States, the number of publicly funded voucher plans remains fairly limited, partly because of obstacles under constitutional law.[19] The most prominent example of contracting out the management of public schools to EMOs are the Edison Schools in the United States, which started in 1995 to take over the management of a public school in Sherman, Texas, and have managed to gain a growing number of management contracts in the United States, partly also in the UK.[20] This highly controversial form of privatization has usually taken place in poorly performing public schools. But experience shows that management by for-profit management organizations, such as Edison Schools, has usually not improved the performance of these schools but led, instead, to further disparities of educational opportunities,[21] which the CESCR-Committee explicitly wishes to avoid. Similarly, assessment reports about charter schools suggest that pupils in public schools performed better in math and reading than those in charter schools.[22]

Voucher systems have also been used in other countries, including Sweden, Chile, and Colombia.[23] In 2001, the Committee on Economic, Social and Cultural Rights urged Sweden in its concluding observations in the state reporting procedure to "ensure that education in independent schools, including those that have been established in form of private companies with shareholders, is in full conformity with Article 13, in particular article 13.1 on educational aims and objectives, of ICESCR and with CESCR General Comment No. 13."[24] But General Comment 13, unfortunately, does not directly address the issue of privatization and its limits. Apart from the warning related to Article 13(4) that states shall ensure that the liberty to establish and direct private educational institutions "does not lead to extreme disparities of educational opportunity for some groups in society,"[25] there are only a few indirect indications about what the Committee thinks about privatization. Section 53 states that the "obligation to pursue actively the 'development of a system of schools at all levels' reinforces the principal responsibility of States parties to ensure the direct provision of the right to education in most circumstances," thereby referring to a well-known observation by UNICEF, *The State of the World's Children*, 1999: "Only the State . . . can pull together all the components into a coherent but flexible education system."[26] The active role of the state is also underlined in § 50, where the Committee stresses the obligation to "fulfil (provide) the availability of education by actively developing a system of schools, including building classrooms, delivering programs, providing teaching materials, training teachers and paying them domestically competitive salaries." Finally, the Committee emphasizes "a strong assumption of impermissibility of any retrogressive measures taken in relation to the right to education, as well as other rights in the Covenant. If any deliberately retrogressive measures are taken, the State party has the burden of proving that they have been introduced after the most careful consideration of all alternatives and that they are fully justified by reference to the totality of the rights provided for in the Covenant and in the context of the full use of the State party's maximum available resources."[27]

Limits of Privatization in the Education Sector

Fons Coomans and Antenor Hallo de Wolf provided a fairly thorough analysis of the limits of privatization of education under international human rights law. After having reviewed different methods of privatizing schools and various practical examples, both authors conclude that "privatization of education services is not prohibited by international human rights law."[28] But the state "should see to it that minimum core obligations are met. This means that privatized education has to be accessible (physically and economically) under all circumstances. . . . It is also crucial that the overall quality level of education (of state organized and privatized institutions) is to be guaranteed, once a process of privatization has started. . . . The creeping development of an impoverished public education system must be avoided."[29] Finally, both authors stress that there are "a number of functions in the area of education, which in our view, cannot be privatized, as they require a single institution to set uniform standards and monitoring procedures in a neutral and objective way. The state is the only institution that should have this legal authority and capacity. These functions relate to the recognition of diplomas, determining and approving the essentials of the curriculum of schools, the recognition of non-public schools, determining and supervising the qualifications of teachers, the monitoring and enforcement of compulsory schooling and the inspection of the quality level of education at individual schools."[30]

In my opinion, these merely standard-setting and monitoring functions are not the only tasks which the state is prevented from delegating to the private sector under present international human rights law. Even Milton Friedman, who compared educational services with services of restaurants, could have agreed with the limits of privatization, as proposed by Fons Coomans and Antenor Hallo de Wolf. But the right to education cannot be compared to the services provided by private restaurants. Of course, the right to food is as important a human right as the right to education. But there are various other means by which human beings can satisfy their right to food than by availing themselves of the services of a restaurant. States have a positive obligation to ensure that everybody has access to food in sufficient quantity and quality to satisfy minimum nutritional needs, but do not have to provide food by means of restaurant services. Educational services, on the other hand, are essential to satisfy the minimum requirements of the right to education. Since a proper school education is a prerequisite for enjoyment of various other human rights and the basis for the empowerment of human beings and the development of our children, international human rights law has laid down a highly ambitious program that needs to be achieved progressively by means of positive state action.

First of all, states have an obligation to ensure to all inhabitants, without any discrimination, free and compulsory primary education of high quality, as required by Article 13(1) CESCR. This means that there should be so many schools in both urban and rural areas that every child between six and approximately fourteen years of age is able to have physical access to such schools. In smaller villages, usually one primary school is sufficient. Since all children have a right to primary education, free of charge, and even have a duty to go to school, it is difficult to see how private schools should be able to make profits by competing with public schools. Of course, private companies may establish for-profit primary schools by charging high tuition fees, which only rich people can afford, but this does not take away the obligation of states to make available to all inhabitants primary education with high quality, free of charge. In principle, the state has no obligation to subsidize private schools, whether established for profit or not.[31] But if the state decides to provide public funding to a particular private school, it is required by the principle of equality and nondiscrimination to also provide equivalent funding to all other private schools.[32] If the state wishes to privatize public primary schools, it would have to fully subsidize these schools in order to ensure that children continue to enjoy their right to free primary education. In addition, it would have to also subsidize all other private schools in that area, including for-profit schools already existing for the rich. A voucher system usually does not cover all the costs, which means parents are expected to add money of their own. If parents are required to pay because the next available public school would be too far away and, therefore, no longer physically accessible for their children, such privatization would definitely constitute a deliberate retrogressive measure in violation of Articles 2(1) and 13(2)(a) CESCR. This conclusion is shared by the UN Special Rapporteur on the right to education, Kishore Singh.[33]

In principle, the same arguments also apply to secondary and higher education. Articles 13(2)(b) and (c) provide for the progressive introduction of free education in order to make secondary education "generally available and accessible to all" and higher education "equally accessible to all, on the basis of capacity." This is an ambitious and costly program for all states that still charge tuition and fees at their public secondary and high schools, colleges, and universities. The reintroduction of school fees would constitute a retrogressive measure. Although the physical accessibility of secondary and high schools seems to be less strict than in primary education, since older children may be more easily required to travel to their schools than six-year-old children, states have an obligation to make secondary education available and accessible (physically and economically) "by every appropriate means." This means that states have to offer a sufficient number of free public schools and universities in order to satisfy the demand within its respective population. Private secondary and high schools, including vocational and technical schools, colleges, and universities may be established in addition to public schools by private religious and other bodies and by the corporate sector, with or without fees, in addition to public schools in order to increase the choice of parents and children, but it is difficult to imagine how states could delegate their obligations to the corporate sector if they are at the same time required to progressively introduce free education. This obligation is also underlined by the UN Agenda 2030 which stipulates in its Sustainable Development Goal 4.1 that by 2030, states shall "ensure that all girls and boys complete free, equitable and quality primary and secondary education leading to relevant and effective learning outcomes." The Covenant is clearly based on the philosophical conviction that education is not a free market commodity which children shall buy by choosing between competing companies offering their respective services, as people choose between restaurants offering different cuisines, but one of the most precious services which the citizens of a respective country, represented by their democratically elected governments, shall offer to their children as a means to develop their "personality, talents and mental and physical abilities to their fullest potential," as required by Article 29(1)(a) CRC. Similarly, when Article 29(1)(c) stipulates that education shall be directed to the "development of respect for the child's parents, his or her own cultural identity, language and values, for the national values of the country in which the child is living," the drafters certainly did not have in mind education as a commodity to be sold by transnational corporations to children around the world, but a holistic public education system that varies from country to country.

In recent years, various UN human rights monitoring bodies have taken a more critical approach to the global trend of privatization in the field of education. The Committee on the Rights of the Child has, for example, requested the governments of Morocco and Ghana to assess the effect of privatization on the right to education and to provide detailed information on the reasons behind the increase in private education and the low quality of public education.[34] In July 2014, the Committee on the Elimination of Discrimination against Women organized a General Discussion on girls' and women's right to education in which the negative consequences of privatization in and of education for women and girls have been highlighted.[35] During this discussion, a wealth of empirical evidence was presented that illustrates that school fees, introduced as part of structural adjustment policies of the World Bank in the 1990s, greatly reduce the enrollment of girls more than boys.[36] In October 2014, the current UN Special Rapporteur on the right to education, Kishore Singh, presented his annual report to the UN General Assembly in which he examined the responsibility of states in the face of the "explosive growth of privatized education, in particular for-profit education."[37] He criticized that in the 1980s and 1990s, developing countries were compelled by the international financial institutions to initiate significant cuts under structural adjustments to their public services, including education. All World Bank education sector strategies, from 1999 to the current strategy for 2020, have stressed the key role of the private sector in education.[38] He also reported that the world's largest education multinational, Pearson, made an income of $7 billion in 2011 and that the top twenty education multinationals are worth a combined $36 billion.[39] The Special Rapporteur concluded that privatization "negatively affects the right to education both as an entitlement and as empowerment."[40] It is therefore "detrimental to education as a public good and vitiates the humanistic mission of education."[41] In March 2016, the Special Rapporteur strongly criticized the plan of Liberia to privatize all primary and pre-primary schools over the next five years by subcontracting these services to a private company, the Bridge International Academies. He warned that "provision of public education of good quality is a core function of the State. Abandoning this to the commercial benefit of a private company constitutes a gross violation of the right to education."[42]

Chapter 4

Right to Health

A Holistic Approach to the Right to Health

Article 25 of the UDHR puts the right to health into the broader context of the right to an adequate standard of living: "Everyone has the right to a standard of living adequate for the health and well-being of himself and his family, including food, clothing, housing and medical care and necessary social services, and the right to security in the event of unemployment, sickness, disability, widowhood, old age or other lack of livelihood in circumstances beyond his control." This broad right, closely related to the umbrella Article 22 on the right to social security and the realization of economic, social and cultural rights "indispensable for his dignity and the free development of his personality,"[1] goes back to the draft prepared by René Cassin in 1947, whose initial focus was on "the right to health, which was understood not only to require access to medical care, but also adequate food and nutrition, clothing and housing."[2] In the original draft prepared by John Humphrey, the different elements of what later became the right to an adequate standard of living had been elaborated in five different provisions. Article 35 of the Humphrey draft had provided for the right to medical care with the corresponding obligations of states to "promote public health and safety."[3] According to Johannes Morsink, this terminology "fits the Latin American socialist tradition within which Humphrey was working."[4] Countries whose constitutions included such a right at that time were either Socialist countries in Europe, including the USSR and Yugoslavia, or Latin American countries, such as Bolivia, Brazil, Cuba, Honduras, Panama, Paraguay, Peru, and Uruguay.[5] During the discussions in the UN Commission on Human Rights, due to opposition from Western countries and the Commission desire for brevity, the right to health was almost lost, but at the insistence of the USSR delegation it was finally mentioned in the context of the right to an adequate standard of living.[6]

Soon after the Commission began the task of transposing the UDHR into binding treaties, it was manifestly apparent that the rights that had been brought together in Article 25 UDHR needed to be segregated again. This led to separate rights on social security in Article 9 and on the "enjoyment of the highest attainable standard of physical and mental health" in Article 12 CESCR.[7] In its practice, the Committee on Economic, Social and Cultural Rights has, however, always emphasized that the right to health "is closely related to and dependent upon the realization of other human rights, as contained in the International Bill of Rights, including the rights to food, housing, work, education, human dignity, life, non-discrimination, equality, the prohibition against torture, privacy, access to information, and the freedoms of association, assembly and movement."[8] The Committee, therefore, adopts a holistic approach to the right to health that "embraces a wide range of socio-economic factors that promote conditions in which people can lead a healthy life, and extends to the underlying determinants of health, such as food and nutrition, housing, access to safe and potable water and adequate sanitation, safe and healthy working conditions, and a healthy environment."[9]

When drafting the right to health, the Commission originally followed the definition of health contained in the preamble to the Constitution of the World Health Organization (WHO) of 1946, which conceptualizes health as "a state of complete physical, mental and social well-being and not merely the absence of disease or infirmity."[10] Although this definition was abolished in the Third Committee of the General Assembly,[11] the CESCR Committee interprets the "highest attainable standard of physical and mental health" in this broad sense, which in any event goes beyond the right to health care. This is also underlined by the enumeration of steps to be taken by states parties to achieve full realization of this right in Article 12(2) CESCR. While much emphasis is put on the prevention of diseases, reduction of infant mortality, and improvement of environmental and industrial hygiene, equal access to medical service and attention in the event of sickness is only mentioned at the end. Whether one can, however, conclude from this list that "medical care gets bottom billing" because of "medicine's modest role in population-wide health," as Gregg Bloche argues in his attempt to downplay privatization of health care as a human rights problem,[12] is doubtful.

Traditionally, health care was primarily the responsibility of families, private charities, and religious organizations. It was only in the nineteenth century that the public health and welfare movement in Europe led to a stronger state role in providing health care.[13] In principle, we can distinguish three models of health care, which Michel Reimon and Christian Felber called the "Bismarck, Beveridge and von Hayek models."[14] The "Bismarck model" goes back to the German health insurance law of 1884 and the social security system based on compulsory contributions by employers and employees. While health care services are provided primarily by private actors such as charities and religious organizations, the state takes responsibility for the organization and financing of the health system as well as regulation, control, and monitoring of private health care providers. Apart from Germany, Austria, and Switzerland, this model has been adopted in a variety of European countries, including France and the Benelux States as well as other countries, such as Japan. The "Beveridge model" is named after the "Plan for Social Security" presented by Sir William Beveridge in 1942 to the British Parliament. It provides for a public health system financed and implemented by the state, which means that health care providers, including doctors and pharmacists, are in principle employed by the state. Apart from the well-known British public health service, this model was followed in Ireland and other European countries, including the Nordic countries, Spain, and Portugal. Most of the former Communist states in Europe also adopted this model after the end of the Cold War. The "von Hayek model" is based on the neoliberal philosophy of leaving financing and implementation of health care primarily to free market forces, that is, private insurance companies and for-profit health care providers. Despite public financing through Medicare and Medicaid, the United States is closest to this model,[15] which has been propagated worldwide in the context of globalization, deregulation, and privatization.

Is the Right to Health "Neutral" Toward Privatization?

In the following, the right to health will be analyzed in relation to the question whether it provides for certain barriers toward privatization of public health care. While the right to education obliges states parties to provide free and compulsory primary education to all children, as well as to take steps to progressively introduce secondary and higher education, free of charge, the right to health does not contain a similar obligation of states to provide for free primary health care and compulsory health insurance coverage. Since most countries, including those that consider health care financing as a public function have relied traditionally on private health care providers, some scholars, including Gregg Bloche, co-director of the Georgetown-Johns Hopkins Joint Program in Law and Public Health, argue that "privatization in itself is no more (or less) likely to fail in this regard than is public provision and financing of health services."[16] In his opinion, "Health care, in short, is a commodity, in the literal sense," and "there is no human rights case against overt commodification of health services."[17] He concludes his analysis of the relationship between the right to health and privatization as follows:

> Neither privatization nor insistence on public provision and financing of medical care offers answers to health care policy's core questions. Nor, for that matter, have efforts to define the human right to health gone far toward yielding such answers. . . . How these matters are resolved is much more important, from a human rights perspective, than whether public or private institutions provide and pay for health care. Debate over privatization risks distracting policy makers and the public from the need to commit enough resources to achieve human rights law's health aims. There is abundant evidence of global failure to make this commitment, even as the wealthiest nations spend remarkable amounts to provide rescue-oriented care near the end of life. This failure is not the fault of privatization. It is a matter of moral indifference of epic scale, given the millions of lives per year that modest investment in health programs would save.

Is it true, as Bloche argues, that the right to health is "neutral" toward privatization and does not offer any answers to health care policy's core questions? In my opinion, he grossly underestimates the normative strength of the right to health and the advanced level of interpretation provided by international human rights monitoring bodies and courts. Of course, General Comment 14, which was adopted by the Committee on Economic, Social and Cultural Rights in 2000, recognizes that health care services can be provided publicly or privately. Indeed, in most countries, health services are provided by private doctors, patients are treated in private hospitals and clinics owned and operated by charities, religious organizations, or private companies, drugs are developed and sold by transnational pharmaceutical corporations and distributed by private drug stores and pharmacies. Nevertheless, under international human rights law, states are the main duty-bearers to ensure that all people under their respective jurisdiction can enjoy the right to the highest attainable standard of health by taking the necessary steps, to the maximum of available resources, aimed at the progressive realization of this right. Like other economic, social, and cultural rights, the right to health was drafted and adopted with the aim of realizing progressively the idea of an advanced welfare state. Under the 4-A scheme, states have an obligation to ensure that health care services and facilities are available in sufficient quality and quantity and are made accessible (both physically and economically) without discrimination to all, especially the most vulnerable or marginalized sections of the population. With respect to availability, General Comment 14 reads as follows: "Functioning public health and health-care facilities, goods and services, as well as programmes, have to be available in sufficient quantity within the State party."[18] The specific obligation in Article 12(2)(d) CESCR to create "conditions which would assure to all medical service and medical attention in the event of sickness," includes, according to the CESCR Committee, the "provision of equal and timely access to basic preventive, curative, rehabilitative health services and health education; regular screening programs; appropriate treatment of prevalent diseases, illnesses, injuries, and disabilities, preferably at the community level; provision of essential drugs; and appropriate mental health treatment and care."[19] With respect to equality of access to health care,

> States have a special obligation to provide those who do not have sufficient means with the necessary health insurance and health-care facilities, and to prevent any discrimination on internationally prohibited grounds in the provision of health care and health services, especially with respect to the core obligations of the right to health. Inappropriate health resource allocation can lead to discrimination that may not be overt. For example, investments should not disproportionately favour expensive curative health services which are often accessible only to a small, privileged fraction of the population, rather than primary and preventive health care benefiting a larger part of the population.[20]

The obligation of states parties to the CESCR to protect the right to health against interference by private parties requires states to "ensure that privatization of the health sector does not constitute a threat to the availability, accessibility, acceptability and quality of health facilities, goods and services; to control the marketing of medical equipment and medicines by third parties; and to ensure that medical practitioners and other health professionals meet appropriate standards of education, skills and ethical codes of conduct." The Committee also emphasized that "States parties which are members of international financial institutions, notably the International Monetary Fund, the World Bank, and regional development banks, should pay greater attention to the protection of the right to health in influencing the lending policies, credit agreements and international measures of these institutions."[21] With respect to the core obligations under the right to health, the Committee made reference to the Alma-Ata Declaration, adopted by the International Conference on Primary Health Care in 1978, which stresses, inter alia, the right of access to primary health care by vulnerable and marginalized groups, provision of essential drugs, and adoption and implementation of a national public health strategy and plan of action.[22]

Selected Case Law and Practice Relating to the Right to Health

In states in which the right to health is directly applicable and justiciable, domestic courts, as the following cases illustrate, have not hesitated to compel their respective governments to live up to their obligations to respect, protect, and fulfill the right to health.[23] In *Mariela Visconte v. Ministry of Health and Social Welfare*, a court in Argentina ordered the government to take protective measures against hemorrhagic fever, which threatened 3.5 million people. According to the court, it was the government's responsibility to make health care available in a situation where the existing health care system, including the private sector, was not protecting individuals' health. Since the private sector saw the production of the WHO-certified vaccine Candid-1 as unprofitable, the court ruled that the government had not fulfilled its obligations under the right to health and ordered the government to produce Candid-1.[24] In *Minister of Health v. Treatment Action Campaign*, the South African Constitutional Court ruled on the economic accessibility of Nevirapine, an antiretroviral drug used to treat HIV, which could be obtained either from private medical providers or from two public research and training sites per province. The court held that the state's limited provision of Nevirapine was unreasonable and ordered the government to act without delay to provide the drug in public hospitals and clinics when medically indicated.[25] The case of *Paschim Banga Khet Mazdoor Samity v. State of West Bengal* concerned a man who had fallen from a train and suffered serious head trauma, but was refused treatment at six successive state hospitals because the hospitals had inadequate medical facilities or did not have a vacant bed or trauma and neurological services. The Supreme Court of India found that denial of timely medical treatment necessary to preserve human life in government-owned hospitals constitutes a violation of the right to life. It ruled that providing adequate medical facilities for the people is an essential part of the obligations undertaken by the government in a welfare state and it was, therefore, the duty of the state to ensure that medical facilities for emergency treatment were adequately available. It required the state to ensure that primary health care centers were equipped to provide immediate stabilizing treatment for serious injuries and emergencies. In addition, the court ordered the state to increase the number of specialists and regional clinics around the country available to treat serious injuries, and to create a centralized communication system among state hospitals so that patients could be transported immediately to the facilities where space is available.[26]

In 2001, thirty-nine pharmaceutical companies initiated legal action in the High Court of Pretoria against the government of South Africa, claiming that amendments to the Medicines Act permitting the government to override or evade existing patent rights in respect of certain essential medicines, above all antiretroviral HIV/AIDS drugs, transgressed the state's obligations under the WTO intellectual property rights regime, known as TRIPS (Trade-Related aspects of Intellectual Property rights). After a worldwide outcry ensued at the perceived rapacity of the companies in the face of a government trying to tackle an HIV/AIDS epidemic of potentially terrifying proportions, they were forced to drop the case barely two months later.[27] The companies seemed to have overlooked an exception in the TRIPS agreement that authorizes states in the case of a national emergency or other circumstances of extreme urgency to override existing patent rights, and which the government of South Africa could have successfully invoked had the case proceeded to trial. In addition, the government could have argued that the right to health, as stipulated in Article 12(2)(d) CESCR, which required it to create conditions which would assure to all medical service and medical attention in the event of sickness, must be given precedence over intellectual property rights.[28]

In September 2013, the High Court of Madrid accepted a complaint brought by a medical association against a decision by the health authorities of Madrid that in fact paralyzed the privatization process of the health system in the region of the capital of Spain.[29]

In my opinion, it is difficult to imagine how the comparably high standards of the right to health, as developed by the United Nations in accordance with the vision of an advanced welfare state and interpreted by the UN Committee on Economic, Social and Cultural Rights, the UN Special Rapporteur on the Right to Health, and other international human rights bodies, as well as domestic courts, can be fully realized in a system where the public health services are to a considerable extent privatized. In his 2012 report to the General Assembly, the Special Rapporteur on the Right to Health, Anand Grover, explicitly addressed the risks of privatization. In his judgment, "the global trend towards privatization in health systems poses significant risks to the equitable availability and accessibility of health facilities, goods and services, especially for the poor and other vulnerable and marginalized groups. In many cases, privatization has led to increased out-of-pocket payments for health goods and services, disproportionate investments in secondary and tertiary care sectors at the expense of primary health care, and increased disparity in the availability of health facilities, goods and services among rural, remote and urban areas."[30] The Special Rapporteur also stressed that state financing for health should be informed by the core obligations of the right to health, as defined by the Committee on Economic, Social and Cultural Rights in General Comment 14. In this sense, "core obligations establish a funding baseline below which States would be considered in violation of their obligations under the right to health."[31] In order to meet this funding baseline, the Special Rapporteur advocated the pooling of health funds collected through prepayment schemes:

> Pooling allows for the cross-subsidization of financial risks associated with health care among different groups across large populations and the transfer of health funds from the rich to the poor and the healthy to the sick. Cross-subsidization of financial risks thus

protects vulnerable or marginalized groups, such as the poor, from catastrophic health expenditures and ensures access to good quality health facilities, goods and services that may otherwise be financially inaccessible. Pooling of funds for health in order to facilitate the cross-subsidization of health and financial risks is thus an essential method by which States may ensure the equitable allocation of health funds and resources as required under the right to health.[32]

The Special Rapporteur also criticized individual states for their privatization policies. For example, in 2012 he recommended to the government of Vietnam to complete an official assessment of the effects of privatization on the health system, including its impact on the right to health and the accessibility of health goods and services for the poor, near poor, and ethnic minorities; to expand the scope of health insurance coverage for the poor and consider alternative revenue-generating mechanisms for health service providers, such as progressive taxation; and to ensure that children under six receive free health care in accordance with the existing government policy.[33]

Similarly, UN treaty monitoring bodies have repeatedly expressed concern about privatization of health care. The Committee on the Elimination of All Forms of Discrimination against Women (CEDAW Committee) already in 1997 expressed its "deep concern" with the Armenian government's plan to consider proposals for privatization of the health system and emphasized the "adverse effects for women and other vulnerable groups of privatization in the health area, even in highly developed countries."[34] It also recommended, for example, to India in 2007 to monitor privatization of health care and its impact on the health of poor women.[35] In 2013, it urged the government of Pakistan to "ensure that the privatization of the health sector and the devolution to the provinces of the main health competence do not reduce further the already limited health services accessible to women."[36] Similarly, the CEDAW Committee recommended to Hungary in 2013 to "ensure that the policy of the privatization of health, education and other services does not deprive women of continuous access to good quality basic services in the field of economic, social and cultural rights."[37] The Committee on Economic, Social and Cultural Rights had already in 2001 expressed concern at the privatization of health care in countries as diverse as Venezuela and Sweden.[38] In 2008, it expressed its concerns to India "that the quality and the availability of the health services provided under the scheme have been adversely affected by the large-scale privatization of the health service in the State party, impacting in particular on the poorest sections of the population."[39] It recommended to the Indian government in this context to increase funds allocated to public health, to prevent further loss of medical professionals from the public health services, to ensure universal access to affordable primary health care, and to regulate the private health care sector.[40] In 2009, it recommended to Poland to "ensure that privatization of the health system does not impede the enjoyment of the right to health, in particular for the disadvantaged and marginalized individuals and groups."[41] In line with its criticism of the structural adjustment policies of the international financial institutions with regard to the protection of the right to health,[42] the Committee also urges individual states, such as Sweden, as members of these organizations in the state reporting procedure to "do all it can to ensure that policies and decisions of those organizations are in conformity with obligations of States parties."[43]

The Inter-American Court of Human Rights held in a number of judgments that the protection of the rights to life and personal integrity in Articles 4 and 5 ACHR supposes the regulation of the health care services in the domestic sphere, as well as the implementation of a series of mechanisms designed to ensure the effectiveness of this regulation. In *Ximenes-Lopes v. Brazil*, the court ruled in 2006 that since "health is a public interest the protection of which is a duty of the States, these must prevent third parties from unduly interfering with the enjoyment of the rights to life and personal integrity, which are particularly vulnerable when a person is undergoing health treatment. The Court considers that the States must regulate and supervise all activities related to the health care given to individuals under the jurisdiction thereof, as a special duty to protect life and personal integrity, regardless of the public or private nature of the entity giving such health care."[44] This jurisprudence was further developed in *Suárez Peralta v. Ecuador* by explicitly referring to General Comment 14 of the UN Committee on Economic, Social and Cultural Rights and the respective case law of the European Court of Human Rights.[45] The European Court has held, for example, in *Storck v. Germany*, that the state is under an obligation to secure to its citizens the right to physical integrity under Article 8 ECHR (right to privacy): "For this purpose, there are hospitals run by the State which coexist with private hospitals. The state cannot completely absolve itself of its responsibility by delegating its obligations in this sphere to private bodies or individuals."[46]

Limits of Privatization in the Health Sector

One of the standard arguments of the international financial institutions and others who advocate the privatization of the health sector is that private corporations provide their health services in a more cost-effective manner than the public sector. The United States, which is not a party to the CESCR and therefore not legally bound to implement the right to health, is the country most advanced in the privatization of its health care system. Since the 1990s, private corporations, such as Columbia/HCA and Tenet, have systematically bought community-based hospitals and drastically reduced costs through rationalization measures.[47] Similarly, the health insurance scheme was privatized by the creation of so-called managed care organizations (MCOs), which manage the distribution of funds provided by the government through its Medicare and Medicaid programs.[48] One would, therefore, expect that the U.S. government spends less public money on its largely privatized health care system than countries that still follow the "Bismarck" or "Beveridge" models. The opposite is true, however. The U.S. system, with all its well-known weaknesses and disparities, seems to be the most expensive health care system in the world, both in absolute and relative terms. According to statistician Nate Silver, federal spending on health care increased between 1972 and 2011 at a rate of 6.7 percent per year, which is much higher than the rate of gross domestic product, which grew at a rate of 2.7 percent, or the rate of increase in tax revenues.[49] Economist Eduardo Porter argues that the U.S. for-profit system "delivers worse value for money than every other in the developed world. We spend nearly 18 percent of the nation's economic output on health care and still manage to leave tens of millions of Americans without adequate access to care."[50] It is projected to rise to over 20 percent of the GDP by 2021, while Great Britain, Germany, and France provide universal health coverage for between 10 and 12 percent of their GDP.[51]

The reasons why the "von Hayek model" of privatizing the health care system led to an economic disaster in the United States are manifold. Apart from the profits, which private health and insurance corporations make at the expense of public funding, the high administrative costs of private health insurers and managed care organizations (MCOs) are often cited.[52] The fact that MCOs exercise a monopoly over a beneficiary's access to health care[53] certainly is not conducive to cutting costs. Another reason is the high level of corruption[54] and the close cooperation between private health care providers and pharmaceutical corporations. A study by the School of Pharmacy at the University of Wisconsin-Madison, for instance, discovered that patients in private for-profit nursing homes received roughly four times as much medication as patients at church-affiliated non-profit homes.[55] Similar studies also found for-profit hospitals concentrating on more expensive and profitable procedures such as open-heart surgery rather than on less profitable services like home health care and psychiatric emergency care.[56]

This brings us to the more principal question whether the free market model can actually work effectively in the field of health care. In their highly critical, and sometimes a little polemical, book against privatization, Michel Reimon and Christian Felber argue in accordance with economist Kenneth Arrows that the basic requirements for a functional market system, such as the rules of supply and demand, are simply lacking.[57] Nobody wishes to be sick. The patients never go voluntarily to a hospital but because they are sick. In most cases, they are not free "clients" to choose whether they would like to avail themselves of the services of one or an other private health care provider, but are forced by accidents and illnesses to go to the next hospital or primary health care center. In addition, there is an extremely asymmetrical relationship between doctors and their patients, as doctors have the expertise and patients depend on the advice of their doctors. Optimal health care, therefore, requires a relationship of trust between the doctor and the patient, which can only work if the doctor is not forced by for-profit considerations to prescribe a certain medication or deny a certain treatment. Of course, costs also play an important role in public health care systems, and most governments in the world are today struggling with the rising costs of their health care systems. But in countries that are based on the so-called "Bismarck model," such as Germany, Austria, and Switzerland, charities and religious organizations as owners of hospitals and other health services find economic conditions that are not based on maximizing profits. They are reimbursed for their high-quality services with reasonable amounts out of public health insurance funds.[58] As soon as this limited and heavily regulated market is opened to for-profit corporations, charities and religious organizations are forced to apply the same rationalization strategies in order to be able to compete with the corporate sector, usually at the expense of the quality of their services. The U.S. health care provider Kaiser, which was a nonprofit-oriented organization founded by industrialist Henry Kaiser in 1945 in California and used to be a symbol of high quality health care in the United States, had to change its orientation during the 1990s toward for-profit in order to be able to compete with the big for-profit corporations. As a result, the quality of its services deteriorated rapidly because of serious cost-cutting measures.[59]

Taking into account the experiences in various rich and poor states, as expressed in numerous reports, conclusions, and recommendations of the UN Special Rapporteur on the Right to Health, UN treaty bodies, domestic courts, and academic literature, that privatizing public health systems by opening up the market to for-profit corporations, usually leads to a deterioration of the quality of health care and increasing disparities that often exclude poor, marginalized, and discriminated groups from access to health care providers, it seems obvious that the hypothesis of Gregg Bloche and others that international human rights law was "neutral" in relation to privatization cannot be maintained. The problem is not that health care is provided by private doctors or in privately owned hospitals, as these functions were traditionally exercised by private charities or religious organizations, whose services were paid, according to the model of the advanced welfare state, out of public funds and state-administered (usually compulsory) health insurance funds based on the cross-subsidization of financial risks.[60] The only part of the health system that has for a long time been in the hands of the corporate sector is the development, production, and sale of drugs and medical equipment by pharmaceutical and similar companies. This may lead to serious problems in relation to the right of equal access to essential medicines, as the dispute about intellectual property rights in the context of provision of antiretroviral HIV/AIDS drugs in South Africa and other countries vividly illustrates. But the high costs involved in research and development of modern drugs and high-tech medical equipment seem to justify private investments, albeit under strict state regulatory power, in order to ensure equal access to essential medicines as an important component of the right to health.

The further privatization of health care providers and insurance involves, however, substantial risks of retrogressive measures. At the very least, states parties to the CESCR who consider such a step are under an obligation to conduct a thorough human rights impact assessment, which must look in particular into the core obligations arising from Article 12 CESCR, as elaborated by the CESCR Committee,[61] the consequences for poor, marginalized, and discriminated groups and their access to primary health care facilities. Privatization in the absence of such an assessment or contrary to such assessments by independent experts has to be considered as a deliberate retrogressive measure in violation of Articles 2 and 13 CESCR and General Comment 14 of the CESCR Committee. As with the right to education, the right to health does not exclude the corporate sector from operating hospitals and clinics and rehabilitation centers for those who can afford them as long as the state and its public health insurance and financing system ensures that everyone has equal access to publicly funded health care and is guaranteed the right to the enjoyment of the highest attainable standard of physical and mental health.

Chapter 5

Right to Social Security

History, Significance, and Content of the Right to Social Security

The right to social security constitutes the central right of defining the advanced welfare state as it developed since the late nineteenth century.[1] Starting with Otto von Bismarck's social insurance legislation in Germany during the 1880s as a tool to secure political stability, social insurance and social welfare systems developed during the first half of the twentieth century, actively promoted by the International Labour Organization (ILO), in most industrial societies, above all in Europe and Latin America, and were intensified in reaction to the Great Depression of the early 1930s. The term "social security" goes back to the U.S. Social Security Act 1935,[2] which formed a central component of President Franklin D. Roosevelt's New Deal legislation aimed at securing freedom from want.[3] It was in the same spirit that Lord Beveridge, the British minister of social affairs, in 1942 "assigned to social security systems the role of guaranteeing basic egalitarian protection to the whole population."[4] Bård-Anders Andreassen, with reference to Max Weber's interpretation of the state, argues that this "development reflects a shift in the nature of State legitimacy from its liberal sources to the fulfillment of welfare State provisions."[5]

This was the predominant thinking, underscored by the economic theories of state intervention developed by John Maynard Keynes,[6] when the UDHR was drafted in the aftermath of World War II. Article 41 of the Secretariat draft prepared by John Humphrey in 1947 read as follows:

> Everyone has the right to social security. The State shall maintain effective arrangements for the prevention of unemployment and for

insurance against the risks of unemployment, accident, disability, sickness, old age and other involuntary or undeserved loss of livelihood.[7]

This original draft was only slightly changed by René Cassin and other members of the Working Group on the Declaration in the Commission on Human Rights.[8] But during the third session of the Commission in June 1948, the right to social security was conflated with the desire to include an umbrella article on state obligations in relation to economic, social, and cultural rights.[9] The proposed text in the Commission was as follows:[10]

Every one has the right to social security. This includes the right to a standard of living and social services adequate for the health and well-being for himself and his family and security in the event of unemployment, sickness, disability, old age.

During the ensuing discussion in the Commission, the representative of the ILO proposed to delete the reference to "social security" completely because "the Commission was placing a new definition on the words 'social security' and was giving it the same meaning as the right to a standard of living and adequate social services."[11] Consequently, the term "social security" was deleted from the draft, but was later included again on the insistence of René Cassin, who argued that it would be "a grave error to omit from the Declaration the modern and widely accepted concept of social security."[12] It seems that Eleanor Roosevelt was equally interested in saving the idea of social security, which had been so dear to her late husband. As chairwoman of the Commission, she suggested beginning the umbrella article with the sentence, "Every person has the right to social security," which was then adopted by 12 votes with 5 abstentions.[13] But the discussion came up again in the Third Committee of the General Assembly. The Chilean social democrat Hernán Santa Cruz expressed concern that the term "social security" in the chapeau's opening sentence "was apt to be misconstrued. In some states it had a technical sense, limited to the situation of persons unable to work because of incapacity, whereas its function here was to introduce a series of articles aimed at protecting individuals against a variety of social and economic risks including unemployment."[14] When Syria proposed to replace the term "social security" with "social justice," Eleanor Roosevelt, "though conceding the term social security might not be perfect, said she hoped the chapeau would be adopted without modifications."[15] After Article 22 had been adopted by thirty-nine votes against one, with three abstentions, the representative of Saudia Arabia explained his abstention, as he had been disappointed by the failure of the Syrian motion to substitute "social justice" for "social security": "The former term conformed better to the Saudi system, where 'zaka, a voluntary tax levied for the purpose of assisting the poor and unemployed, was one of the five pillars of Islam. Social security was a recent historical development in western society, while 'zaka had been an article of faith in actual operation in Moslem communities for almost fourteen centuries.' "[16] The final text of the umbrella Article 22 UDHR reads as follows:

> Everyone, as a member of society, has the right to social security and is entitled to realization, through national effort and international co-operation and in accordance with the organization and resources of each State, of the economic, social and cultural rights indispensable for his dignity and the free development of his personality.

This short history of the drafting of Article 22 illustrates very well the concept of the right to social security as it was understood in different societies in the period immediately after World War II. Of course, Hernán Santa Cruz, the Syrian and Saudi representatives, and Bård-Anders Andreassen were right in arguing that the appropriate term for the Commission would have been "social justice."[17] The confusion was created when the Commission wished, all of a sudden, to combine an umbrella article on economic, social, and cultural rights with the right to social security. It is only thanks to the determination of René Cassin and Eleanor Roosevelt that the term "social security" was saved in the text of the UDHR. But Article 22 has to be read in conjunction with the other umbrella right to an adequate standard of living in Article 25,[18] which includes the "right to medical care and necessary social services, and the right to security in the event of unemployment, sickness, disability, widowhood, old age or other lack of livelihood in circumstances beyond his control."[19] The combined reading of both articles shows that the right to social security is intimately linked with the right to an adequate standard of living, which also includes the right to health.

During the drafting of the Covenants, it soon became clear that such an overall right to "livelihood security" would be too broad. What is covered in Articles 22 and 25 UDHR has been split up in the CESCR into four different rights to social security (Article 9), protection to the family (Article 10), an adequate standard of living (Article 11), and the right to health (Article 12). Article 9 is the shortest provision and reads as follows:

> The States Parties to the present Covenant recognize the right of everyone to social security, including social insurance.

Why did the drafters of the Covenant refrain from further defining this important social right? The travaux préparatoires suggest a combination of reasons. While some states, such as Italy, Yugoslavia, and Uruguay, proposed a definition of the pillars of social security, similar to Article 25 UDHR, and Israel argued for an explicit reference to ILO Convention No. 102 concerning Minimum Standards of Social Security, others, including Chile and Syria, preferred a statement of general principle, which would allow states the freedom to develop its precise scope.[20] Most important, many states, such as France, Iran, the UK, and Canada, felt that it was unnecessary to go into details, since the ILO had already defined the minimum standards of social security and the UN should avoid interfering with the work of its specialized agency.[21] There is, therefore, some evidence in the drafting history of an intention for ILO standards to operate as a kind of *lex specialis* for Article 9 CESCR.[22] In January 1957, shortly before the adoption of the final text in the Third Committee, the ILO representative had explained that the term social security had

> originated in the United States of America, had been adopted in Europe and had gradually made its way into international terminology. In that connection, he referred to the International Labour Convention (No. 102) concerning Minimum Standards of Social Security, which had been adopted in 1952. The replacement of the term "social insurance" by the term "social security" reflected, as the Yugoslav representative had noted, a broadening of the notion itself."[23]

The ILO Convention 102 concerning the Minimum Standards of Social Security of 1952 requires states parties to comply with certain general obligations and a minimum of three of the following nine pillars of social security: medical care, sickness, unemployment, old age, employment injury, family, maternity, invalidity, and survivors' benefits. In its monitoring work relating to Article 9 CESCR, the Committee on Economic, Social and Cultural Rights heavily relies on these ILO standards as *lex specialis*.[24] In its General Comment No. 19 on the right to social security, adopted on 23 November 2007,[25] the Committee defines this social right as follows:

> The right to social security encompasses the right to access and maintain benefits, whether in cash or in kind, without discrimination in order to secure protection, inter alia, from a) lack of work-related income caused by sickness, disability, maternity, employment injury, unemployment, old age, or death of family member; b) unaffordable access to health care; c) insufficient family support, particularly for children and adult dependents.[26]

This definition clearly reflects the nine pillars of ILO Convention 102, most of which had already been anticipated in the original Humphrey draft for the UDHR, cited above. When discussing the availability of the right to social security, the Committee explicitly refers to the "nine principal branches" of social security as defined in ILO Convention 102, "which was confirmed by the ILO Governing Body in 2002 as an instrument corresponding to contemporary needs and circumstances."[27] The Committee further stresses the redistributive character of social security, which "plays an important role in poverty reduction and alleviation, preventing social exclusion and promoting social inclusion."[28] The measures to provide social security benefits include contributory or insurance-based schemes such as social insurance, and noncontributory schemes such as universal schemes or targeted social assistance schemes.[29] The right to social insurance is explicitly mentioned in Article 9 CESCR and generally involves compulsory contributions from beneficiaries, employers, and, sometimes, the state, in conjunction with the payment of benefits and administrative expenses from a common fund.[30] Universal social assistance schemes provide the relevant benefit in principle to everyone who experiences a particular risk or contingency, whereas targeted social assistance schemes provide benefits to those in a situation of need. The Committee emphasizes that in "almost all States parties, non-contributory schemes will be required since it is unlikely that every person can be adequately covered through an insurance-based scheme."[31]

Other forms of social security are also acceptable to the Committee, including privately run schemes and self-help or other measures, such as community-based or mutual schemes, as long as they "conform to the essential elements of the right to social security."[32] In this respect, the Committee further specifies that where social security schemes, whether contributory or noncontributory, are operated or controlled by third parties, "States parties retain the responsibility of administering the national social security system and ensuring that private actors do not compromise equal, adequate, affordable and accessible social security. To prevent such abuses an effective regulatory system must be established which includes framework legislation, independent monitoring, genuine public participation and imposition of penalties for non-compliance."[33] In addition to these obligations of states to protect their people against abuses by private actors, including private insurance corporations, the Committee also stresses the obligation of states to fulfill the right to social security by at least establishing noncontributory schemes or other social assistance measures to provide support to those individuals and groups who are unable to make sufficient contributions for their own protection.[34] Special attention should be given to times of emergency and to disadvantaged and marginalized groups. As with other rights, the Committee repeats the "strong assumption" that retrogressive measures taken in relation to the right to social security are prohibited under the Covenant.[35]

With respect to the core obligations under Article 9 CESCR, the Committee adopts a broader definition of the right to social security, including the basic elements of the right to an adequate standard of living. It requires the state party "to ensure access to a social security scheme that provides a minimum essential level of benefits to all individuals and families that will enable them to acquire at least essential health care,[36] basic shelter and housing, water and sanitation, foodstuffs, and the most basic forms of education."[37] In addition, the core obligations contain the right of access to social security systems or schemes on a nondiscriminatory basis, as well as the obligations of states to respect existing social security schemes and protect them from unreasonable interference, to adopt and implement a national social security strategy and plan of action, to take targeted steps to implement social security schemes, particularly those that protect disadvantaged individuals and groups, and to monitor the extent of the realization of the right to social security.[38] As in other General Comments, the Committee also urges the international financial institutions and individual member states of these institutions to take into account the right to social security in their structural adjustment programs and similar projects, "so that the enjoyment of the right to social security, particularly by disadvantaged and marginalized individuals and groups, is promoted and not compromised."[39]

Privatization in the Field of Social Security

The language of General Comment 19 is fairly strong and reacts to certain criticism in the academic literature as having been too vague in relation to neoliberal policies of privatization in the field of social security.[40] If one reads the General Comment in context, there can be no doubt that the Committee is highly critical to any privatization measures in relation to social security schemes, and in particular to the structural adjustment policies adopted by the IMF and the World Bank, which have forced many poor countries to cut social assistance systems and to privatize their social insurance schemes. One of the earliest and most striking examples of these neoliberal policies was the total privatization of the social pension system under the influence of the "Chicago Boys" during the military dictatorship in Chile, which led to an economic and social disaster and produced the most expensive pension system with the lowest benefits, while a few private corporations made huge profits.[41] Nevertheless, the World Bank considered Chile as a positive model and introduced in 1994 the individualized mandatory defined contribution (DC) model to replace the classical defined benefit (DB) pension schemes, which led to a proliferation of initiatives aimed at transferring to the person the cost and the responsibility of his or her own financial, as well as physical security.[42] Countries affected by this structural adjustment program include many Latin American countries, but also various transitional countries in Central and Eastern Europe, such as Hungary, Poland, Latvia, Macedonia, Bulgaria, and Croatia. Kazakhstan is the second country that was forced to totally privatize its old age pension system.

But also many Western countries with a highly effective social security and welfare system started to move from public social insurance schemes with mandatory contributions from (employed or self-employed) beneficiaries and employers toward private insurance schemes. For old-age pensions this means in essence that the pooling of funds, where the actively employed population of a particular society pays the pensions of the retired population, is gradually replaced or at least supplemented by a system where everybody is responsible for his or her old age pension. The respective contributions are paid to private pension funds, often funds administered by the employer, which are sometimes even used for speculation on the global financial markets. If these private pension funds (or the respective employers) go bankrupt, the contributions are lost, until saved by the state out of its general budget. This happened in many cases, such as the well-known bankruptcy of the U.S. energy corporation Enron in 2001.[43]

In the UK, a country known for one of the best social security systems in the world, based on the "Beveridge model," the possibility of contracting out to private pension funds started in 1961, and was accelerated during the Tory government of Margaret Thatcher and later under the Labour government of Tony Blair, who in 1999 introduced so-called "shareholder pensions."[44] This meant that by the beginning of the new millennium, some 40 percent of pension funds were held by private funds and investors. In principle, the state remains responsible under international law to respect, protect, and fulfill human rights, even if the implementation of traditional government functions is delegated to the private sector. In order to ensure that the obligations under the ECHR would also apply when public functions were implemented by private companies, Section 6(3)(b) of the Human Rights Act of 1998 was introduced to make sure that "any person certain of whose functions are functions of a public nature" were to be considered as "public authorities." But Section 6(5) added that such a person "is not a public authority . . . if the nature of the act is private."[45] This, of course, raises the question whether a function that was traditionally considered a public function can become a function of a "private nature" thanks to the growing influence of neoliberalism and privatization. This question was put to the House of Lords in the well-known case of YL v. Birmingham City Council, decided in 2007.[46] Mrs. YL was a resident in a care home run by Southern Cross Healthcare Ltd., under a contract between Southern Cross and Birmingham City Council, in fulfillment of the council's statutory duty, under Sections 21 and 26 of the National Assistance Act 1948, to arrange for the provision of residential care for the elderly who lack the means to provide for their own care. The council paid Southern Cross out of public funds for the provision in one of Southern Cross's nursing homes, of residential care for Mrs. YL, who suffered from Alzheimer's disease. Because of various disputes, Southern Cross gave notice to terminate Mrs. YL's right to remain in the care home. Her lawyers argued that this amounted to a violation of her right to respect of her home under Article 8 ECHR, as implemented by the British Human Rights Act. In a highly disputed majority decision of 3–2, the majority rejected the claim of Mrs. YL on the ground that Southern Cross was a private company "carrying on a socially useful business for profit . . . in a commercial market with commercial competitors," and "where the actual accommodation is provided by a private contractor on commercial terms, for profit, that is not a function of a public nature, even though it may fulfil the statutory duty of the local authority to arrange care and accommodation." Lord Bingham and Baroness Hale strongly dissented from the majority, holding that the provision of residential care for the elderly was a function of a public nature and that Southern Cross Ltd. was accordingly a public authority within the meaning of Section 6(3)(b). Lord Bingham noted, in particular that "for the past 60 years or so, it has been recognized as the ultimate responsibility of the state to ensure that . . . those who, by reason of age, illness, disability or other circumstances are in need of care and attention which is not otherwise available to them . . . are accommodated and looked after through the agency of the state and at its expense if no other source of accommodation and care and no other source of funding is available."[47] This case illustrates in a drastic manner how the principle of core government functions in the advanced welfare state has been eroded even in the mind of high court justices by neoliberalism and the notion of new public management.

In the Netherlands, a country that also has been known for its excellent social security system, a case concerning the privatization of social security benefits was even litigated before the UN Committee on the Elimination of All Forms of Discrimination against Women, which in February 2014 decided in favor of the applicants: *Elizabeth de Blok et al. v. the Netherlands*.[48] Under the Discontinuity of Access to Incapacity Insurance (Self-Employed Persons) Act of 2004, the public mandatory incapacity insurance for self-employed workers, professional workers, and coworking spouses ceased to exist. Consequently, self-employed workers such as the six applicants were no longer entitled to receive public maternity benefits and were required to turn to private insurance companies to cover the loss of income resulting from pregnancy and delivery. The applicants sought to take out such insurance privately, but all but one were dissuaded from doing so by the costs of the insurance in light of their relatively low income. When the act was discussed in the Dutch Parliament, the government had even "asked itself whether these benefits must be the subject of a public law arrangement," but had come to the conclusion that international "treaties do not give an obligation to do so."[49] According to Article 13(2)(b) CEDAW, states parties have an obligation, in order to prevent discrimination against women on the grounds of marriage or maternity, to take appropriate measures to "introduce maternity leave with pay or with comparable social benefits without loss of former employment, seniority or social allowances." The Committee rejected the argument of the government that Article 11(2)(b) does not apply to self-employed women as well as the holding of the District Court of The Hague that CEDAW was not directly applicable and contained only a "best-efforts obligation." It also recalled that during the consideration of the Netherlands' fourth periodic report, the Committee had specifically called upon the Dutch government to reinstate maternity benefits for all women, to include self-employed women.[50] It found that "the reform introduced in 2004 by the State party did negatively affect the authors' maternity leave benefits, as protected under article 11(2)(b), if compared with those existing under the previous public coverage scheme," and therefore "constitutes direct sex and gender-based discrimination against women and a violation of the obligation of the State party to take all appropriate measures to eliminate discrimination under article 11 of the Convention."[51]

In the United States, which is not party to CEDAW or to CESCR, the privatization of social security or social welfare seems to be most advanced, as Gillian Metzger reports: "Even more dramatic expansion in privatization is evident in the welfare context, which is also characterized by extensive and longstanding private involvement. Private organizations run homeless shelters and food banks; provide treatment services; operate Head Start programs; and work closely with child welfare agencies."[52] The 1996 welfare legislation, which replaced Aid to Families with Dependent Children (AFDC) with the Temporary Aid to Needy Families (TANF) program, paved the way for greater privatization by expressly permitting private administration of state TANF programs. Wisconsin provides the prime example of a government putting operation of its welfare system in private hands. Private contractors are "responsible for substantial aspects of program administration, such as determining applicants' eligibility for benefits, assessing their ability to work, developing employment plans, and sanctioning beneficiaries for noncompliance with program requirements."[53] Such wholesale privatization of public welfare programs has "increased reliance on for-profit contractors, as nonprofits often lack the capacity and financial resources to undertake such large-scale contracts, where payment is often significantly delayed and contingent on program outcomes."[54] The results are similar to the Medicare and Medicaid privatization discussed in the context of the right to health.

Limits of Privatization in the Field of Social Security

The CESCR Committee only received the competence to consider individual complaints in accordance with the Optional Protocol in 2013 and has not yet handed down final views in individual cases relating to the right to social security. But in the context of the state reporting procedure, it had plenty of opportunities to comment on the privatization of social security schemes by the states parties, in both North and South. In 1998, it adopted a statement on globalization and economic, social, and cultural rights criticizing

> specific trends and policies including an increasing reliance upon the free market, a significant growth in the influence of international financial markets and institutions in determining the viability of national policy priorities, a diminution in the role of the state and the size of its budget, the privatization of various functions previously considered to be the exclusive domain of the state, the deregulation of a range of activities with a view to facilitating investment and rewarding individual initiative, and a corresponding increase in the role and even responsibilities attributed to private actors, both in the corporate sector, in particular to the transnational corporations and in civil society.[55]

In the following, only a few examples of concluding observations relating to privatization will be provided.[56] Starting in the early 1990s, for example, with respect to Argentina,[57] the Committee has expressed concern about the inaccessibility of private schemes to certain vulnerable groups of workers, including agricultural or domestic workers and women, and those who cannot contribute, such as the unemployed, underemployed, lower-paid workers and those in the informal sector.[58] It criticized Nigeria for not interfering at all in the private sector where social security benefits are voluntary,[59] and expressed concern to Zambia where privatized systems are financially unsustainable, leading to inadequate protection. The government was urged to guarantee an adequate standard of living, including through provision of social safety nets for most disadvantaged and marginalized groups, in particular those "women and children who had been hardest hit by structural adjustment programmes, privatization and debt servicing."[60] Afghanistan and the Democratic Republic of Congo were criticized for not having established any basic social security system, and the Committee stressed that budgetary constraints should not be invoked as the only justification for the lack of progress toward the establishment of a social security system.[61] The Committee also expressed concern to many countries where privatization had an adverse effect on pension schemes.[62] In 2010, it called on Kazakhstan to "provide detailed information on the ongoing privatization of the pension system, in particular its effects on the right to social security of the most disadvantaged and marginalized individuals."[63]

The CESCR Committee also frequently called on states parties to increase funding to social security,[64] and strongly criticized Canada in 1998 for having reduced social security coverage:[65]

> The Committee is concerned that newly introduced successive restrictions on unemployment insurance benefits have resulted in a dramatic drop in the proportion of unemployed workers receiving benefits to approximately half of previous coverage, in the lowering of benefit rates, in reductions in the length of time for which benefits are paid and in increasingly restricted access to benefits for part-time workers. While the new programme is said to provide better benefits for low-income families with children, the fact is that fewer low-income families are eligible to receive any benefits at all. Part-time, young, marginal, temporary and seasonal workers face more restrictions and are frequently denied benefits, although they contribute significantly to the fund . . . These cuts appear to have significant adverse impact on vulnerable groups, causing increases in already high levels of homelessness and hunger.

In a similar vein, the Committee encouraged Sweden in 1995 "to continue to take adequate measures to ensure that the reduction of the Government's social welfare programmes do not result in a violation of the State party's obligations under the Covenant."[66] It also expressed concern to the Czech Republic "that the inadequacy of the social safety nets during the restructuring and privatization process has negatively affected the enjoyment of economic, social and cultural rights, in particular by the most disadvantaged and marginalized groups."[67] Israel was requested in 2011 to address the problem of poverty and social exclusion by "scaling down of the privatization of social services."[68] The Committee also regretted that Senegal spent more on its military and servicing its debt than on basic social services.[69]

On the basis of a comprehensive analysis of state obligations under Article 9 CESCR and the respective practice of the CESCR Committee, Ben Saul, David Kinley, and Jacqueline Mowbray recently arrived at the following conclusions:[70] "Privatization raises special difficulties for the accessibility and comprehensiveness of social security protection. Commercial private entities (as opposed to private non-profit organizations) are understandably concerned to profit from their business. To this end, they will instinctively prefer to selectively cover those workers from whom they are able to make money, and to avoid those who are either unprofitable or potentially loss-making. State intervention may be necessary to ensure that their profit imperative is balanced with social obligations to ensure the accessibility and affordability of social security, without imposing such burdensome requirements that their private schemes are no longer financially viable. Given that private providers may also be restricted to the social insurance of workers, they may play no role at all in assisting those out of the workforce, including the unemployed, young people or family members. Thus, even adequate regulation of private entities may still require the state to provide complementary universal public social security, in order to fill the gaps left by private arrangements."

Already in 2005, Lucie Lamarche strongly advocated to put the state back in social protection issues.[71] In her opinion, the human right to social security is based on the model of the welfare state, whereas the "realities as well as the mythology of globalization and global poverty" weakened this important role of the state.[72] Monitoring social protection in a human rights perspective "rules out certain trends actually promoted by the actors of globalisation."[73] In interpreting the core content of the right to social security, she stressed that social security and social protection, "as rights, express the human need for predictability and security." Therefore, social security as a human right is not a commodity and relies on collective funding.[74] As to the argument that the private sector can deliver in a more efficient way "social risks" products, she claims that "no convincing evidence had been so far produced to show the viability of this approach."[75]

In fact, the CESCR Committee, in its General Comment 19 of 2008, expressed concern "over the very low levels of access to social security with a large majority (about 80 per cent) of the global population currently lacking access to formal social security. Among these 80 per cent, 20 percent live in extreme poverty."[76] According to the *World Social Security Report* issued by the ILO in 2010/11, only about "20 per cent of the world's working-age population (and their families) have effective access to comprehensive social security."[77] The report continues by emphasizing that "contrary to earlier beliefs, no negative effects on economic growth of increased social spending during and after crises have been found. On the contrary, well-designed unemployment schemes, social assistance and public works programs effectively prevent long-term unemployment and help shorten economic recessions." The report concludes that the

> current crisis has once more proved how important a role social security plays in society in times of crisis and adjustment, working as an irreplaceable economic, social and political stabilizer in hard times. Social security plays this role in addition to its other functions—providing mechanisms to alleviate and also to prevent poverty, to reduce income disparities to acceptable levels, and to enhance human capital and productivity. Social security is thus one of the conditions for sustainable economic and social development. It is a factor in development. It is also an important factor in a modern democratic state and in society.

It is indeed not very encouraging to realize that almost one century after the creation of the ILO, and more than seventy years after the United Nations was established with its goals of promoting development and an international social order in which all human rights can be fully realized by all human beings, that only 20 percent of the world's population have effective access to formal social security. This massive failure of the international community is not the result of a lack of economic resources. It is the result of a deliberate policy of introducing a neoliberal economic model by the countries of the Global North in an age of rapid globalization and by enforcing this model, through the international financial institutions, the World Trade Organization, bilateral and international investment treaties and regional organizations, including the European Union, on the Global South. This situation does not only reflect a fundamental failure of global development policies. It constitutes a systematic violation of states' obligations to respect and ensure the human right to social security for the vast majority of the global population and many closely related human rights, such as the rights to health and to an adequate standard of living, including the rights to food, water, clothing, and housing. The Covenant on Economic, Social and Cultural Rights is an international treaty legally binding on almost 90 percent of all states, including all states of the Global North with the one exception of the United States. The Convention on the Rights of the Child, which has been ratified by all states of the world with the exceptions of the United States and Somalia, contains in Article 26 a clear, legally binding obligation of all states parties to recognize for every child the right to benefit from social security, including social insurance, and to take the necessary measures to achieve the full realization of this right in accordance with their national law.

The right to social security illustrates better than most other human rights that privatization of social security schemes, that is, transferring governmental obligations to the corporate sector, in principle constitutes a violation of the respective state obligations. The notion of "social security" symbolizes the core of social justice, freedom from fear and want, which can be achieved in a market economy only through state intervention aimed at protecting individuals against certain risks and vulnerabilities, such as sickness, disability, accidents, old age, unemployment, or emergencies. The term "security" implies that human beings should not have to be afraid to drift into poverty if they get sick, old, unemployed, or disabled. They should be able to rely on a social safety net if they are, for whatever reason, no longer able to care for themselves and their families. The term "social" underlines that in a market economy, only the advanced social welfare state can provide the necessary safety nets by means of pooling such risks and by redistribution from the wealthy to the poor, from the healthy to the sick, from the younger and actively employed generation to the elderly. The corporate sector by definition cannot provide such a safety net. By aiming at maximizing profits, private insurance companies and service providers necessarily tend to exclude from their services those who are most in need of their services—the most vulnerable and marginalized groups.

Under the CESCR and other human rights treaties providing for economic, social, and cultural rights, states have an obligation to take steps, to the maximum of available resources, to progressively realize the right to social security for all people under their jurisdiction, above all the most vulnerable. This means that the status quo at the time of ratification should be considered as the base line from where states should start and further develop toward an advanced welfare state. They should broaden existing social safety nets by including those groups that were not yet fully covered, such as the homeless, long-term unemployed persons, migrant workers, refugees, those working in the informal sector of the economy, persons with disabilities, and so on. In addition, they shall deepen and improve the services provided in the past, and rich states also have an obligation to assist the people in poor states, by means of development cooperation, to have equal access to social security benefits. On the basis of the experience during the last decades, privatization of social security schemes, whether in rich or poor countries, must be considered as deliberate retrogressive measures in violation of the right to social security. As members of the international financial institutions, rich states also have an obligation to prevent structural adjustment policies which lead to cuts in the social security systems of poor countries. By supporting such policies, they also violate their obligations to provide international assistance and cooperation in accordance with Articles 2(1) and 11 CESCR.

The development of the world economy since the 1980s clearly illustrates that the neoliberal policies in times of globalization, above all privatization and deregulation, have had a negative impact on social security and social justice in a more general sense. On the basis of a considerable amount of statistical data, Richard Wilkinson and Kate Pickett have proved that "only in its early stages does economic development boost life expectancy," happiness and other indicators of well-being.[78] The role of their book "is to point out that greater equality is the material foundation on which better social relations are built."[79] A comparison of rich countries shows that states with a high level of privatization, such as the United States and the UK, are much more unequal than states where the traditional policies of the advanced welfare state, including social security and social justice programs, such as Japan and the Nordic states in Europe, have been less affected by the global trend toward privatization and the diminishing role of the state.[80] It also shows that the gap between rich and poor has been on the rise since the Thatcher and Reagan governments.[81] By putting statistical data on income equality in 23 rich states, where the relevant data are available,[82] in relation to data on health and social problems,[83] child well-being,[84] the level of trust toward other people,[85] the percentage of persons with mental illness,[86] the use of illegal drugs,[87] life expectancy and child mortality,[88] obesity,[89] educational performance,[90] teenage births,[91] homicides,[92] children's experience of conflict,[93] incarceration,[94] social mobility,[95] or annual work hours,[96] the study reached the conclusion that countries with higher income equality are almost always performing better than those with a high level of inequality. Recent economic studies show that inequality of income and wealth has slowly risen during the last decades of neoliberal politics in most countries. On the basis of a unique collection of historical data relating to income from labor and income from capital in many countries, Thomas Piketty shows that income inequality in the United States has reached roughly the same level as in Europe before the outbreak of World War I.[97] Such extreme inequalities and concentration of capital are "potentially incompatible with the meritocratic values and principles of social justice fundamental to modern democratic societies."[98]

The data analyzed in Wilkinson's and Pickett's study are at the core of the concept of social security, social justice, and an adequate standard of living. The study was not written from a human rights perspective, but the authors realized very well that their findings touch upon the fundamental question of the relationship between freedom and equality:[99]

> The idea that we can't have both liberty and equality seems to have emerged during the Cold War. What the state-owned economies of Eastern Europe and the Soviet Union seemed to show was that greater equality could only be gained at the expense of freedom. An important ideological cost of the Cold War was that America gave up its historical commitment to equality. For the first Americans, as for Tom Paine, you couldn't have true liberty without equality.

Another important philosopher who argued that freedom and equality are two sides of the same coin, is Immanuel Kant.[100] The right to equality and the principle of nondiscrimination are at the heart of the universal human rights framework, and the right to social security in the broader sense of social justice embodies this principle more than any other human right. If states wish, as they are legally required by Article 9 CESCR and similar provisions in international human rights law, to progressively realize the right to social security, they should understand that further privatization, deregulation, and similar policies of the neoliberal political and economic agenda will necessarily lead to more inequality and, therefore, to less social security, social justice, and standard of living.

Right to Water

Trend Toward Privatization of Water

"Water is a limited natural resource and a public good fundamental for life and health."[1] While education, health care, social security benefits, or the protection by the police and courts are services to be provided by governments in order to ensure some of the more basic human rights, water is a natural resource and, therefore, considered as a public good. Whereas other natural resources, such as oil, gas, and minerals, need to be explored and extracted by sophisticated technologies, water has been available and accessible to most human beings on the surface or by using simple tools, such as digging wells. Since water was throughout history not perceived as a scarce natural resource, but "considered to be available as freely as is the air to breathe,"[2] access to water was not even explicitly recognized as a human right during the drafting of the two Covenants in the 1950s and 1960s. But in special circumstances where water was considered scarce and essential for survival, health, or an adequate standard of living, such as in prisons,[3] women in rural areas,[4] children,[5] or workers,[6] access to clean drinking water and sanitation was emphasized. The general right to water discourse[7] only started when water was beginning to be perceived as a scarce resource and when transnational water corporations, with the assistance of the international financial institutions, made huge profits by exploiting the "water market," often to the detriment of the poor. In 1977, the United Nations Water Conference in Mar del Plata, Argentina, issued an Action Plan on "Community Water Supply," declaring for the first time that "all peoples . . . have the right to have access to drinking water in quantities and of a quality equal to their basic needs."[8] In the same year the United Nations declared the 1980s as the International Water Supply and

Sanitation Decade.[9] The principle of a universal right of access to drinking water was also reaffirmed in the Agenda 21 adopted during the Earth Summit in Rio de Janeiro 1992.[10] But six months earlier, in January 1992, the experts who gathered at the International Conference on Water and Environment in Dublin had stressed that "managing water as an economic good is an important way of achieving efficient and equitable use, and of encouraging conservation and protection of water resources."[11] The Dublin Principles, on the one hand, had recognized the right to clean water, and on the other hand, emphasized a link between pricing water appropriately and environmentally sustainable water usage. They were adopted only a few years after the Washington Consensus 1989 and after Margaret Thatcher had privatized the public water services in England and Wales in 1989. Managing water as an economic good was a highly controversial principle as it would pave the way for greater commodification and privatization, placing control over a vital resource in the hands of a few who would sell it for a price.[12] From then on, the international attempts of recognizing a universal right to water were seen in the context of the universal fight against the privatization of water and its exploitation by a few, primarily European, water corporations.

In fact, the global water industry is characterized by a high level of concentration, dominated by three European corporations. In 2009, the French company Veolia Environnement (formerly Vivendi) operated in over one hundred countries and provided water services to 110 million people; the French company Suez operated in 130 countries and provided water services to 115 million people; and the German RWE Group, which had bought British Thames Water, provided water services to over 70 million people.[13] In her well-known book *Blue Covenant*, published in 2007, Maude Barlow, who was named Senior Advisor on Water Issues by the UN General Assembly, reported that Suez, with 160,000 employees worldwide, had accrued revenues of almost $60 billion; Veolia Environnement, with 272,000 employees, had accrued revenues of just under $34 billion; and Thames Water, with 12,000 employees, had accrued revenues of more than $2 billion! Other big players are Saur (France), Agbar (Spain), AquaMundo (Germany), and a few British corporations.[14] According to different sources, "the combined revenue potential of the three largest corporations was close to three trillion dollars."[15]

The Washington Consensus of 1989 was a major factor in the development of the global water industry. Until the 1980s, the World Bank and

IMF had financed many public water projects. Thereafter, under the influence of neoliberal policies, as articulated in the Washington Consensus, the financial institutions became the main factor pushing the global privatization of water systems.[16] In 1990, only 51 million people in France, England and Wales bought their water from private companies, while in 2002 this figure had risen to almost 300 million.[17] Under the structural adjustment programs of the World Bank and the IMF, international aid or loans were conditioned on involving the private sector in the water management of poor countries. As Maude Barlow reports, by the early 1990s, the World Bank, the IMF, and regional development banks "were encouraging poor countries to let the big European water corporations run their water systems for profit. A country's ability to choose between public or private water systems was steadily eroded, and by 2006 the vast majority of loans for water were conditional on privatization. In fifteen years, reports Public Services International, there was an 800 percent increase in African, Asian and Latin American water users purchasing water from transnational water companies."[18] According to other sources, between 1996 and 2002, the World Bank conditioned approximately one-third of its water-related loans on the privatization of the water utility.[19] Despite the "water war in Cochabamba"[20] and other evidence that treating water as a commodity leads to conflicts and exclusion of the poor, the international financial institutions are still pursuing these policies today. The Special Rapporteur of the UN Human Rights Council on the human right to safe drinking water and sanitation, Catarina de Albuquerque, reported in 2013, for example, that during the current economic crisis, "private sector participation in public service delivery, including in water provision, has been a condition for bailout packages signed with indebted countries," including Greece.[21]

Despite this enormous pressure on poor countries, the actual full privatization of water, that is, the full-scale divestiture of assets, is rare. Only the United Kingdom under Margaret Thatcher with respect to England and Wales in 1989, and Chile in 1998 have employed full-scale water privatization.[22] But a substantial number of countries, above all in the Global South and in Central and Eastern Europe, follow the "French model" involving public-private partnerships whereby the state continues to own the assets and is involved in the monitoring and decision making of the service delivery, while the actual operations and planning of water services are undertaken by private companies. On the other hand, in Japan, Canada, Egypt, Pakistan, and many European countries, such as the Nordic countries or

Austria, water management is still considered a genuinely public responsibility. Even in the United States, only a small percentage of the population
is served by private water companies, and the state treats water, in principle,
as a public good.[23] As the Special Rapporteur on the right to water and
sanitation has reported after her mission to the United States in 2011, the
vast majority of people in the United States (268 million) receive their water
from a community water system, that is, a public water system that serves
people year-round in their homes.[24] In addition, she reported that there are
53,000 rural water utilities in small communities, and 46 million Americans
rely on their own private drinking water supplies, usually wells.

According to World Bank estimates, in 2007 about 270 million people
worldwide received water from private companies in more than 40 countries, including about 160 million in developed countries and 110 million
in developing countries.[25] The *Pinsent Masons Water Yearbook 2011–2012*,
which uses a broader definition and includes wastewater services, estimated,
however, that 909 million people in 62 countries or 13 percent of the world
population were served by the private sector in one form or another:[26] This
includes 309 million people in China, 61 million in the U.S., 60 million in
Brazil, 55 million in the UK, 46 million in France, 23 million in Spain, 15
million in India, and 14 million in Russia. In addition, in Chile, the Czech
Republic, Armenia, Côte d'Ivoire, Ghana, Gabon, and Senegal, private
companies provide water services to the entire urban population. In his
report on the implementation of the Millennium Development Goals, UN
Secretary-General Ban Ki-moon reported that over 2.3 billion people
gained access to an improved source of drinking water between 1990 and
2012, out of which there were 1.6 billion people who had gained access to
a piped drinking water supply on the premises.[27]

Opposition to the Privatization of Water

Opposition to the privatization of water has gained ground at almost the
same speed as the international financial institutions had promoted it
around the world.[28] There are many examples where the "water warriors"
finally won the battle against business interests.[29] The best known is certainly the "water war" of Cochabamba, Bolivia's third largest city.[30] In 1998,
under World Bank supervision, the Bolivian government had passed a law
privatizing Cochabamba's water system and concluded a contract with the

U.S. engineering corporation Bechtel, which immediately tripled the price of water, cutting off those who could not pay. The company even charged them for rainwater they collected in cisterns. Under the leadership of Oscar Olivera, the Coalition in Defence of Water and Life, one of the first coalitions against water privatization in the world, organized a successful referendum demanding that the government cancel its contract with Bechtel. Since the government did not wish to give in, many thousands took to the streets in nonviolent protest and were met with army violence that wounded dozens and killed a seventeen-year-old boy. In April 2000, the government finally backed down, told Bechtel to leave the country, and transferred ownership of the water company back to public control. Since Bechtel had inserted three tiers of Dutch companies into the chain of ownership between itself and its subsidiary in Bolivia, it claimed violation of the Netherlands-Bolivia Bilateral Investment Treaty (BIT) and requested arbitration before the International Centre for the Settlement of Investment Disputes (ICSID), the arbitration tribunal of the World Bank.[31] Bolivia objected on various grounds to the jurisdiction of the ICSID, but lost this legal battle. Under the pressure of public opinion, Bechtel, which had originally claimed 25 million dollars of damages, in 2006 finally settled their claims for a token payment amounting to thirty cents. Nevertheless, in May 2007 the government of Bolivia formally withdrew from the ICSID Convention since, in its opinion, ICSID favors multinational corporations over governments.[32]

Other Latin American countries such as Nicaragua and Venezuela threatened that they would follow the example of Bolivia.[33] In 2004, the people of Uruguay had decided in a popular referendum to amend the constitution to include a human right to water, which means that the service of water supply may be controlled exclusively and directly by state legal persons and not by for-profit companies.[34] This referendum resulted from a failed contract with a subsidiary of Suez and might become a trend in Latin American countries, which are dissatisfied with their experiences with water privatization under the supervision of the World Bank.[35] In reporting on her mission to Uruguay in 2012, the UN Special Rapporteur on the right to water and sanitation noted with satisfaction that "Uruguay was the first country in the world to recognize the rights to safe drinking water and sanitation at the domestic level" and that "the Constitution provides a sound legal basis for guiding public action to comply with the obligations on the human rights to water and sanitation."[36] She also reported that

"Uruguay has one of the highest rates of access to safe drinking water in Latin America," reaching 98.1 percent of the population in urban areas and 94.2 percent in small locations.[37]

Argentina also had very negative experiences with transnational water corporations and in 2006 had even lost an arbitration case against Azurix before the ICSID under its BIT with the United States.[38] Under the Conservative government of Carlos Menem, the water management of Buenos Aires had been outsourced, with the financial assistance of the international financial institutions, to Aguas Argentinas, a daughter of the two French TNCs Suez and Veolia.[39] In 1996, the first protests started because of high tariffs. Since Aguas Argentinas expanded the water net without equally investing in the sewage system, the environmental pollution of the Rio de la Plata increased dramatically. In 2002, during the economic crisis, the new government was freezing the water tariffs and in 2006, the government finally rescinded the contract with Aguas Argentinas because the company had repeatedly raised tariffs and dumped nearly 90 percent of the city's sewage into the river and thereby broken its promise to treat wastewater. With the backing of the French government, Suez tried to recoup $1.7 billion from the state of Argentina before the ICSID.[40] But in this case, the ICSID, for the first time, accepted amicus curiae briefs from civil society organizations, even in the face of objections from the disputing parties, on the ground that "these systems provide basic public services to millions of people and as a result may raise a variety of complex public and international law questions, including human rights considerations."[41] In 2005, an Argentinian court, by directly applying the right to water derived from the CESCR, ordered the private water company Aguas de Buenos Aires S.A. (ABSA) to resume the provision of water services to a woman whose failure to pay for the potable water service for several months had led to the complete termination of the water service and the removal of the water meter by the private service provider.[42] Similar disputes over water privatization have led to strong civil society reactions in Mexico, Chile, Ecuador, and other Latin American countries.[43]

With only 36 percent of its population having access to basic sanitation and almost 300 million people lacking access to safe drinking water, the African continent faces some of the greatest challenges with respect to equal access to water and sanitation.[44] In 2003, Tanzania was awarded $143 million by the World Bank and other development institutions for the purpose of repairing and expanding the water and sewage infrastructure of Dar es

Salaam under the condition of privatization. The government made a contract with the British water corporation Biwater. From the beginning, serious problems were encountered, and in 2005, the government terminated the contract, seized the company's assets, and installed a new management. In 2006, Biwater started arbitration proceedings before the ICSID demanding $25 million from Tanzania. Although the ICSID ruled that the various actions of Tanzania amounted to an expropriation of Biwater's investments, its claims for damages were finally dismissed.[45]

Although South Africa was also heavily criticized for relying too much on private investments,[46] it is seen by many as a success story as the post-Apartheid government under Nelson Mandela succeeded in providing safe water to 15 million people between 1994 and 2005. The 1996 Constitution of South Africa is one of the most human rights sensitive constitutions in the world and, therefore, even contains a right to water.[47] It has been argued that the constitutional duty to provide access to water cannot be transferred to a private party.[48] The National Water Act of 1998 provides that all water, whether surface or underground, belongs to the nation, and the minister of water affairs must ensure that the water is protected, used, developed, conserved, managed, and controlled for the benefit of all persons. In 2001, the minister of water affairs announced that the government had decided to provide a basic supply of 6,000 liters of safe water per month to poor households free of charge. For a household of eight people, this amount corresponds to the WHO standards of 25 liters per person per day.[49] This free basic water is often coupled to the not always popular prepaid meters.[50] Under pressure from the World Bank, Suez was brought in to manage Johannesburg's water services and immediately implemented a full-cost system of payment and installed water meters in people's homes.[51] This led to strong protests by the South African Coalition Against Water Privatization, consisting of many human rights and environmental groups. In April 2008, the High Court of South Africa ruled in the well-known Mazibuko case that the city of Johannesburg's forced installation of prepayment water meters was unconstitutional and ordered the city to provide local residents with 50 liters of free basic water per person per day rather than the limit of 25 which had been in existence.[52] The court also explicitly ruled against the background of international law that the state is obliged to provide free basic water to the poor. Similarly, in the Bon Vista case, the court held that if a local authority disconnects an existing water supply to consumers, this is a prima facie breach of its constitutional duty to respect the right of existing access to water, and requires constitutional justification. Where a person proves that he or she is unable to pay for basic services, the service may not be discontinued.[53]

Water privatization was also applied in various Asian countries, including China, India, the Philippines, and Indonesia.[54] With the blessing of and funding from the World Bank and the Asian Development Bank, Suez and Thames Water used their connections to the regime of former Indonesian dictator Suharto to secure concessions to Jakarta's water, which was privatized in 1998.[55] Connections for those who could pay increased, while the situation for the poor, who no longer had access to public water, got worse. After the fall of the Suharto regime, the new government wanted to cancel the contracts with the two transnational corporations, but the threat of litigation before the ICSID prevented such action.

Development of the Right to Water
as Reaction to Privatization

These and many other experiences with water privatization under pressure from the international financial institutions and strong opposition against these policies by human rights groups, environmental groups, indigenous groups, religious groups, and other civil society actors and "water warriors" are the political background for the development of a human right to water under international law. Most important, in 2003 the UN Committee on Economic, Social and Cultural Rights published its well-known General Comment 15 on the Right to Water.[56] Although the right to water is not explicitly mentioned in the text of the Covenant on Economic, Social and Cultural Rights, the Committee argued that the right to an adequate standard of living in Article 11 CESCR is an umbrella right and that the word "including" indicates that the catalogue of rights (to food, clothing, and housing) listed in this Article was not intended to be exhaustive: "The right to water clearly falls within the category of guarantees essential for securing an adequate standard of living, particularly since it is one of the most fundamental conditions for survival."[57] In addition, the Committee stressed that the right to water was also inextricably related to the right to health in Article 12 CESCR and the rights to food and housing in Article 11. In other words, the Committee did not create a new right, it simply interpreted Article 11 (and to some extent also Article 12) CESCR as having contained a right to water from the outset without explicitly mentioning it, since water was not yet considered a scarce good when the Covenant had been drafted. The Committee also stressed that water is a "public good," and that the human right to water is "indispensable for leading a life in human dignity."[58]

General Comment 15 follows other General Comments by applying the 4-A scheme, explaining states parties' obligations, including core obligations, violations, and implementation at the national level. As in other General Comments, the Committee avoids addressing the controversial question of privatization directly. But it emphasizes that water should be treated "as a social and cultural good, and not primarily as an economic good. The manner of the realization of the right to water must also be sustainable, ensuring that the right can be realized for present and future generations."[59] With respect to availability, the Committee notes that the water supply for each person must be sufficient and continuous for personal and domestic uses, including drinking, personal sanitation, washing of clothes, food preparation, personal and household hygiene. The quantity of water available for each person should correspond to WHO guidelines.[60] Accessibility means that water must be within safe physical reach and economically affordable for all sections of the population, including the most vulnerable or marginalized ones.[61] States parties, therefore, should give special attention to women, children, homeless persons, indigenous peoples, refugees, asylum seekers, internally displaced persons, prisoners and detainees, older persons, persons with disabilities, victims of natural disasters, and so on.[62] The Committee further repeats its "strong presumption that retrogressive measures taken in relation to the right to water are prohibited under the Covenant."[63] With respect to state obligations to protect, the Committee notes that where "water services (such as piped water networks, water tankers, access to rivers and wells) are operated and controlled by third parties, states parties must prevent them from compromising equal, affordable, and physical access to sufficient, safe and acceptable water."[64] This indicates that the Committee, in principle, accepts a certain privatization of water management, but under conditions that are very difficult to meet for both states and for-profit water companies. The Committee also calls on states parties that are members of the international financial institutions, and to such institutions directly, to take the right to water into account in their lending policies and structural adjustment programs.[65] Finally, reading the core obligations, which include ensuring access to the

minimum essential amount of water on a nondiscriminatory basis, especially for disadvantaged or marginalized groups, adopting and implementing a national water strategy and plan of action addressing the whole
population, and adopting "relatively low-cost targeted water programs to
protect vulnerable and marginalized groups,"[66] it is difficult to see how
states should carefully implement these core obligations with a view to
achieving progressively the full realization of the right to water to the maximum of their available resources, if they privatize the water management
to for-profit corporations with totally different goals and preferences.
When the Committee finally spells out that the adoption of retrogressive
measures incompatible with the core obligations outlined above constitutes
a violation of the right to water,[67] the experiences in so many countries of
the world during the last two decades illustrate that privatization, at least in
the long term, almost always turned out to be retrogressive and, therefore, a
violation of the core obligations of the respective governments. It is difficult
to imagine how the huge profits of transnational water corporations, which
have been financed either by public funding or through contributions by
the beneficiaries, could be interpreted as being in compliance with states'
obligations to progressively implement the right to water for all.[68]

In 2006, the former UN Sub-Commission on the Promotion and Protection of Human Rights adopted Guidelines for the Realization of the
Right to Water and Sanitation, which had been drafted by its Rapporteur
El Hadji Guissé.[69] These guidelines stress, inter alia, that states should give
priority in water and sanitation policies and programs to the persons without any basic access; adopt and implement a plan of action for the full
realization of the right to water and sanitation which establishes specific
targets, indicators, and time frames; formally recognize the right to water
and sanitation in relevant laws and regulations; refrain, and ensure that
private persons and organizations refrain, from interfering with the enjoyment of the right to water and sanitation or any other human rights, unless
such interference is permitted by law and includes appropriate procedural
protection.[70]

In 2007, the UN High Commissioner for Human Rights, in accordance
with a request by the Human Rights Council of 2006,[71] submitted a report
on the scope and content of the relevant human rights obligations related
to equitable access to safe drinking water and sanitation, in which she
concluded that "it is now time to consider access to safe drinking water

and sanitation as a human right, defined as the right to equal and non-discriminatory access to a sufficient amount of safe drinking water for personal and domestic uses—drinking, personal sanitation, washing of clothes, food preparation and personal and household hygiene—to sustain life and health."[72] With respect to the controversial issue of privatization, the High Commissioner noted that "further elaboration is needed regarding the human rights response and requirements concerning the private provision of water and sanitation services."[73] On the basis of this report, the UN Human Rights Council in 2008, "deeply concerned that over one billion people lack access to safe drinking water and that 2.6 billion lack access to basic sanitation," unanimously appointed an Independent Expert on the issue of human rights obligations related to access to safe drinking water and sanitation to examine the status of both rights.[74] It is interesting to note that the Council in the preamble to this resolution emphasized that the CESCR entails "obligations in relation to access to safe drinking water and sanitation" and thereby implicitly confirmed the interpretation of the CESCR Committee in General Comment 15. The Independent Expert was requested to develop a dialogue with governments and other stakeholders on best practices, to undertake a study on the further clarification of the content of human rights obligations in relation to access to safe drinking water and sanitation, and to submit a report with conclusions and recommendations to the Council.

Does the Right to Water Prohibit Privatization?

The Independent Expert on the right to water and sanitation, the Portuguese expert Catarina de Albuquerque, on 1 July 2010 presented a report on the compilation of good practices.[75] She explained the normative content of this right by applying the 4-A scheme as developed by the Special Rapporteur on the right to education and adapted by the CESCR Committee to other rights contained in the Covenant, including the right to water. Despite the highly contested role of transnational corporations in water management, the Independent Expert fully recognized the role of the private sector: "Beyond their role in service provision, private actors are active in many areas related to the rights to water and to sanitation. The private sector includes companies and business, and they can contribute by including the respect and realization of the rights to water and sanitation in their core business operations and decision-making processes."[76]

Only a few days earlier, Catarina de Albuquerque had issued a special report on human rights obligations related to non-state service provision in water and sanitation.[77] She had addressed this question because the High Commissioner had left it open in her 2007 report and because she had noted "a constant interest and curiosity in a human rights analysis of private sector participation. While the debate surrounding private sector participation has often been polarizing, the independent expert observes that concrete situations are rarely 'black or white,' but instead are characterized by varying shades of grey."[78] She continues by describing the history of privatization, the role of the international financial institutions and the widespread opposition to water privatization. But then she tries to downplay the role of big business:[79]

> The intensity of the debate between advocates and critics, which is sometimes ideological and emotional, may have partially obscured the actual extent of private sector participation. While such participation is very common in some countries, on a global scale, other forms of service provision predominate. It has been estimated that, as of 2003, only 5 percent of the world's population was being served by the formal private sector. Moreover, the debate sometimes conveys the impression that the private sector is largely dominated by transnational corporations. This does not reflect present reality. Some transnational corporations have started to withdraw from developing countries, they are increasingly developing local partnerships, and, in a number of countries, local private actors are also very active.

To the argument that the right to water may rule out privatization of water services, she responds by repeating the neutrality argument of human rights:[80] "Yet, the two issues are separate. Human rights are neutral as to economic models in general, and models of service provision more specifically." She continues by referring to the human rights responsibilities of the corporate sector under the UN Global Compact, the Ruggie framework of "respect, protect and remedy," and other international standards of corporate social responsibility. In particular, she takes up the idea of a human rights impact assessment:[81]

States are encouraged to build human rights impact assessments into the process of deciding on the means of service provision and monitoring such provision, as well as to adopt legislation that imposes on service providers the obligation to carry out a human rights impact assessment. Service providers have a responsibility to undertake these assessments as part of exercising due diligence to become aware of the actual and potential impact of their action on the human rights to water and sanitation. On that basis, the state and service providers can work together to integrate human rights into water and sanitation policies, thereby ensuring compliance with human rights law, preventing human rights violations and maximizing positive effects.

She concludes her report by repeating that

a more nuanced approach is needed in the debate on the participation of non-state actors in water and services provision, namely, one that overcomes the simplistic public versus private debate and acknowledges the existence of a wide variety of actors and arrangements for the delivery of water and sanitation services. These are rarely exclusively public or private, and they also involve both the formal and informal sectors.[82]

She repeats the dogma of the neutrality of human rights by stating that the

human rights framework does not call for any particular form of service provision. It is well established that, from a human rights perspective, States can opt to involve non-State actors in sanitation and water services provision. But the State cannot exempt itself from its human rights obligations and hence remains the primary duty-bearer. Therefore, also when involving other actors in services provision, the role of the State is crucial. The obligations of States and the responsibilities of non-State actors are complementary. The latter can and should support the State in the realization of human rights.[83]

This report came as a blow to those who had been fighting for the right to water and against the power of the transnational water corporations and the global privatization of water services. Only a few days after the release of her report, Bolivia, on the basis of its negative experiences with privatization and water justice struggles, introduced a resolution on the human right to safe drinking water and sanitation to the General Assembly. It seems that many states were caught by surprise, and the resolution was adopted on 28 July 2010 by 122 votes in favor, none against, and 41 abstentions, primarily from Western countries.[84] The resolution was silent on the role of the corporate sector and privatization and recognized the "right to safe drinking water and sanitation as a human right that is essential for the full enjoyment of life and all human rights." The concerns of Western states were, however, taken into account in a consensus resolution on human rights and access to safe drinking water and sanitation, adopted by the Human Rights Council only two months later.[85] This resolution is much more specific and affirms that "the right to safe drinking water and sanitation is derived from the right to an adequate standard of living and inextricably related to the right to the highest attainable standard of physical and mental health, as well as the right to life and human dignity."[86] This language confirms the interpretation of the CESCR Committee in General Comment 15. In order to support the interests of the transnational water corporations, Western states, in conformity with the recommendations of the Independent Expert, had, however, insisted on including the explicit recognition of the possibility of privatization and outsourcing of water management to the corporate sector. In this respect, the Council reaffirmed that "States have the primary responsibility to ensure the full realization of all human rights, and that the delegation of the delivery of safe drinking water and/or sanitation services to a third party does not exempt the State from its human rights obligations."[87] More precisely, the Council even recognized that "States, in accordance with their laws, regulations and public policies, may opt to involve non-State actors in the provision of safe drinking water and sanitation services and, regardless of the form of provision, should ensure transparency, non-discrimination and accountability."[88] In addition, states were requested to "ensure that non-State providers fulfil their human rights responsibilities throughout their work processes, contribute to the provision of a regular supply of safe, acceptable, accessible and affordable drinking water and sanitation services of good quality and sufficient quantity, integrate human rights into impact assessments in order to identify and help address human rights challenges, develop effective organizational-level grievance mechanisms for users, and refrain from obstructing access to

State-based accountability mechanisms."[89] Although the resolution does not mention the corporate sector, it is clear that transnational water corporations were addressed as "non-State providers." While in the health or education sector, charities, religious institutions, and other nonprofit organizations play an essential role, this is not the case in the water sector despite the efforts of the Independent Expert to emphasize the role of small-scale providers. "Non-State providers" in principle means big business.[90] This link between human rights and business is also underlined by a reference in the preamble to the Principles on Business and Human Rights developed by Special Representative John Ruggie.

In her more recent reports to the Human Rights Council, the Independent Expert, who has been promoted in March 2011 to a Special Rapporteur on the human right to safe drinking water and sanitation,[91] seems to have become more critical toward water privatization. In a 2013 report on sustainability and non-retrogression in the realization of the rights to water and sanitation, Catarina de Albuquerque expressed concern that often "profits made by private operators are almost fully distributed among shareholders, rather than being partly reinvested in maintaining and extending service provision, the result being increased prices for consumers, continued need for public investment, and potentially unsustainable services."[92] In her opinion, private service provision "can also create concerns for other important human rights principles and standards, such as the principles of participation and accountability. During the current crisis, private sector participation in public services delivery, including in water provision, has been a condition for bailout packages signed with indebted countries. Once the decision to privatize has been made, and especially in the context of economic crisis, the process of selling the assets often does not include sufficient opportunities for meaningful public participation."[93]

From these more recent developments one can conclude that the United Nations have officially recognized the existence of a human right to water and sanitation as an essential element of the right to an adequate standard of living in Article 11 CESCR, as originally suggested by the Committee on Economic, Social and Cultural Rights in its General Comment 15 of 2002.[94] None of the relevant UN human rights bodies, including the CESCR Committee, the Human Rights Council, the former Sub-Commission, and the Independent Expert and later Special Rapporteur on the right to water and sanitation, has argued, however, that the right to water would prevent states parties to the CESCR from privatizing or outsourcing water management to the corporate sector. On the contrary, the Special Rapporteur explicitly stressed that international human rights law was neutral in this respect, and the Human Rights Council has explicitly recognized that states "may opt to involve non-State actors in the provision of safe drinking water and sanitation services."[95] The (core) obligations of states to ensure, to the maximum of their available resources, the progressive realization of equal access to water to all inhabitants, with particular attention to the most disadvantaged and marginalized groups, and to protect their people against violations by private service providers, means, however, that states have an obligation to carry out a human rights impact assessment when considering privatization measures, to closely regulate and monitor private water companies, and to terminate contracts in case of violations of the right to water. Otherwise, taking the experiences with water privatization into account, states would have to be considered as deliberately taking retrogressive measures in violation of their obligations under the Covenant. In the state reporting procedure, the CESCR Committee regularly reminds states parties of these obligations when considering privatization measures.[96] Similarly, the Independent Expert/Special Rapporteur on the right to water and sanitation has expressed concern to individual states that in considering the granting of concessions to private companies, they are obliged to establish regulations that private or semiprivate entities do not infringe human rights.[97]

In reality, full privatization has only occurred in England and Wales and in the cities of Chile. After negative experiences with water privatization on the pressure of the international financial institutions, a growing number of governments cancelled their contracts with transnational water corporations and returned to public water management. Others tried to protect themselves against this international pressure by adopting the right to water in their respective constitutions or national laws. Uruguay was the first country that recognized in 2004 the right to water in its constitution (Article 47) and prohibited water privatization. The Constitution of South Africa (Section 27(1)(b)) provides for a right to access to sufficient food and water and has partly been interpreted as prohibiting privatization. Other countries followed by including an explicit or at least implicit recognition of the right to water, such as Argentina (Article 41), Bolivia (Article 16), the Democratic Republic of Congo (Article 48), Ecuador (Article 12), Kenya (Article 43(1)d), the Maldives (Article 23(a)), Nicaragua (Article 105), and Niger (Article 20).[98] Again other countries, including Algeria, Brazil, France, Hungary, the Netherlands, Peru, Uganda, and Ukraine, passed laws recognizing a domestic right to water[99] and, at least partly, banning water privatization. In Italy, a law in favor of water privatization was repealed in June 2011 by an overwhelming majority of Italians through a referendum. In Austria, the efforts of the EU to push privatization of water services met with fierce resistance.[100]

Domestic courts and regional human rights monitoring bodies have been fairly creative in deducing a human right to water from various human rights provisions in the respective constitutions or regional human rights treaties. In India, various courts have interpreted the right to life in Article 21 of the constitution as encompassing the right to water as one of the "attributes of the right to life, for these are the basic elements which sustain life itself."[101] The Belgian Court of Arbitration invoked the right to the protection of a healthy environment under Article 23 of the constitution to establish that there existed a right of everyone to a minimum supply of drinking water.[102] In Argentina and South Africa, domestic courts have ruled that constitutional guarantees of access to adequate water prevent private sector water providers from cutting off supply to customers in the event of the latter's inability to pay for the service.[103] In *Free Legal Assistance Group et al. v. Zaire*, the African Commission on Human and Peoples' Rights had already in 1996 held that the failure to provide safe drinking water constituted a violation of the right to health under Article 16 of the African Charter of Human and Peoples' Rights.[104] In the landmark case of *SERAL v. Nigeria* regarding the violation of various rights of the Ogoni people in the Niger Delta by operations of the Nigerian military, in close cooperation with Shell, the African Commission also found violations of the right to water, as protected by the rights to health and a clean environment in Articles 16 and 24 of the African Charter.[105] The African Commission has also adopted in 2010 and 2011 reporting guidelines and principles for states parties to the African Charter, which contain a comprehensive interpretation of the right to water and sanitation, derived from different provisions of the African Charter.[106] In a case involving the Mapuche indigenous people in Argentina, the Inter-American Commission on Human Rights found Argentina in breach of the right to a judicial remedy in Article 25(2) ACHR by not complying with domestic court orders to supply safe and permanent drinking water to the Paynemil Mapuche community whose water sources had been contaminated with heavy metals, including lead and mercury.[107] In *Zander v. Sweden*, the European Court of Human Rights had found in 1993 a violation of the right to fair trial in Article 6

ECHR on the ground that Sweden had denied the applicants access to a legal remedy for the threatened pollution to a water source they used for drinking purposes.[108]

Sometimes, transnational corporations realize themselves that it is difficult to make profits in states where the governments take their obligations under the right to water and sanitation seriously by establishing appropriate regulatory frameworks, monitoring bodies, and accountability mechanisms, and leave such countries. In particular, private companies have retreated from the water supply sector in lower-income countries and show an increasing reluctance to engage in the long-term concession contracts that had become typical of the private sector participation projects of the 1990s.[109] Although the UN seems to treat the rights to water and sanitation as two sides of the same coin, there are substantial differences between them. Sanitation has traditionally been considered a core public function, similar to waste disposal, the provision of gas, electricity, and other public utilities. But sanitation is not a public good. Water, on the other hand, is a natural resource and, therefore, considered a public good. Human beings usually are willing to pay a reasonable price for being connected to a communal water pipe system and receiving clean water from the state, but many find it difficult to pay high tariffs for a public good in order to enable transnational water corporations to make huge profits with "their" public good. In my opinion, human rights are not "neutral" toward the privatization of water.[110] If private water companies make huge profits, whether from public funds (taxpayers' money) or through water tariffs, for providing water to the people, the respective governments have not taken the necessary steps, to the maximum of their available resources, as required by Article 2(1), to make this public good available to their people. States may resort to the private sector for certain services, such as repairing or expanding the water pipeline or sewage systems, or for the purification of water. The construction of water pipelines by private companies also contributed to the fact that a total of 2.3 billion more people worldwide have gained access to clean drinking water between 1990 and 2012.[111] Nevertheless, the delivery of clean drinking water as such, including the responsibility of equally servicing the poor and other marginalized groups, is a core public function which shall not be delegated to for-profit providers. I, therefore, agree with Miloon Kothari, former UN Special Rapporteur on the right to housing, when he said in October 2005 at the Berlin Conference organized by the German government in cooperation with the UN High

Commissioner for Human Rights, that "Water, essential for human life and all life on Earth, is part of the global commons and arguably the most quintessential of all collective resources. It is *not* a private commodity to be bought, sold or traded for profit—an exclusive luxury accessible to the few and elusive to the many."[112]

Chapter 7

Right to Personal Liberty and Rights of Detainees

Privatization of Prisons

The administration of justice, including access to the courts, investigation and prosecution of criminal offenses, the right to a fair trial before an independent court, law enforcement, arrest and detention, as well as the operation of prisons and other detention facilities are usually considered core functions of the state, which has the monopoly on the legitimate use of force. Nevertheless, neoliberal economic and political theories have also deeply penetrated these inherent governmental functions, which have a direct bearing on various human rights, including the rights to personal liberty and security, personal integrity and dignity, as well as the rule of law and the right to a fair trial. As in other areas, the United States since the Reagan administration and the United Kingdom since the Thatcher government were the forerunners. In this chapter, the focus will be on the privatization of prisons, while other aspects, above all the delegation of governmental powers to private military and security companies (PMSCs), will be dealt with in the following chapter.

In the United States, certain services in prisons, such as laundry, food, vocational training, and health delivery, have been outsourced to private companies for quite some time. In addition, we should not forget that historically, "prisons were typically privately run."[1] But the private interest was primarily the exploitation of prison labor. With the gradual development of the rule of law, human rights, and the modern welfare state in the twentieth century, the management of correctional facilities was considered even in the United States as an inherent governmental function.[2] The move back to private prisons started with the Weaversville Intensive Treatment Unit for juveniles, opened in 1976 as the first modern privately operated prison in Pennsylvania.[3] However, contracting for the operation of an entire prison or delegating both the construction and operation of a prison to a private company for purely economic reasons only started during the 1980s and was triggered by the dramatic increase of the number of prisoners and prison overcrowding caused by the "war on drugs" and similar "tough on crime policies."[4] The largest private prison company, Corrections Corporation of America (CCA), was founded in 1983 by Thomas Beasley, a former chair of the Republican Party in Tennessee,[5] where prison overcrowding was so rampant that a court had ordered the state to reduce overcrowding.[6] After winning a first contract in 1984 to run an immigration detention center in Houston, Texas,[7] CCA in 1984 entered into a contract with the state of Tennessee to run its Hamilton County facility. In the same year, Wackenhut Corrections Corporation, a Florida-based corporation founded by the former FBI agent George Wackenhut in the 1950s with three decades experience in the security industry,[8] won a contract to build a detention center in Denver, Colorado. Since then, the private prison industry has grown considerably, operating prisons, jails, juvenile and immigration detention centers, and other closed facilities under contract with the federal government and many state and local governments. By 1996, thirteen states had outsourced some portion of their penal systems and by 2004, thirty-four states had embraced the privatization trend.[9] Other companies, such as Esmor Correctional Services, had entered the market. The total number of beds in private prisons rose from 5,000 in 1988 to almost 95,000 in 2001.[10]

At the same time, the total prison population in the United States (including jails) had been skyrocketing from less than 300,000 in 1972 and less than 320,000 in 1980 to 600,000 in 1988, 1 million in 1994, 2 million in 2001, and 2.3 million in 2009. For most of the period between 1925 and 1972, the prison population (excluding jails) had fluctuated between 100,000 and 200,000 inmates, and the incarceration rate between 100 and 150, that is, comparable to Western Europe and other highly industrialized states.[11] During the 1970s, the prison population grew by 53 percent, during the 1980s by 115 percent, and in the 1990s by a further 77 percent![12] At the same time, the total spending on corrections has gone from $4 billion in

1975 to over $68 billion in 2006.[13] With over 2.2 million detainees, the United States presently has by far the highest number of prisoners world-wide (almost 25 percent of the world prison population as compared to about 5 percent of the world's population) and the highest incarceration rate (roughly 700 prisoners per 100,000 inhabitants) in the world.[14] According to the most recent statistics from the U.S. Department of Justice, which only includes state and federal prison facilities, not county jails and pretrial detention facilities, the number of sentenced prisoners increased from 294,400 in 1978 to over 1,511,500 in 2012 with an absolute peak of 1,555,600 in 2009.[15] By the end of 2012, a total of 137,200 inmates (40,446 federal and 96,774 state prisoners) were in the custody of private prisons, a 5 percent increase over the 131,000 inmates in 2011. This means that the U.S. prison population housed in private prisons further increased from 8.2 percent in 2011 to 8.7 percent in 2012. The states with the highest number of inmates in private prisons were Texas (18,617), Florida (11,701), and Georgia (7,900).[16] On the other hand, the following nineteen states had no private prisoners reported: Arkansas, Delaware, Illinois, Iowa, Maine, Massachusetts, Michigan, Minnesota, Missouri, Nebraska, Nevada, New Hampshire, New York, North Dakota, Oregon, Rhode Island, Utah, Washington, and West Virginia. Of these states, New York and Illinois have enacted legislation expressly barring private prison contracts.[17] The Reeves County Detention Complex in Pecos, Texas, operated by the GEO Group (formerly known as Wackenhut Securities) with a capacity of 3,763 prisoners, is reported to be the largest private prison in the world. According to journalist Matt Taibbi, the prison industry as a whole took in over $5 billion in revenue in 2011.[18]

The reasons for prison privatization and the rise of the prison industrial complex in the United States are manifold. One of the most common explanations is prison overcrowding, caused in the United States by the "war on drugs" dating back to Richard Nixon, tough policies on crime, racism, and a highly retributive criminal justice ideology that favors locking away of prisoners, many of them drug addicts, rather than their rehabilitation. Statistically, there is no correlation between the crime rate and the incarceration rate in the United States. It is interesting to note that the most dramatic increase in the prison population, from 1 to 2 million prisoners, occurred during the Clinton administration, that is, at a time when the crime rate was decreasing.[19] Statistically, this was also the high time of prison privatization, with the number of prisoners in privately operated prisons increasing from 45,000 to 95,000. Those who run the prison industry, who are themselves usually politicians of the far right with a highly retributive penal philosophy, offered to quickly build and operate cheaper prison facilities at a time when the majority of states in the United States were even under court orders to remedy cruel prison conditions as a result of overcrowding.[20] In other words, it is the same ideology that causes prison overcrowding and then offers free market solutions.[21] Other explanations are globalization in a time of neoliberal economic policies, which have led to a powerful global prison industrial complex with a strong influence on state and federal governments. Nossal and Wood argue, "what matters in the last instance in terms of the political choices that are made is not economic efficiency, historical precedent, global pressures or shifts in the prevailing political and ideological wisdom, but rather the ability of the private prison companies to organize and wield political influence and insert themselves directly into the corrections policy-making process."[22] They continue to argue that even within the United States, there are huge disparities with the prison industrial complex strongly rooted in the South, whereas more liberal states in the North, such as New York and Illinois, have even enacted laws that ban the privatization of prisons. This theory might also explain why the U.S.-based global prison industry, after initial successes in the UK and Australia, soon experienced difficulties on the global prison market with different criminal justice philosophies and stricter regulatory regimes.

The United Kingdom was the first European country to use prisons run by the private sector. During the government of Margaret Thatcher, who was herself, interestingly enough, not enthusiastic about the idea of prison privatization, the British Home Office conducted a series of feasibility studies into the practicability of prison contracting, first "as an experiment" for remand prisons.[23] The Criminal Justice Act of 1991 introduced legislation for contracted remand prisons, but later amendments ensured that privatization could be applied to all prisons. Wolds Prison opened as the first privately managed prison in the UK in 1992. It was a newly constructed 320-bed prison for male remand prisoners managed by Group 4 Corrections Services. During the Conservative government of John Major, three further prisons (Doncaster, Blakenhurst, and Buckley Hall) were opened that had been built with public funds but were privately managed. Although the Labour Party at that time opposed the Conservatives' policy on private prisons, it reversed its policy as soon as Tony Blair took office in 1997 and Jack Straw became home secretary.[24] Between 1992 and 2012, a total of thirty prisons were tendered, and between 1997 and 2003, fully eight private prisons were opened, some of them young offenders' institutions.[25] As a result, there were fourteen prisons in 2013 run by private companies, such as G4S, Sodexo Justice Services, and Serco, on behalf of the state, equivalent to 15.3 percent of the total UK prison population.[26] The UK has the second largest market for prisons in the world and the highest proportion of private prisoners, as compared to less than 10 percent in the United States.[27] Under the government of David Cameron, Birmingham became the first existing public prison to be transferred to contracted management. Three of the first privately managed prisons, Wolds remand prison, Blakenhurst, and Buckley Hall, were, however, returned to the public sector.

In Australia, prison privatization started even before it did in the UK. The first private prison, Borallon, opened in Queensland in 1990 on the initiative of the National Party against strong opposition by the Labour Party and trade unions.[28] Over the next eleven years, eight more private prisons were opened in New South Wales, Victoria, and other federal states and territories, run by Australasian Correction Management (ACM), a subsidiary of the U.S. Wackenhut Corrections Corporation, Corrections Corporation of Australia, Group 4, or Australian Integrated Management Systems (AIMS) Corporation. By reaching 20 percent of all prisoners, and in Victoria almost 50 percent accommodated in private prisons, Australia had a higher privatization rate than even the UK.[29] Similarly, illegal immigrants and asylum seekers have been detained for many years in special immigration detention centers, many of which were outsourced to private companies, such as Australasian Correction Management (ACM).[30] This includes the infamous Woomera Immigration Detention Centre, built in 1999 for up to 2,000 detainees, from where more than 500 refugees escaped in 2001 after a prison riot.[31]

The UN Human Rights Committee has found various violations of the right to personal liberty because of excessive length of immigration detention in Australia.[32] The case of *Cabal and Pasini v. Australia* concerned two Mexican citizens whose extradition from Australia had been requested by Mexico.[33] Both applicants were held, inter alia, together with convicted prisoners in the Sirius East high protection unit of Port Phillip maximum security prison in Victoria. Port Phillip was a privately operated prison, run by Group 4 and regulated by the law of the State of Victoria. They complained about a high level of violence, sexual assaults, and widespread communicable diseases. The Human Rights Committee held "that the contracting out to the private commercial sector of core State activities which involve the use of force and the detention of persons does not absolve a State party of its obligations under the Covenant, notably under articles 7 and 10, which are invoked in the instant communication. Consequently, the Committee found that the State party was accountable under the Covenant and the Optional Protocol of the treatment of inmates in the Port Philip Prison facility run by Group 4."[34] On the merits, the Committee found a violation of the right of detainees under Article 10(1) CCPR to be treated with humanity and dignity. The formulation "core State activities" indicates the Committee's disapproval of the privatization of prisons. At the same time, the Committee has not used this opportunity to rule on the compatibility of prison privatization with Article 10 CCPR as such.

In 2002, however, the UN Human Rights Committee criticized New Zealand in the state reporting procedure in fairly strong words.[35] It noted

> with concern that the management of one prison and prison escort services have been contracted to a private company. While welcoming the information that the state party has decided that all prisons will be publicly managed after the expiry of the current contract in July 2005 and that the contractors are expected to respect the United Nations Minimum Standards for the Treatment of Prisoners, it nevertheless remains concerned about whether the practice of privatization, in an area where the State is responsible for protecting the rights of persons whom it has deprived of their liberty, effectively meets the obligations of the State party under the Covenant and its own accountability for any violations.

The decision to privatize had been made in 1998 by the National Party government under Jenny Shipley.[36] The government had announced that the management of three new prisons would be put out to tender, starting with the new Auckland Central Remand Prison. This prison opened in July 2000 and was run by Australasian Correctional Management (ACM), a subsidiary of Wackenhut. But in 1999 the National Party lost the elections, and the new Labour government of Helen Clark decided it would halt the prison privatization program of the Conservatives immediately without terminating the contract with Wackenhut. Although the government of New Zealand had promised to the Human Rights Committee to return to the public management of prisons in 2005, this issue was again raised by

Japan during the Universal Periodic Review of New Zealand's human rights performance in 2009.[37] One year later, the Human Rights Committee again recommended to the government of New Zealand that all measures of privatization of prison management should continue to be closely monitored with a view to ensuring that under no circumstances can the state party's responsibility for guaranteeing to all persons deprived of their liberty all Covenant rights, in particular those under Article 10, be impeded.[38] This formulation illustrates again the principal concern of the Committee with the privatization of prisons.

The situation in Canada is similar to that in New Zealand.[39] In the mid-1990s there was some discussion of prison privatization in Nova Scotia, Alberta, and Ontario. Under the Conservative government of Mike Harris in Ontario, a plan was developed to establish twelve "super-jails" that would replace all forty-five prisons operated by the Ontario government.[40] When the "super-jails" were first announced, it was not anticipated that the private sector would be involved. But after the reelection of the Conservatives in 1999, the Ontario government in 2001 opened the maximum-security Central North Correctional Centre in Penetanguishene, run by the Management and Training Corporation (MTC), based in Utah, under a five-year contract.[41] The other identical "super-jail," the Central East Correctional Centre in Kawartha Lakes, opened in 2002 under public management. When the Conservatives in Ontario were ousted by a Liberal government in 2003, enthusiasm over privatization of prisons soon declined. The only other private prison in Canada was the New Brunswick Miramichi Youth Detention Centre; after strong public protests both private prisons have later been reverted to government control.

Selected Domestic Case Law

In Israel, the Supreme Court, in a landmark judgment of 2009, has put an end to experiments with prison privatization. In 2004, the Israeli Knesset passed the Prisons Ordinance Amendment Law (no. 28) permitting the establishment of private prisons in accordance with the "English model," in which the management of the prison is entrusted to a private enterprise operating under the supervision of the state. In 2005, the Human Rights Division of the Academic Center of Law and Business, acting as a public petitioner, together with a retired senior officer in the Israeli Prison Service and a prisoner, filed a petition to the Israeli Supreme Court challenging the constitutionality of this law on the ground that it violated the constitutional rights of prison inmates. On 19 November 2009, the Supreme Court decided in *Academic Center of Law and Business v. Minister of Finance* that this amendment violated the human rights to personal liberty and human dignity disproportionately and was therefore unconstitutional.[42] The judgment was delivered by a majority of eight judges against one dissenting opinion. The main majority opinion was written by President Dorit Beinisch and is worth being cited at length. She did not take up the factual arguments of the applicants that, based upon experience in other countries, there is a serious risk that in a private prison there will be more human rights violations than in state managed prisons, because this is speculation about the future. For the same reasons, she did not discuss the main argument of the government, namely that private prisons are more cost-effective than public prisons. Even under the assumption that private prisons are cheaper than public prisons and that they provide better protection of human rights than public prisons, President Beinisch arrived at the conclusion that private prisons nevertheless violate the constitutional rights of personal liberty and human dignity. Her argument is an argument of principle and not a pragmatic argument. It has to do with the very purpose of the modern democratic state, as envisaged by John Locke, and the for-profit motivation of the corporate sector on the other hand:[43]

According to modern political philosophy, one of the main factors that led to the organization of human beings in society, whereby invasive powers—including the power to send convicted offenders to prison—were given to the authorities of that society and especially the law enforcement authorities, is the aspiration to promote the protection of personal security and public order . . . Although, naturally, many changes and developments have occurred since the seventeenth century in the way in which the nature and functions of the state are regarded, it would appear that the basic political principle that the state, through the various bodies acting in it, is responsible for public security and the enforcement of the criminal law has remained unchanged throughout all those years, and it is part of the social contract on which the modern democratic state is also based." In order to carry out this important function, the state of Israel "has exclusive authority to resort to the use of organized force in general, and to enforce the criminal law in particular.[44]

Running prisons for profit would undermine this basic principle of state responsibility and legitimacy:[45]

> Imprisoning persons in a privately managed prison leads to a situation in which the clearly public purposes of imprisonment are blurred and diluted by irrelevant considerations that arise from a private economic purpose, namely the desire of the private corporation operating the prison to make a financial profit. There is therefore an inherent and natural concern that imprisoning inmates in a privately managed prison that is run with a private economic purpose *de facto* turns the prisoners into a means whereby the corporation that manages and operates the prison makes a financial profit. It should be noted that the very existence of a prison that operates on a profit-making basis reflects a lack of respect for the status of the inmates as human beings, and this violation of the human dignity of the inmates does not depend on the extent of the violation of human rights that actually occurs behind the prison walls.

The judgment of the Supreme Court of Israel, which also compares the situation, literature, and case law on prison privatization in other countries,[46] was issued at a time when prison privatization was being strongly criticized globally on the basis of increasing evidence of serious human rights violations and mismanagement in private prisons, above all in the United States. In this respect, it might also have influenced political decision makers in other countries, where private prisons were returned to public management. In Germany the privatization started during the 1990s with immigration detention centers in Glasmoor and Wuppertal. The first prison built by a private company was opened in 1996 in Waldeck near Rostock in the eastern part of Germany, while the private management of prisons was only started in this century. In 2001, the federal state of Hessen decided a partial privatization of the Hünfeld prison with some 500 inmates, followed by the prison Burg in Sachsen-Anhalt and the prison Bremervörde in Niedersachsen.[47] But the privatization of prisons faces limits under the German "Grundgesetz" (GG), the federal constitution of Germany. Although the right to human dignity plays an important role in

Article 1 of the German constitution, the Federal Constitutional Court so far has not followed the Supreme Court of Israel in this respect. But Article 33 GG contains an institutional guarantee of public civil servants (Funktionsgarantie des Berufsbeamtentums). According to Article 33(4), the exercise of sovereign powers has to be entrusted, as a permanent function, in principle to public civil servants with a fiduciary relationship to the state. The words "permanent function" show that nonpermanent tasks may be entrusted to others, and the formulation "in principle" (in der Regel) illustrates that there might be exceptions. But the exception must not become the rule.[48] More difficult is the interpretation of the term "sovereign powers" (hoheitsrechtliche Befugnisse), since the German constitution does not contain a catalogue of inherent governmental functions or core state responsibilities. But Article 33 GG has been interpreted in combination with the principles of democracy, the rule of law, and human rights to contain certain core state responsibilities which are essential for the functioning of the state and where an interference with human rights is highly probable. These functions concern the democratic organization of the state, defense and foreign relations, taxes, currency, as well as internal security and order, including the prevention of dangers and violence, the administration of justice, execution of court judgments, and prisons.[49] In addition, the fulfillment of human rights by means of positive measures, such as providing social security benefits and education, has been interpreted as an essentially public state function.[50] In December 2008, the State Court of Niedersachsen held that the partial privatization of psychiatric institutions, where mentally ill offenders are detained (Maßregelvollzug), violated the principle of democracy.[51]

In January 2012, the Federal Constitutional Court of Germany had to decide a similar question concerning the privatization of a special psychiatric prison in Hessen.[52] The court confirmed that the use of force which directly interferes with human rights is an essential public power.[53] The court also confirmed that carrying out of a prison sentence belongs to the core state functions, irrespective of whether it takes place in a regular prison or in a special psychiatric prison.[54] Nevertheless, in the particular circumstances of this case, taking into account the close organizational connection between psychiatric prisons and other psychiatric institutions, which were managed by the same company, and the fact that this company was owned by the state and was not operating for profit, the court decided that this purely formal type of privatization was still covered by the exception provided for in Article 33(4) GG. With this judgment, the Constitutional Court developed fairly clear standards which show that the management of prisons by for-profit companies would be prohibited under the German constitution. The margin, in which private companies may make profits in the public prison sector under the constitution, seems to be fairly small and, therefore, not interesting for the global prison industry. In 2009, the management of a prison in Offenburg was partly delegated to a for-profit company based in Essen, Kötter Security.[55] In fact, the 101 Kötter Security employees were not in charge of security in the prison (for which the 130 public officials were responsible), but were responsible for the provision of health, education, food, and work for prisoners. Nevertheless, the new coalition government of Social Democrats and the Green Party in Baden-Württemberg decided that this prison was again fully managed by the state as of June 2014.[56]

In Austria, there had been no experiments with privatization in the prison sector. But during the coalition government between the Conservatives and the far-right Freedom Party during the first decade of this century, the minister of the interior decided to privatize care for asylum seekers, a function that had been carried out by charities and nonprofit organizations, such as Caritas, Evangelische Diakonie, or Volkshilfe. The German company European Homecare was entrusted to advise asylum seekers that they had no chance to stay in Austria and should, therefore, voluntarily return to their country of origin (Rückkehrberatung). In addition, European Homecare was in charge of running the camps where asylum seekers were housed immediately after having arrived in Austria. Although these asylum seekers had certain duties to be present in these asylum centers, they were not detained there. The detention centers for refugees and immigrants pending deportation remained in the responsibility of the Ministry of Interior and the police. In fact, in most federal states, the former police jails are used to detain "illegal" immigrants and refugees. Since these police jails are not well suited for this type of detention, the Human Rights Advisory Council at the Ministry of Interior and its six visiting commissions had advocated for quite some time that a modern, human, and more open immigration detention center should be built. After many years of political discussions, the ministry finally announced that this immigration detention center (Schubhaftzentrum) would be built in the small and fairly remote municipality of Vordernberg in the state of Styria. In 2013, the media uncovered that the management of this detention center, for the first time in the history of Austria, would be partly outsourced to the Austrian subsidiary of the transnational security company G4S, whose management has excellent contacts to senior staff in the ministry. In fact, the ministry made a public contract to delegate running of the detention center to the mayor of Vordernberg, who again contracted the management to G4S. According to these contracts, G4S shall be primarily responsible for the cleaning, food, health care, and similar services, while the police would remain in charge of security. In spite of strong criticism by experts, the media, and the Austrian Ombuds-Institution, the detention center was opened at the beginning of 2014.[57]

As in the case of Germany, the question arises whether this type of privatization is compatible with the Austrian constitution and human rights. In 1996, the Austrian Constitutional Court in its well-known Austro Control judgment defined the limits of privatization under the Austrian federal constitution.[58] The Austro Control Law of 1993 had authorized the federal minister of public economy and traffic, together with the minister of finance, to replace the Austrian Federal Agency for Civil Aviation with the private Austro Control Company, of which the federal government had to remain majority owner. In addition to the ownership structure, the minister of public economy and traffic kept far-reaching monitoring and control functions, including issuing direct orders to the company. Taking these special circumstances into consideration, the Constitutional Court decided that the merely formal privatization of Austro Control had not violated the Austrian federal constitution. In this respect, the court held that the core functions of the public administration, which included the maintenance of public order and security, defense, and the administration of justice, including administrative penal sanctions, have not been delegated to Austro Control.[59] Therefore, neither the organizational system of the Austrian public administration nor the provisions of the constitution relating to the final responsibility of the government for public administration had been violated.[60] This leading judgment was reaffirmed in a number of later judgments.[61] Most important, the Constitutional Court decided in 2004 that the mandatory civilian service, which provides an alternative to the mandatory military service for conscientious objectors, belongs to the core functions of the state that must not be privatized.[62] By this judgment, the court declared the respective provisions in the Austrian Federal Law on Civilian Service of 2001, which had authorized the federal minister of the interior to delegate the administration of the civilian service, which includes possible interferences with human rights of persons subject to civilian service, as unconstitutional. Taken together, this jurisprudence seems to indicate that the privatization of prisons and immigration detention centers is unconstitutional, as it infringes a core state function.

Pros and Cons of Prison Privatization in Academic Discourse

In principle, we can distinguish between two major types of privatization of prisons. What is often called the "British model"[63] means that the full management of a prison, including maintenance of security, is entrusted to a private enterprise operating under the supervision of the state, which retains for itself only a limited number of powers, most notably the power to try and sentence persons to deprivation of liberty. In England and Wales, prisons were often financed, built, and run by private companies under contract with the government.[64] Nevertheless, "as a rule, the scope of powers given to private enterprises that operate prisons is more limited in the British model than in the American model."[65] This seems to be also a reason why the U.S.-based global prison industry had problems operating in Europe, including the UK. In the United States, the level of state supervision is only marginal, and the state sometimes even guarantees the private prison industry a certain number of prisoners, which is usually close to the full capacity of the respective prisons. Payment to the prison company is partly based on the number of prisoners detained, which is of course not an incentive to early release as a reward for good behavior of the person concerned.[66]

The other major model, often called the "French model," is a mixed system of public-private partnership in which custodial functions remain the responsibility of state employees while everything else is outsourced.[67] In addition to France, this model has been tried, for example, in Germany and Chile. This seems at first hand more acceptable from a human rights perspective, as the major sovereign power of using force to uphold public order and security in the prison remains with the state. However, experience around the world shows that this division of responsibility and powers between state prison guards and private security personnel causes many problems in the actual operation and management of the prison.[68] In particular, the separation of the security functions from the administrative functions makes it difficult to create a uniform policy and to define goals, and the global prison industry is not that interested in investing in a public-private partnership with an unclear division of labor and powers.

The main arguments in favor and against the privatization of prisons can be summarized as follows. Proponents of privatization argue that privately managed prisons are more efficient and less costly, because perpetual "competition and survival requires efficiency day in and day out; making a profit for shareholders requires it. Income sheets and balance sheets are the constant measure of revenues, expenses, profit, and return on investment in the private sector. Costs are closely followed, evaluated, and minimized. Present and future profits are an important basis for attracting investors in equity and in debt. Try as it may to measure, discipline, and motivate itself similarly, the public sector has nothing comparable."[69] In addition, flexible hiring, promotions, moving staff around, where and when needed, firing and the ability to quickly expand and contract help achieve efficiency in the private sector, as compared to the slow and bureaucratic public sector with long-term employed law enforcement officials.[70] This latter argument seems to have been decisive in states faced with overcrowding of prisons and even court orders to reduce overcrowding. A "final—and significant—anticipated benefit of privatization is decreased liability of the government in lawsuits that are brought by inmates and prison employees."[71]

The arguments against the privatization of prisons are more elaborate, as illustrated by the list of arguments provided by Martin E. Gold, who himself is in favor of prison privatization.[72] First of all, many people feel that operating prisons and other detention facilities, whether for convicted offenders, for persons accused of having committed a crime, for irregular migrants, asylum seekers, juveniles, drug users, and others, is an inherently governmental function which the state simply should not delegate to the for-profit private sector. Second, there might not be enough professional private companies able and willing to do the job. Third, the profit motive itself may prevent contracted-out services from being provided properly. Fourth, the procurement process for privatization may be difficult, slow, and open to risks, such as bias, heavy lobbying, conflicts of interest, and corruption. Fifth, the drafting, negotiation, monitoring, and enforcement of the contract may be expensive and difficult. Finally, in case of breach of contract, there may be difficulties in terminating the contract, leading to expensive and slow arbitration proceedings, and so on. Interestingly enough, neither Gold nor most other writers have mentioned human rights concerns when discussing the pros and cons of prison privatization.[73] Is privatization compatible with the right of detainees under Article 10(1) CCPR to be "treated with humanity and with respect for the inherent dignity of the human person"? Furthermore, how can a prison run by a for-profit enterprise be reconciled with the obligation of states parties under Article 10(3) CCPR, which stipulates that the "penitentiary system shall comprise treatment of prisoners the essential aim of which shall be their reformation and social rehabilitation"?

Both provisions of the Covenant are briefly mentioned in the contribution of Ira P. Robbins, professor of law and justice at the American University in Washington, D.C., to the book *Privatisation and Human Rights in the Age of Globalisation*, edited by the well-known human rights scholars Koen De Feyter and Felipe Gómez Isa in 2005.[74] Although the title of his contribution, "Privatisation of Corrections: A Violation of U.S. Domestic Law, International Human Rights, and Good Sense," promises an in-depth legal investigation on the limits of privatization under the U.S. Constitution and international human rights law, the author does not live up to this expectation. He seems personally to be convinced that privatization of prisons is not a "good thing" and violates "good sense," but his legal analysis is extremely weak and cautious. The only legal question he clearly answers on the basis of U.S. case law concerns the responsibility of the state under U.S. constitutional law for the conduct of private prison operators, who are considered to act "under color of state law."[75] But that the state cannot avoid its responsibility by delegating its functions to non-state actors is fairly uncontested under both international and domestic law in most states. The much more difficult and controversial question is whether international or constitutional law in fact prohibits the privatization of prisons as such. Robbins is aware of this question but, in the absence of relevant case law in the United States, feels unable to provide a clear legal answer:[76]

> There comes a point, however, at which concerns about the fairness of decision-making that affects the interests of individuals in what is so clearly a governmental function must outweigh the need for unchanneled exercises of expertise and claims of efficiency and reduced costs. Whether that point is reached with privatisation of corrections is a very difficult question, without any good, clear,

recent help from the case law. But it is important to distinguish among different types of privatisation. Privatisation of airports, for example, or air-traffic controllers, or mass transit, or firefighting services, or water-treatment services, or garbage-collection services all clearly involve the provision of services. Privatisation of prisons and jails, on the other hand, involves more than the simple provision of services; it also involves the *doing of justice*. Just as it would almost certainly violate the federal and state constitutions in the United States to privatize our criminal courts, it should similarly be unconstitutional to privatize our prisons and jails.

In a footnote, Robbins also raises the question why there is no U.S. case law on this important issue after so many years of privatization. His answer is worth quoting:[77] "My strong suspicion is that when a plaintiff raises that question in a credible way, the private company is quick to reach a confidential settlement of the lawsuit. Moreover, access to this information is deemed by the private company to be 'proprietary information,' and, therefore, is not required to be disclosed in corporate filings with the government."

With respect to international human rights law, the analysis of Ira Robbins is not much more revealing.[78] He refers to binding treaty obligations of the United States under Article 10 CCPR in the same way as to the Standard Minimum Rules for the Treatment of Prisoners and other soft law instruments adopted by the UN or the Maastricht Guidelines adopted by experts. His overview of these standards as compared to the practice in private U.S. prisons, and juvenile and asylum seeker detention facilities is useful to illustrate many instances in which these standards have been actually violated in private institutions, but one would probably be able to find as many cases in which they have been violated in public U.S. prisons. As the Supreme Court of Israel has so eloquently emphasized, this is, however, not the decisive question.[79] Even if we assume that the level of human rights violations is the same in private and public prisons and that private ones are more cost-effective than public ones, we still have to ask whether the privatization of prisons per se violates the right of detainees under Article 10 CCPR to be treated with humanity and respect for human dignity. Rather than providing an analysis of this important legal provision, Robbins arrives at the following moral or political rather than legal conclusion:[80]

I believe that certain functions within the prison setting—such as food service, medical service, educational service, and vocational training—can appropriately be privatized, assuming . . . that the overall level of quality regarding these services is not diminished. But other functions of the incarceration system—those in which accountability to the public is essential and inexorable—i.e., justice-based government functions—go well beyond what Professor Graham calls "essential services" and which the European Union refers to as "services of general interest." They are, and properly should be, so uniquely governmental in nature that contracting them out should be viewed as both bad policy and unlawful.

It is not clear which legal (or moral) standard Robbins applies when he speaks of "unlawful." In addition, one might question why the administration of security and discipline in a prison is more "governmental" than the provision of food, medical, and educational services to prisoners whom the state has deprived of their liberty. When Article 10(3) CCPR requires states to organize their correctional system in a way that is aimed at the "reformation and social rehabilitation" of offenders, why are then educational services less governmental than a disciplinary punishment? If a prisoner is punished by depriving him or her of food or essential medical services, why should this be less governmental than putting him or her for three days in isolation?

The second contribution to the volume of De Feyter and Gómez, written by Alfred C. Aman, professor of law at Indiana University, on "Privatisation, Prisons, Democracy and Human Rights," does not at all address the question of the permissibility of privatization of prisons under constitutional or international law. The author takes the existence of private prisons simply for granted, because historically private prisons are not a new phenomenon.[81] Rather, he is interested in the following questions:[82] "how best can non-state actors be involved in decision making processes; how can we maximize the flow of information involving these decisions; and how can we mitigate conflict of interest concerns that arise from the fusion of public and private that typify many markets and market approaches to policy issues—issues ranging from private prisons to welfare eligibility." His analysis provides useful information about the practice of operating private prisons in the United States,[83] but despite its promising title any human rights analysis is missing.

Limits of Prison Privatization Under
International Human Rights Law

During my mandate as UN Special Rapporteur on Torture between 2004
and 2010, I visited hundreds of prisons and other detention facilities in all
world regions.[84] In most countries, in both the Global North and South,
the conditions of detention are so terrible that I spoke at the conclusion of
my mandate of a "global prison crisis" and recommended the drafting and
adoption of a UN Convention on the Rights of Detainees, similar to other
special treaties for vulnerable groups, such as the UN conventions on the
rights of children or persons with disabilities.[85] Unfortunately, there is no
lobby for prisoners and detainees, and only a few nongovernmental organizations specialize in the rights of this particularly marginalized group of
human beings. There is very little empathy among the general public, politicians, and civil society for persons behind bars and very little knowledge
about the appalling conditions in most detention facilities. Prison walls
have a double function: they lock people in and at the same time they lock
the public out. Most people have never seen a prison from inside and have
very little interest in knowing more about this secret world. There is a
general assumption that persons deprived of their liberty by the state, for
whatever reason, have done something wrong and, therefore, "deserve" to
be locked away. This perception overlooks that many persons behind bars,
such as migrants and asylum seekers, pretrial detainees, patients in psychiatric institutions and facilities for persons with mental disabilities, or children in orphanages, have not committed any crimes or done anything
"wrong." In addition, in many countries, the administration of criminal
justice is fairly dysfunctional, nonindependent, and corrupt, which means
that even in correctional institutions there are usually many innocent and
"forgotten" prisoners. But even those of us who, for whatever reason, have
committed crimes, and therefore have been rightfully sentenced to a prison
term, have a human right to be treated with humanity and respect for their
dignity as human beings. They are lawfully deprived for a certain period of
their right to personal liberty, but not of other liberties and human rights.
The prison authorities have a responsibility to ensure, to the best of their
abilities, that prisoners are capable of enjoying and actively exercising all
human rights in order to use their time in prison in a way that most effectively contributes to their social reformation and rehabilitation as well as
reintegration into society after their release. The aim of rehabilitation, as

foreseen in Article 10(3) CCPR, is not only in the interest of the individual prisoner but in the interest of the society at large. The better a prisoner is rehabilitated during serving his or her prison term and reintegrated into society after release, the smaller the risk of recidivism and the lower the overall crime rate in the respective society.

This simple logic is underlined by the empirical fact that countries with the highest standards of prison conditions, such as the Nordic countries in Europe, usually also have the lowest recidivism, crime, and incarceration rates. On the other hand, countries with low standards of prison conditions, such as the United States, usually also show a high recidivism, crime, and incarceration rate.[86] This also has to do with the philosophy of justice prevailing in different countries. In general, societies that are based on a retributive philosophy of criminal justice usually show a higher crime and incarceration rate and tend to have lower standards of prison conditions, where inmates are simply locked away and not provided with extensive rehabilitation services. On the other hand, societies that are based on a restorative philosophy of criminal justice usually show a lower crime and incarceration rate and tend to have higher standards of prison conditions, where prisoners have access to meaningful work, education, social and psychological rehabilitation, and recreational facilities, where good behavior may lead to earlier release or release on probation, where prisoners are already during their sentence gradually prepared for a life after prison and are also further taken care of by probation officers and social workers after release. Countries with high prison standards apply the "principle of normalization," which means that conditions in detention should as much as possible resemble life outside prison.[87] Prisoners should not be locked away most of the time in their cells, but should be as free as possible and make their own autonomous decisions within the limits of a closed institution. The director of a prison I visited in Sweden referred to the "inmates" as her "clients." This is again not only in the interest of her "clients." She considered her task as treating her "clients" as well as possible, which was also in her own interest, as prisoners would cause fewer problems, would not try to escape, would have fewer fights among themselves and with prison guards, and so on. To provide prisoners with "full services" aimed at their social reformation and rehabilitation requires the necessary financial and personnel resources, including psychologists, social workers, teachers, vocational trainers, pastoral care providers, mediation experts, probation officers, and so on. On first sight, a prison with "full services" is, of course, more expensive than one that simply locks inmates away. But in the long term, because of contributing to better rehabilitation and social reintegration of offenders, which in turn leads to a lower recidivism, crime, and incarceration rate, high-standard prisons might turn out to be cheaper.

There can be no doubt that international human rights law, as provided for in Article 10 CCPR and a broad variety of soft law instruments, such as the UN Standard Minimum Rules for the Treatment of Prisoners of 1955, the UN Standard Minimum Rules for the Treatment of Prisoners of 2015 (Mandela Rules), or the Body of Principles for the Protection of All Persons under Any Form of Detention or Imprisonment of 1988, is based on the philosophy of restorative justice.[88] States have an obligation to treat prisoners with humanity and respect for the dignity inherent in every human being and to provide them with all services required for their social reformation and rehabilitation, as well as enabling them to enjoy and exercise all human rights, including the rights to food, education, health care, work, privacy, freedom of expression, information, and religion. Such an approach toward treating prisoners is simply not compatible with the very idea of privatization, which treats prisoners as commodities for making profit. Outsourcing the prison management to for-profit companies may reduce costs by reducing staff and services for prisoners, but these cost-saving measures are incompatible with the purpose of prisoner rehabilitation, as required by Article 10 CCPR and other human rights provisions. The privatization of prisons is, therefore, contrary to the right of detainees to be treated with respect for their human dignity, as held by the Supreme Court of Israel. To treat prisoners as an economic commodity violates their basic human right to human dignity.

Chapter 8

Right to Personal Security

·

History, Significance, and Content of
the Right to Personal Security

The human right to personal security goes back to the origins of human rights in the social contract theories of the seventeenth and eighteenth centuries. It is closely related to the legitimacy and sovereignty of the modern nation state. When John Locke wrote in 1690 that the "great and chief end . . . of men uniting into commonwealths, and putting themselves under government, is the preservation of their property,"[1] he meant the preservation of the natural rights of human beings, namely, their lives, liberties, and estates.[2] In other words: states were created by human beings for the purpose of securing the natural rights of human beings and overcoming the state of nature, where human beings had to fight against each other in order to protect their rights which were "constantly exposed to the invasion of others, . . . very unsafe, very unsecure."[3] These ideas were directly transformed into the human rights documents adopted during the American and French revolutions of the late eighteenth century. According to the American Declaration of Independence of 1776, "Governments are instituted among Men, deriving their just powers from the consent of the governed" for the single purpose "to secure these rights," above all "Life, Liberty and the pursuit of Happiness." Similarly, Article 2 of the French Declaration of the Rights of Man and of the Citizen 1789 defines the aim of every political association as "the preservation of the natural and inalienable rights of man; these rights are liberty, property, security and resistance to oppression."[4] The Jacobin Declaration of the Rights of Man and Citizen of 1793 is even more explicit:

Article 1: The aim of society is the common welfare. Government is instituted in order to guarantee to man the enjoyment of his natural and imprescriptible rights.

Article 2: These rights are equality, liberty, security, and property. . . .

Article 8: Security consists in the protection afforded by society to each of its members for the preservation of his person, his rights, and his property.

When human beings move from the state of nature to the political association which we call "states," they keep their substantive natural rights but transfer their procedural rights and powers to defend and protect these substantive rights to the government.[5] According to John Locke, these powers were primarily the right of everybody to punish criminals and the right of victims of crime to demand reparation.[6] The human right to security therefore requires the state to protect the life, liberty, property, and other human rights by means of criminal and civil law and its enforcement against those who violate these rights. It also means that human beings, by giving up their right to punish criminals themselves and force them to grant reparation for the harm inflicted, entrust the state with the monopoly of using force for the proper enforcement of their right to personal security and other human rights. According to the German sociologist Max Weber, whose sociology of the state became highly influential for the understanding of the functioning of the modern nation state and its public civil servants, this monopoly on the legitimate use of force constitutes the decisive criterion for defining the modern state.[7] The human right to personal security can, therefore, be defined as an umbrella right for the protection of other human rights, such as the rights to life, personal liberty, property, privacy, and health, against interference by other human beings, through means of criminal law, civil law, and the enforcement of these laws, based upon the monopoly of the legitimate use of force.

This particular significance of the right to security as an umbrella right has been reaffirmed in Article 3 of the Universal Declaration of Human Rights 1948: "Everyone has the right to life, liberty and the security of person." In the legal commentaries on Article 3 UDHR, the right to personal security has been described as "the right of being protected against certain intensive interferences from the State or from non-State actors (integrity rights)" without, however, attaching much importance to this right.[8] The reference to "integrity rights" illustrates that the right to personal security is also closely related to the prohibition of torture and other forms of ill-treatment, the prohibition of slavery, servitude, and forced labor, as well as to the right to human dignity. In essence, the right to personal security means protection against any form of violence, which is closely related to "freedom from fear" as articulated by President Franklin D. Roosevelt. The idea that security means freedom from internal and external violence was further developed by the UN with the notion of "human security" as an umbrella concept of protecting human beings against a variety of threats and forms of violence, including armed conflicts, organized crime, terrorism, natural disasters, and so on.[9] Although the UN General Assembly has emphasized that the "notion of human security is distinct from the responsibility to protect,"[10] both concepts are closely related. While human security is based on national ownership,[11] the failure of states to provide human security to their populations, that is, to protect them against the worst forms of violence and threats, such as genocide, ethnic cleansing, war crimes, and crimes against humanity, which can also be defined as gross and systematic violations of human rights to life, personal integrity, liberty, and security, triggers the concept of the Responsibility to Protect (R2P) by the international community, represented by the UN Security Council.[12] Some authors even argue that the responsibility to protect vulnerable populations "can be seen as a first step in the *normative grounding* of human security."[13]

In the European Convention on Human Rights 1950, the right to life in Article 2 was separated from the other two rights in Article 3 UDHR, which were codified together in Article 5(1) ECHR: "Everyone has the right to liberty and security of person." The remainder of Article 5 only deals with the right to personal liberty and its restrictions. This has prompted the European Court of Human Rights to divest the right to personal security of any independent significance beyond personal liberty.[14] Article 9(1) of the International Covenant on Civil and Political Rights literally follows the wording of Article 5 ECHR and is based on a British proposal in the Commission on Human Rights of 1952.[15] In the Third Committee of the General Assembly, the Israeli delegate expressed the opinion that the right to personal security would "rather represent a general heading for all the rights in Articles 6 to 17 guaranteeing the security and inviolability of the person."[16] Despite the identity of the formulation in Articles 5 ECHR and 9 CCPR, the UN Human Rights Committee did not follow the restrictive interpretation of the European Court of Human Rights and attaches an independent meaning to the right to personal security, in accordance with the historical significance of this right. In the landmark case of *Delgado Páez v. Colombia*, the Committee held in 1990 that an "interpretation of article 9 which would allow a State party to ignore threats to the personal security of nondetained persons within its jurisdiction would render totally ineffective the guarantees of the Covenant."[17] The applicant, a Colombian teacher, had to leave Colombia and ask for political asylum in France after having received death threats and having been attacked by private militias without any protection afforded by the Colombian government and its security forces. The Committee found a violation of Article 9(1) CCPR on the ground that Colombia had not taken, or had been unable to take, appropriate measures to ensure Mr. Delgado's right to security of his person. This remarkable jurisprudence was confirmed in a number of further cases concerning death threats, assassination attempts, harassment, and intimidation in a variety of countries, such as the Dominican Republic, DRC (formerly Zaire), Zambia, Equatorial Guinea, Angola, Jamaica, and Sri Lanka.[18]

In its more recent jurisprudence, the European Court of Human Rights, without changing its approach to Article 5 ECHR, has derived from the rights to life and personal integrity in Articles 2 and 3 ECHR a special procedural obligation of states to protect individuals against threats or interference with these rights by private parties.[19] In fact, this jurisprudence comes very close to accepting a right of human beings to be protected by the state against private violence, which constitutes the essence of the human right to personal security.

Of course, the right to personal security, like any other human right which demands from the state positive measures for its protection, must be applied by taking into account the principle of "due diligence." Not every private act of violence against another human being can be interpreted as a violation of the right to personal security by the respective state, and public law enforcement authorities do not have an obligation to provide every citizen who feels unsecure with a personal bodyguard. But states have an obligation to take all measures that can reasonably be expected from them in the particular circumstances to protect their inhabitants against all forms of violence. To enjoy freedom from fear and to feel secure constitutes one of the most important elements of quality of life and is closely related to the notion of the modern welfare state. Human beings should be able to rely on their governments to warn them in time about environmental disasters and to evacuate them, if need be; to protect them against wars and other forms of armed conflicts, terrorism, and similar types of organized violent crime; and they should be able to call the police and rely on a quick response by the police if they feel threatened by burglars, armed robbers, or violent husbands. Since the government has the monopoly on the legitimate use of force, it is the obligation of state security forces to protect their inhabitants against the use of force by others. If governments fail to protect their people against violence and crime, and the people lose the trust in their governments to protect them against such threats, they will increasingly take the law into their own hands, buy firearms to protect themselves, or hire private security guards if they can afford them. Such reactions soon develop their own dynamics and undermine the monopoly of the state on the legitimate use of force which may soon lead to the phenomenon of the fragile or failed state as we observe in a growing number of African and other states in our rapidly globalizing world. Since the protection of human rights constitutes the main legitimacy of the modern state, and taking into account the particular importance of the right to personal security as an umbrella right for the protection of many other rights, including the rights to life, personal integrity, private property, privacy, and health, the failure of governments to effectively prevent violence and provide protection against violence seriously undermines their legitimacy as states.

Protection of Personal Security as a Core Function of the State

We have to keep this historical, philosophical, and sociological background and importance of the right to personal security in mind when we assess the current trend toward privatization of the police, intelligence, and military forces, as well as the legitimacy of private military and security companies (PMSC).[20] Many states accept a concept of core state responsibilities, and the protection of external and internal security is without doubt one of the most important core responsibilities of states. This has, for example, been underlined by the Constitutional Court of Germany when interpreting the institutional guarantee of public civil servants in Article 33 of the German Federal Constitution in the context of the privatization of prisons.[21] Similarly, the Austrian Constitutional Court, when declaring the privatization of the compulsory alternative civilian service unconstitutional, has clearly stated that military and police functions are among the core functions of the public administration which must not be privatized.[22] In addition to its landmark judgment which declared the privatization of prisons as a violation of the right of detainees to human dignity,[23] the Supreme Court of Israel has held that it is "clear and certain that maintaining order at public events which involve a realization of constitutional rights, such as demonstrations, falls within the very heart of the police's functions."[24] This case concerned various conditions which the Israeli police had demanded from the petitioners who had applied to hold a public demonstration, including that they should arrange themselves to have security, first aid, and fire extinguishing services present at the demonstration. The Supreme Court held unanimously that the police have the duty to provide security and maintain order at demonstrations, and that they may not impose this responsibility on the persons organizing the demonstration.

Despite the fact that the concept of inherently governmental functions is not alien to U.S. law,[25] the Supreme Court of the United States, on the other hand, ruled in the well-known case of *Castle Rock v. Gonzales* that the police had no obligation to enforce a restraining order against a violent ex-husband because under the Due Process Clause of the Fourteenth Amendment to the U.S. Constitution, Colorado's law on the police enforcement of restraining orders did not give the petitioner, whose three daughters had been killed by her violent ex-husband in violation of the restraining order, a "property interest in the enforcement of the restraining order against her former husband."[26] The ex-wife and mother of the three murdered girls, Jessica Lenahan (formerly Gonzales), filed a petition against this judgment to the Inter-American Commission on Human Rights, which decided in 2011 that the U.S. authorities had failed to act with due diligence to protect the applicant and her daughters from domestic violence, which constituted violations of the rights to life, equal protection of the law, the right of special protection as girl-children, and the right to judicial protection under Articles 1, 2, 7, and 18 of the American Declaration on the Rights and Duties of Man.[27]

In a similar approach, the Working Group on Mercenaries of the UN Human Rights Council has repeatedly stressed its task of examining "the role of the State as the primary holder of the monopoly of the use of force, and related issues such as sovereignty and State responsibility to protect and ensure respect for human rights by all actors."[28] With respect to the rights to life, personal integrity, liberty, and security in Articles 6, 7, and 9

CCPR, the UN Human Rights Committee in the state reporting procedure, for example, with respect to Guatemala, "regrets the growing delegation of citizens' security functions to private companies without adequate registration or control." It thus recommended to the government to "ensure the subordination of private to public security, and provide access to justice and effective reparation mechanisms for the victims of acts committed by private security companies."[29]

The Rise of Private Military and Security Companies

Despite the danger for the state monopoly of legitimate use of force and its legitimacy in protecting human rights, certain states, above all the United States and the UK, have gone very far in privatizing their military, intelligence, and security sectors. Private security companies, such as the one of George Wackenhut in the United States or the operations by Sir Percy Sillitoe, a high-ranking British counterespionage expert from the Second World War, developed during the 1950s and 1960s.[30] Their services were hired for the protection of homes, real property, installations such as oil pipelines, companies, nongovernmental and intergovernmental organizations, and individuals in countries and in situations where the traditional protection by the state security forces was deemed insufficient, above all in Africa,[31] Asia, and Latin America. While mercenaries as the traditional "universal soldiers" fighting for profit in armed conflicts have existed throughout history, they had almost disappeared between the middle of the nineteenth and twentieth centuries.[32] But they reappeared again after World War II when colonial powers hired them to fight against anticolonial movements and liberation struggles in Africa and Asia. As the United Nations has outlawed in Article 2(4) of its Charter the use of force for the settlement of disputes (with the only exceptions of self-defense in Article 51 and collective military action authorized by the Security Council under Article 42), it also took steps to prohibit mercenaries under international law.[33] These attempts by the world organization in reaction to the rise of white mercenaries involved in attempts of European powers and the white minority regimes in Southern Africa to uphold colonialism and apartheid were, however, never fully supported by the West. This is one reason for the rapid development of private military companies during the 1990s and 2000s.

The decisive reason for the explosion of private military and security companies (PMSCs) seems, however, to be that the end of the Cold War coincided historically with the global spread and promotion of neoliberal deregulation and privatization policies.

The global disarmament, demilitarization, and demobilization as a consequence of the end of the Cold War led to the demobilization of roughly 6 million soldiers in a time span of only five years.[34] The collapse of the Soviet Union led to tens of thousands of former soldiers becoming mercenaries or serving in many of the private security companies that have proliferated in Russia.[35] But demobilization also occurred in other parts of the world, such as the demobilization of soldiers and guerrilla fighters after the peace deals in Central America. A direct connection between demobilization and the rise of mercenaries and PMSCs can be observed after the end of apartheid in South Africa. Former members of the South African military and police forces engaged in mercenary activities, such as the attempted overthrow of the Obiang regime in 2004 in Equatorial Guinea,[36] or joined private military companies, such as the South Africa-based Executive Outcomes, which played a decisive role in fighting rebel groups during the 1990s in countries such as Angola or Sierra Leone.[37]

But demobilization of soldiers is only one consequence of the end of the Cold War which had an impact on the rise of PMSCs. The ideological vacuum created by the collapse of Communist systems led to a feeling of insecurity after the end of the Cold War in Central and Eastern Europe. New nationalist movements in the Russian Federation, the Balkans, and other countries in this region emerged from this ideological vacuum directly leading to armed conflicts, in which many mercenaries and private military companies, such as the U.S.-based Military Professional Resources Incorporated (MPRI) were involved.[38] The feeling of insecurity, not only in post-Communist societies, was increased by the rapid globalization driven by neoliberal market forces and threats to human security posed by fragile states, rebel movements, transnational organized crime, and terrorism.[39] In other words, we see a dangerous vicious circle: the neoliberal ideology, by means of deregulation, privatization, and deliberately weakening state structures, creates a feeling of insecurity, from which the private military and security industry is benefitting. The World Bank, which has through its privatization and structural adjustment policies contributed more than others to the weakening of state structures in the global South, seems now to be concerned about the growing number of fragile states and has started in

2002 initiatives to assist "low income countries under stress" (LICUS) with state-building measures.[40]

The explosive growth of the private military and security industry, which today earns globally more than $100 billion per year, has been particularly pronounced in the United States and the United Kingdom, where 70 percent of the companies are registered.[41] According to a recent study by Corinna Seiberth, "the United States and the United Kingdom, as the largest providers and clients of PMSCs, have developed a culture of outsourcing that goes beyond what many other states find acceptable in view of the traditional notion of sovereign statehood. The United States and the United Kingdom each have a state structure that is practically hollowed out through privatization."[42] The Austrian brigadier and military expert Walter Feichtinger notes, however, an important difference between outsourcing of military functions in the United States and the UK: while U.S.-based PMSCs receive 95 percent of their contracts from the U.S. government, official contracts between the British government and UK-based PMSCs only amount to 5 percent of their revenues.[43] This shows that British PMSCs are much more export-oriented, primarily to the African "market" of fragile states and armed conflicts, than U.S.-based PMSCs.[44]

Under the present Conservative government of David Cameron, there seems to be a new wave of privatizing the British police. According to a 2012 report in the *Guardian*, West Midlands and Surrey have invited bids from G4S and other major security companies on behalf of all forces across England and Wales to take over the delivery of a wide range of services previously carried out by the police. This transformation program with a potential value of £1.5 billion is the largest-ever plan on police privatization in the UK, with strong backing from Home Secretary Theresa May. If successful, it would completely redraw the accepted boundaries between public and private and the definition of frontline and back-office policing.[45] Around the same time, the head of G4S for the UK and Africa, David Taylor-Smith, had predicted that most UK police forces would sign up to privatization by 2017.[46] According to its website, G4S is the "leading global integrated security company specialising in the provision of security products, services and solutions. The group is active in more than 120 countries, is the largest employer quoted on the London Stock Exchange with more than 618,000 employees, and has a secondary stock exchange listing in Copenhagen."[47] After strong opposition by police officers and unions, this ambitious privatization programme was put on hold shortly after it was revealed by the *Guardian*.[48] The public relations disaster of G4S, which failed to fulfill its contract of providing security during the Olympic Games in summer 2012 with the result that 3,500 British Army soldiers had to step in,[49] might be a reason why this gigantic privatization program has not been implemented so far.[50]

Shortly after the terrorist attacks of 11 September 2001, the Pentagon under Donald Rumsfeld published a new defense strategy which undermined the doctrine of inherent government functions[51] by stating that "any function that can be provided by the private sector is not a core government function."[52] The war initiated by the Bush administration and the Blair government against Iraq in 2003 had been described by the British *Observer* as the "first privatized war."[53] The United States and UK are also in the forefront of proposals of outsourcing international peace operations to the private sector.[54] In a 2009 report, the UN Working Group on the Use of Mercenaries strongly criticized the common perception among UK authorities of the private military and security industry as "business as usual."[55]

In a growing number of countries, the number of private security personnel is greater than the number of active state police.[56] A 2005 report on Kenya showed that there have been twice as many private security personnel operating in the country as public police.[57] During my fact-finding mission as UN Special Rapporteur on Torture to Papua New Guinea, I was told by the head of the police that the British security company G4S had about four times as many security personnel in the country as he had under his command.[58] It was, therefore, no surprise that even the UN availed itself of the services of G4S to provide security to our mission! In this respect, we can observe another vicious circle: rather than assisting fragile states in their capacity to build effective national security services, international actors, such as the United Nations and its various agencies, humanitarian organizations, diplomats, and transnational corporations take it for granted that their security needs cannot be effectively protected by the state and, therefore, need to be contracted out to PMSCs. This in turn leads to a further erosion of the already weak national security structures in fragile states.[59] The head of the police in Papua New Guinea also frankly (and in a certain resigned mood) admitted that G4S was paying about three times the salary he could offer to his police staff, and that his best officers were increasingly hired by G4S. At the end of their book on private security and public order, Simon Chesterman and Angelina Fisher provide us with another fairly telling story:[60] "It is striking that industry has taken such a lead role in debates over regulation, except when governments are forced to act by scandal. And even in response to scandal the industry may play an outsize role. Three weeks after the Nisour Square incident, half a dozen FBI investigators prepared to fly to Baghdad to examine the crime scene and interview witnesses. Under its State Department contract, initial plans provided for the investigators' security and transportation outside the Green Zone to be provided by . . . Blackwater. Following protests, the FBI announced that in order to avoid 'even the appearance' of a conflict of interests their agents would be protected by US government personnel."

Consequences of Privatizing Public Security Functions

The consequences of outsourcing the military and security sector to private business are well known, above all from the many scandals with Blackwater, CACI International, DynCorp, and other PMSCs in Iraq, Afghanistan, Colombia, and a variety of other countries.[61] First of all, there is a clear discrepancy between the public interest of preventing armed conflicts, organized crime, and other threats to human security and the private interests of PMSCs. Like other for-profit organizations, their main interest is to make a profit, and the personnel of PMSCs may earn up to $1,000 a day.[62] In order to further increase their profits and share values, PMSCs have a vested interest in prolonging armed conflicts and other unstable situations like fragile states. Powerful transnational PMSCs and the lobbyists for this rapidly growing industry, such as the U.S.-based International Peace Operations Association (IPOA) and the British Association of Private Security Companies (BAPSC)[63] play today a significant role in world politics and military decision-making processes.[64] Since PMSCs are primarily working for their own interest and not in the public interest, their staff sometimes simply desert if their operations, such as supporting the soldiers at the front line in the North of Baghdad with water, food, munition, and gasoline, turn out too dangerous.[65] Second, as the chairperson of the UN Working Group on the Use of Mercenaries, José Gómez del Prado has illustrated with various examples, "in their search for profit, PMSCs often neglect security and put their employees in dangerous and vulnerable situations that may have disastrous consequences," such as the well-known Blackwater disasters in the Iraqi town of Fallujah in 2004 and in Nisour Square of Baghdad in 2007.[66] Third, the lack of public regulation and oversight over the recruitment policies of PMSCs means that many "black sheep" are recruited, including military personnel from the Pinochet dictatorship in Chile or security officers from the former apartheid regime in South Africa, who had been responsible for gross and systematic human rights violations.[67] Fourth, governments, most notably the United States and the UK, often use PMSCs for operations that violate international or domestic law and can, therefore not be carried out by their public military and security forces.[68] Typical examples are the operations of DynCorp on behalf of the U.S. government in the "war on drugs" in Colombia, which included large-scale aerial fumigation with herbicides to eradicate the coca bush,[69] the violation of the UN arms embargo against Sierra Leone by the British government by using the UK-based military company Sandline International during the late 1990s,[70] or the use of privately chartered aircrafts of U.S. companies, such as Jeppesen Data Plan, by the CIA for so-called extraordinary rendition flights of terrorism suspects by the Bush administration in clear violation of International Aviation Law.[71] Finally, PMSCs are often exempted from legal accountability when committing serious violations of international humanitarian and human rights law, as the well-known torture practices of U.S.-based PMSCs, such as CACI, in the U.S. prison Abu Ghraib in Iraq have revealed.[72] When I interviewed the victims of U.S. torture in Abu Ghraib in Amman, Jordan, in 2006, many alleged that the most brutal torture methods had been applied by personnel of PMSCs, followed by CIA officers, and "only" in third place by military officers, who were, however, the only ones who were brought to justice in the United States.

Mercenary Activities Under International Law

It is, therefore, not surprising that the United Nations, which had outlawed the use of force in its Charter and promotes international human rights as one of its major aims and objectives, took a fairly critical approach toward mercenaries. In reaction to the reappearance of mercenaries during the colonial wars of the 1960s and 1970s, the international community regulated mercenaries in Article 47 of Additional Protocol 1 to the Geneva Conventions of 1977 (AP 1) by providing that they should neither have the right to be a combatant nor to be treated as prisoners of war.[73] This provision was adopted by consensus at the Diplomatic Conference of 1977. According to Article 47(2), a mercenary is defined as "any person who

(a) is specially recruited locally or abroad in order to fight in an armed conflict;

(b) does, in fact, take a direct part in the hostilities;

(c) is motivated to take part in the hostilities essentially by the desire for private gain and, in fact, is promised, by or on behalf of a Party to the conflict, material compensation substantially in excess of that promised or paid to combatants of similar ranks and functions in the armed forces of that Party;

(d) is neither a national of a Party to the conflict nor a resident of territory controlled by a Party to the conflict;

(e) is not a member of the armed forces of a Party to the conflict; and

(f) has not been sent by a State which is not a Party to the conflict on official duty as a member of its armed forces.

As can be seen from this definition, the two most important criteria for defining a mercenary are the foreign component, that is, they should not be nationals of any party to the conflict, and the financial motivation—the desire for private gain.[74] The phrase "does, in fact, take a direct part in the hostilities" in Article 47(2)(b) was included in the definition in order to exclude foreign advisers and military technicians recruited to train or maintain weapons.[75] However, Article 47 of AP 1 only applies to international armed conflicts whereas most of the present armed conflicts, where mercenaries take part, are noninternational ones. In addition, Article 47 does not explicitly prohibit mercenaries and, in particular, does not make mercenary activities or the recruitment, use, and financing of mercenaries a war crime. It only deprives mercenaries of the privileges of the status of combatants and prisoners of war. In reality, it is very difficult to prove that a person has cumulatively fulfilled all six requirements of the definition of mercenaries in Article 47(2), in particular the motivation by private gain.[76]

In order to address these two obstacles, the UN adopted in 1989 a special UN Mercenary Convention.[77] The definition of mercenaries under Article 1 of the Mercenary Convention covers all the criteria of Article 47(2) of AP 1 cited above, with the exception of "does, in fact, take a direct part in the hostilities." This means, as outlined above, that also foreign advisers and military technicians recruited to train or maintain weapons are considered as mercenaries, provided that the other definition criteria apply. The

Convention applies both to international and noninternational armed conflicts. But according to Article 3, only those mercenaries who participate directly in hostilities or in a concerted act of violence, commit an offence for the purposes of the Convention. In addition, any "person who recruits, uses, finances or trains mercenaries, as defined in article 1 of the present Convention, commits an offence for the purposes of the Convention," as stipulated in Article 2. This illustrates that the Convention aims primarily at those state or non-state actors who recruit, use, finance, or train mercenaries. States parties have an obligation to criminalize these activities and to apply broad jurisdiction, including universal jurisdiction, similar to the various antiterrorism treaties or the UN Conventions against Torture or Enforced Disappearances. However, the UN Mercenary Convention has only been ratified so far by 33 states, primarily in the Global South. Of Western States, only Belgium, Croatia, Cyprus, Italy, and New Zealand are parties, as well as Germany and Poland as signatories. The difficulties of proving in a criminal court all definition requirements of a mercenary apply to the Convention as well and deprive it of much practical relevance. In addition to the UN Convention, the Organization of African Unity, the predecessor of the African Union, had adopted in 1977, as a reaction to mercenary activities in Africa during the 1960s and 1970s, a Convention for the Elimination of Mercenaries in Africa, which entered into force in 1985.[78]

Can the PMSCs and their staff be considered "mercenaries of the 21st century"? A closer analysis of the definition criteria shows that, apart from the difficulties of proving that somebody is in fact a mercenary, many private contractors clearly do not fall within this definition.[79] For example, U.S. citizens recruited by U.S.-based PMSCs to fight in Iraq would not meet the foreign component of the mercenary definition. Some of the private contractors might fight not only for the purpose of private gain, but because of adventurism, patriotism, or simply because they are highly qualified military, security, or intelligence experts, who lost their jobs in the regular armed forces and wish to find another job. Most commentators would, therefore, agree that PMSCs act in an environment that is not sufficiently regulated by international law as well as by domestic law in most countries.

The UN General Assembly already in 1976 took a strong stance against the use of private force and repeatedly called mercenaries criminals.[80] Similarly, the former UN Commission on Human Rights has been examining the question of private force since the early 1980s and established a Special Rapporteur on Mercenaries in 1987.[81] The Peruvian expert Enrique Bernales Ballesteros, who carried out this mandate between 1987 and 2004, strongly argued that there was no effective difference between mercenaries and PMSCs.[82] In 2004, when the Commission appointed Ms. Shaista Shameen from Fiji as Special Rapporteur, it requested

> the Special Rapporteur to continue taking into account in the discharge of his/her mandate that mercenary activities are continuing to occur in many parts of the world and are taking on new forms, manifestations and modalities and, in this regard, requests him/her to pay particular attention to the impact of the activities of private companies offering military assistance, consultancy and security services on the international market on the exercise of the right of peoples to self-determination.[83]

Ms. Shameen acknowledged that there may be a difference between mercenaries and PMSCs and argued that companies that engage in combat ought to be included in a new international regulation dealing with mercenaries and other private contractors.[84] The Special Rapporteur also tried to promote the ratification of the UN Mercenary Convention, as well as the adoption of national legislation specifically targeting mercenary activities.

In 2005, the Commission decided to end the mandate of the Special Rapporteur on Mercenaries and to establish a Working Group on the Use of Mercenaries consisting of five independent experts.[85] The Working Group actively investigates human rights violations committed by PMSCs on a global scale, including summary executions, torture, arbitrary detention, trafficking of persons, and so on.[86] For example, the Working Group recommended that the government of Iraq clarify as a matter of urgency the legal situation of PMSCs operating in the country, in particular whether they are entitled to immunity. At the same time it recommended to the U.S. government to strengthen oversight mechanisms in any contracts with PMSCs.[87] The government of Afghanistan was requested to maintain transparent registers of private security companies covering all matters relating to ownership, statutes, purposes, and functions, as well as a system of regular inspections.[88] With respect to Ecuador, the Working Group emphasized the need for rigorous national legislation, to regulate and monitor the activities of national and transnational PMSCs, in order to ensure the responsibilities of the state to effectively protect and promote human rights.[89] The government of Chile was requested to establish at the highest level of government a body charged with monitoring both private security companies and new forms of mercenary activity. Steps should also be taken to guarantee the "universal right of all people to security as a public good" through the adoption of a new private security act, which must incorporate the principles of efficiency—in relations between public and private sectors—and transparency, responsibility and accountability.[90] Particularly harsh criticism was addressed to the British government for approaching PMSCs through the prism of "business as usual."[91]

Draft UN Convention on Private Military and Security Companies

The Human Rights Council extended the mandate of the Working Group in 2008 and 2011 and explicitly tasked it to "elaborate and present concrete proposals on possible complementary and new standards aimed at filling existing gaps, as well as general guidelines or basic principles encouraging the further protection of human rights, in particular the right of peoples to self-determination, while facing current and emergent threats posed by mercenaries or mercenary-related activities."[92] In addition, the Working Group was requested to "monitor mercenaries and mercenary-related activities in all their forms and manifestations in different parts of the world," to "study and identify sources and causes, emerging issues, manifestations and trends regarding mercenaries or mercenary-related activities and their impact on human rights," and to "monitor and study the effects on the enjoyment of human rights, particularly the right of peoples to self-determination, of the activities of private companies offering military assistance, consultancy and security services on the international market, and to prepare a draft of international basic principles that encourage respect for human rights by those companies in their activities."

In the course of its first five years of activities, the Working Group found a clear regulatory legal vacuum covering the activities of PMSCs, as well as a lack of common standards for the registration and licensing of these companies and for the vetting and training of their staff and the safekeeping of weapons.[93] In the opinion of its former chairperson, the Spanish human rights expert and long-term human rights officer in the United Nations, José Luis Gómez del Prado, the "fact that PMSCs' personnel are not usually 'mercenaries' is also a strong argument for the adoption of a new instrument to deal with a new type of actor. Contrary to the 'dogs of war' mercenaries of the past, private military and security companies are legally registered, and the definition used in international instruments . . . typically does not apply to their personnel."[94] In 2010, the Working Group recommended to the Human Rights Council and the General Assembly principles, main elements, and a text for a possible "Convention on Private Military and Security Companies (PMSCs)" for further consideration and action by the Human Rights Council.[95] The draft Convention on PMSCs[96] attempts to achieve a double purpose.[97] On the one hand, it aims to reaffirm and strengthen the state responsibility for the monopoly on the legitimate use of force by identifying inherent state functions that cannot be outsourced to PMSCs under any circumstances. At the same time, it recognizes that PMSCs are in fact existing and operating in a great number of countries around the world and, therefore, aims at regulating the use of force and firearms by PMSCs under international human rights standards. In particular, it envisages the development of a national regime of licensing, regulation, and oversight of the activities of PMSCs and their subcontractors.[98] In addition, Article 30 of the draft Convention, which would apply in times both of peace and of war, would establish an international register of PMSCs based on information provided by states parties and international organizations[99] to an international expert committee monitoring state compliance. In the words of José Gómez del Prado, the "proposed convention draws a fine line between functions that are permitted but should be regulated, and functions that belong to the state and cannot be privatized."[100]

Inherently state functions are defined in Article 2(i) as

functions which are consistent with the principle of the State monopoly on the legitimate use of force and that a State cannot outsource or delegate to PMSCs under any circumstances. Among such functions are direct participation in hostilities, waging war and/or combat operations, taking prisoners, law-making, espionage, intelligence, knowledge transfer with military, security and policing application, use of and other activities related to weapons of mass destruction and police powers, especially the powers of arrest or

detention including the interrogation of detainees and other functions that a State Party considers to be inherently State functions.

Article 9 contains an explicit prohibition of the delegation or outsourcing
of inherently state functions. This does not mean, however, that the draft
Convention would prohibit every use of force by PMSCs, as Article 18
explicitly provides for the regulation of the use of force by PMSCs.[101]

In October 2010, the UN Human Rights Council decided to establish
an "open-ended working group to consider the possibility of elaborating
an international regulatory framework on the regulation, monitoring and
oversight of the activities of private military and security companies."[102] The
December 2012 report of this intergovernmental working group,[103] meeting
under the chair of South African ambassador Abdul S. Minty, reveals that
there is very little consensus among states on this highly controversial issue.
While the United States and other Western governments emphasized that
there can be no "one size fits all" solution[104] and advocated voluntary codes
of conduct by PMSCs and international "soft law," states from the Global
South stressed the need for a binding Convention.

The Montreux Process as a Soft Law Alternative

In fact, Western states had already worked in parallel to the deliberations
of the UN Working Group on the Use of Mercenaries on alternative "soft
law" instruments for the regulation of PMSCs. In 2005, the government of
Switzerland and the International Committee of the Red Cross had
launched the so-called "Swiss Initiative," an international consultation
process with a group of selected governments, experts as well as representatives of PMSCs, their lobbying groups (IPOA and BAPSC), and civil society.
In September 2008, this consultation led to the adoption of the "Montreux
Document on Pertinent Legal Obligations and Good Practices for States
Related to Operations of Private Military and Security Companies during
Armed Conflict."[105] The Montreux Document was originally endorsed by
17 states, including the UK, United States, France, Germany, and other
Western states, but also by China, South Africa, and selected states where
PMSCs have been operating, including Afghanistan, Iraq, Angola, and
Sierra Leone.[106] The Montreux Document is open to all states and interna-
tional organizations. Its preface reads: "The participating States invite other

States and international organisations to communicate their support for this document to the Federal Department of Foreign Affairs of Switzerland." The Swiss government updates this webpage upon receipt of any such communication. As of June 2014, a total of fifty states, namely, most Western states and a few states from the Global South, including also Ecuador, Chile, Uruguay, Costa Rica, Qatar, Jordan, Kuwait, and Uganda, have expressed their support. In addition, the EU, OSCE, and NATO joined as international organizations.[107] The Montreux Document affirms the international obligations of home states (where PMSCs are based), contracting states (which engage PMSCs), and host states (where PMSCs operate) under existing international humanitarian law and human rights law. It only applies to situations of international or non-international armed conflict. In addition to identifying "hard law" binding under customary or treaty law, the Montreux Document also lists "soft law" standards in the form of seventy-three "good practices." As a "soft law" instrument negotiated and adopted by a carefully selected group of states outside any formal organizational structure, it lacks wider legitimacy[108] and has been criticized as a lobbying tool of home states of PMSCs promoting the private military and security industry.[109] In order to keep the United States on board, nonstate actors were excluded from the final negotiations on the text of the Montreux Document, and the human rights language, including the extraterritorial applicability of human rights law and any direct obligations of PMSCs, had to be considerably watered down, which was strongly criticized by the ICRC, Amnesty International, and other NGOs.[110]

As a supplement to the Montreux Document, the Swiss government also initiated in 2010 a consultation on an International Code of Conduct for Private Security Service Providers (ICoC). The ICoC was drafted during a conference in September 2010 facilitated by the Swiss government, the Geneva Academy of International Humanitarian Law and Human Rights, and the Geneva Centre for the Democratic Control of Armed Forces. The conference involved representatives from PMSCs, industry associations, governments, such as the United States and UK, and nongovernmental organizations. There were 58 original signatory companies, and as of June 2014, 708 PMSCs were signatories to the ICoC.[111] In accordance with the ICoC, in November 2011 members from the three stakeholder communities chose representatives for a temporary steering committee. The committee consists of three participants and one possible auxiliary member from each of three stakeholder groups: governments, PMSCs, and civil society organizations. The main task of the steering committee is to develop documents and arrangements for the governance and oversight mechanism as previewed in the ICoC. The steering committee succeeded in this task and in February 2013 the "Articles of Association" of the International Code of Conduct for Private Military and Security Security Providers were adopted. The Geneva-based ICoC Association (ICoCA) is an independent nonprofit association under Swiss law. According to its website, the "overarching purpose of the Association is to promote the responsible provision of private security services and respect for human rights and national and international law by exercising independent governance and oversight of the ICoC. Under the Articles of Association, the ICoCA has three main functions, namely certification of private security service providers, monitoring their activities, and maintaining a complaints process for alleged victims of ICoC violations. The ICoC Association is a multi-stakeholder initiative uniting PMSCs, States, and civil society organizations."[112] As of June 2014, the website of the ICoCA lists a total of 162 PMSCs, including many well-known companies, such as the UK-based corporations G4S, Titon International, and Aegis, or the U.S.-based corporations DynCorp, Atac, Sterling, Atlas, and the International Protection Group. It also includes many PMSCs registered in other states, including the Dutch Argus, the French GEOS, the Russian Moran, the German Consult Group, or Wackenhut Pakistan.[113]

The Swiss Initiative, which has led to "soft law" standards, such as the "good practices" contained in the Montreux Document and an international code of conduct for PMSCs, and to some form of transparency, self-regulation, and monitoring by a private Swiss association, is certainly a welcome initiative to provide some oversight over the widely unregulated military and security business. In that respect, it can be compared to the Global Compact, corporate social responsibility (CSR) initiatives by transnational corporations, and the so-called Ruggie Guiding Principles on Business and Human Rights,[114] which apply to the corporate sector in general. As the Ruggie Principles, which were developed as an alternative to the former UN Sub-Commission's "Draft Norms on the Responsibilities of Transnational Corporations and Other Business Enterprises with Regard to Human Rights" of 2003,[115] the Swiss Initiative must also be seen as an alternative to the draft Convention on PMSCs submitted by the UN Working Group on the Use of Mercenaries in 2010. During the deliberations in the open-ended working group of the Human Rights Council there was no doubt that many Western states where most PMSCs are based, above all the United States and the UK, praised the Swiss Initiative and the Montreux Document in order to discredit the efforts of adopting a binding international treaty as "premature" or as an expression of a "one size fits all" strategy.[116]

Limits of Privatization of Security Functions Under International Law

However, there are major differences between PMSCs and other corporations, which make a binding international legal instrument in relation to the military and security industry, including clear limits to the privatization of "inherently State functions," much more urgent than in other business sectors. First of all, experience in Sierra Leone, Angola, Afghanistan, Iraq, and other countries provide ample evidence, given the use of armed force, that the risks of serious human rights violations are much higher than in other business sectors. Second, the rise of PMSCs constitutes a serious challenge to the state monopoly on the legitimate use of force and, consequently, to the very essence of the liberal modern welfare state, based on democracy, the rule of law, and human rights. As many fragile states illustrate, it is not difficult to abolish the state monopoly on the use of force, but very difficult to establish it again.[117] Furthermore, the privatization of the use of force even tends to undermine the prohibition on the use of force in Article 2(4) of the UN Charter and, thereby, the first universal peace project in the history of humankind, initiated by the founding of the United Nations in 1945.

A mere regulation of the activities of PMSCs and the respective obligations of home, host, and contracting states vis-à-vis the conduct of PMSCs, as provided for in the Montreux Document, fails to address these fundamental challenges. As outlined above, many constitutions of modern states provide for certain core functions of the state[118] which simply cannot be outsourced to private corporations without violating certain core constitutional principles, including democracy, the rule of law, and human rights.[119] Even authors who are fairly pragmatic toward the pros and cons of PMSCs, such as Surabhi Ranganathan, concede that "as critical investigations of specific services reveal, some services are not appropriate for outsourcing—not just because of dismal previous experience or difficulty of legal oversight, but because they should properly be carried out by public institutions subject to the political process and not by entities driven by the profit motive."[120] Typical examples, in addition to combat operations, are detention,[121] interrogations, intelligence gathering,[122] and peacekeeping.[123] These examples correspond to the inherently state functions outlined in Article 2(i) of the draft Convention on PMSCs proposed by the UN Working Group on the Use of Mercenaries in 2010.[124]

Even in the United States, the concept of "inherently governmental functions" does, in principle, exist.[125] In 1983, the Office of Management and Budget (OMB) issued Circular No. A-76, in which it stated that "certain functions are inherently Governmental in nature, being so intimately related to the public interest as to mandate performance only by Federal employees."[126] These included "management of Government programs requiring value judgments, as in direction of the national defense; management and direction of the Armed Services, activities performed exclusively by military personnel who are subject to deployment in combat, combat support or combat service support role." In the Federal Activities Inventory Reform Act of 1998, the U.S. Congress repeated the language of the OMB Circular by defining an inherently government function as a "function that is so intimately related to the public interest as to require performance by Federal Government employees."[127] While the 1999 revision of the OMB Circular maintained the 1983 language, the 2003 revision "opened up significant loopholes by allowing for activities to be performed by contractors 'where the contractor does not have the authority to decide on the course of action, with agency oversight'."[128] In addition, the Defense Department was authorized to determine if this circular applies to the Department of Defense during times of a declared war or military mobilization. The practice of the U.S. government, and the Defense Department in particular, of increasingly outsourcing combat service support functions and even certain combat functions to PMSCs illustrates the extent to which the concept of inherently governmental functions has been eroded during the time of the Bush administration and thereafter.

In my opinion, there can be no doubt that internal and external security belong to the core functions of the modern constitutional state, based on the rule of law, liberal democracy, and human rights, as it has developed since the late eighteenth century, first in Europe and North America, and after World War II on a global scale. The state monopoly of the legitimate use of force is an essential component of the modern constitutional state, the main legitimacy of which is to protect its inhabitants against external and internal violence and other threats to human security and human rights. This gradual process of reducing the private use of force by a state monopoly, subject to strict judicial, parliamentary, and other forms of political control, has been rightly called a "process of civilization."[129] With the establishment of the United Nations, the use of force has for the first time in history also been prohibited in the external relations of states, with the only exceptions of self-defense and collective military actions authorized by the Security Council.[130] In other words: the idea of the monopoly of the use of force was to a considerable extent transferred in the external relations of states from individual governments to the United Nations, represented by the Security Council. This shift can be described as a process of universal civilization. Unfortunately, states never fully implemented the respective provisions of Chapter VII by establishing a standing UN army, and during the time of the Cold War, the collective security concept was in fact blocked by the veto power of the two superpowers. The end of the Cold War provided a window of opportunity for the United Nations to take the decisive step of making the collective security system work. Unfortunately, there were only a few situations where the Security Council acted in accordance with its historical mandate to prevent unilateral use of force, such as in reaction to the invasion of Kuwait by Iraqi forces under Saddam Hussein in 1990, or in reaction to the massacres by Indonesian militias in East Timor after the people of East Timor had decided in a UN-organized referendum to declare themselves independent from Indonesia.[131] In Somalia, the Security Council even authorized military force for the protection of humanitarian relief operations in a failed state governed by rival war lords.[132] But in most situations of genocide and similar gross and systematic violations of human rights, most notably in Rwanda, Bosnia and Herzegovina, Sierra Leone, the Democratic Republic of Congo, or Sudan, the Security Council failed to take decisive action. This failure by the international community has even been cited as a reason for the rise of PMSCs during the 1990s. For example, the involvement of the South African PMC Executive Outcomes (EO) on the side of the Government of Angola (MPLA) against the rebel movement UNITA or on the side of the Government of Sierra Leone against the brutal rebel movement RUF, supported by Liberia's President Charles Taylor, has been explained by the lack of decisive action by the United Nations and the African Union.[133] This dilemma of the United Nations, willing to provide security to vulnerable groups without the required support of their member states, is also well illustrated by a situation which Kofi Annan, then Under-Secretary-General for Peacekeeping, faced in 1996 in a refugee camp in Goma at the border between then Zaire (now DRC) and Rwanda, where members of Hutu militias were hiding among Rwandan refugees making work very difficult for UNHCR and other humanitarian organizations.[134] When the additional troops requested from member states were not forthcoming, Annan considered the hiring of a PMSC to separate fighters from refugees, but eventually decided not to do so because "the world may not be ready for privatized peace." Nevertheless, it would be difficult to argue that the rapid development of PMSCs was primarily motivated by humanitarian concerns. On the contrary, the rise of PMSCs was the result of a deliberate policy of neoliberalism and privatization by certain governments, above all the United States and UK. Since PMSCs are primarily driven by the desire to make profits, the increasing power of PMSCs has definitely led to a proliferation of armed conflicts during the last decades, not only in Iraq.[135] This is a highly dangerous development, which threatens the very peace architecture of the United Nations. Rather than outsourcing international peacekeeping and peacebuilding operations to the corporate sector and thereby creating another vicious circle,[136] the UN is in urgent need of a fundamental reform in order to live up to its noble aims of securing world peace and protecting human beings against violence, poverty, and serious human rights violations. As Chia Lehnardt has eloquently concluded in her analysis of the trend toward privatizing of peacekeeping, the "question is not only whether the world is ready to privatize peace, but also what would be left of an international community which outsources the first promise of the UN Charter to private companies."[137] From a legal point of view, it is also highly questionable whether a UN force composed of PMSC personnel, at least if acting under an authorization of military force by the UN Security Council in accordance with Article 42 UN Charter, would be compatible with the requirements of Articles 43 and 48 UN Charter.[138]

Former Secretary-General Kofi Annan, in his well-known report "In Larger Freedom," has gone back to the roots of the United Nations by building his report aimed at a fundamental reform of the UN around the Four Freedoms Speech of President Franklin D. Roosevelt and the language of the UN Charter.[139] Freedom from fear, redefined as a concept of human security and elimination of violence, freedom from want, redefined as a concept of human development and elimination of poverty, and human rights (freedom to live in dignity) were declared as the three interdependent pillars of the United Nations,[140] which in his opinion are in urgent need of a fundamental reform, including a reform of the composition of the Security Council and the veto power of its five permanent members.[141] Unfortunately, the reform of the Security Council failed as none of the permanent members showed any willingness to voluntarily give up power. But Kofi Annan was at least successful in introducing the concept of the Responsibility to Protect (R2P) into the Outcome Document of the 2005 Summit Meeting of Heads of State and Government.[142] Learning from the failures of the Security Council in preventing genocides in Rwanda and Bosnia and Herzegovina, and of provoking a NATO-led unilateral humanitarian intervention against Serbia and Montenegro by nonaction, the world leaders unanimously declared that the international community, represented by the Security Council, has not only a right, but also a responsibility to take decisive action, including the authorization of military force as a measure of last resort, in order to protect populations from genocide, ethnic cleansing, war crimes, and crimes against humanity. While the doctrine of R2P was applied in a few situations, such as in Côte d'Ivoire and Libya, the international community, obstructed by the veto power and the lack of a standing UN military force, failed to apply it in other situations, most notably in Sudan and Syria.[143]

Under the UN Charter, war and peace, external and internal security, the eradication of violence, and efforts aimed at achieving human security, are concepts directly related to states.[144] The outsourcing of these essential tasks to private corporations operating for profit is seriously undermining the world order envisaged by the UN Charter, the Universal Declaration of Human Rights, and other human rights instruments, which guarantee to every individual certain basic human rights to life, personal integrity, liberty and security, health, and access to justice. The prevention of armed conflicts, humanitarian disasters, and gross and systematic human rights violations, that is, the implementation of the architecture of peace and protection of human rights envisaged in the UN Charter, can only be achieved if states are willing to defend or reestablish, as the case may be, their monopoly of the legitimate use of force in their own countries, and at the same time are willing to develop an international monopoly of the use of force in their international relations, to be exercised by a well-functioning Security Council with the support of standing UN military and police forces, as envisaged in Article 43 of the UN Charter.[145]

To conclude: the right to personal security in Article 9 CCPR and similar provisions of binding international treaty law is an important umbrella right that requires states to protect their populations, to the best of their abilities, against internal violence (organized crime, terrorism, ethnic and religious conflicts, rebel movements, paramilitary groups, death squads, domestic violence, and so on) as well as external violence (international armed conflicts) and other threats to their security, such as natural disasters. The effective protection of its inhabitants against internal and external violence (freedom from fear) through the monopoly of the legitimate use of force constitutes the major legitimacy of the modern sovereign state and requires governments to establish, train, and maintain professional and effective public security forces. If the state fails to provide this protection and a basic feeling of security to its people, it gradually loses its internal and external sovereignty—its major characteristic as an independent state. In particular, if states are no longer able or willing to protect their populations against genocide, ethnic cleansing, war crimes, and crimes against humanity, this state Responsibility to Protect (R2P) gradually shifts to the international community, represented by the UN Security Council, which should take appropriate action, such as imposing sanctions under Article 41 of the UN Charter or, as a measure of last resort, authorizing military action in accordance with Article 42 UN Charter. The state monopoly of the legitimate use of force is not absolute. As hunters may use rifles, individuals may protect themselves against robbers, burglars, and other criminals and threats. They may also delegate this power of self-defense to other private actors, such as bodyguards or private security companies if they feel that the state does not provide them with effective security. Private security guards may even be authorized to use firearms. But the state has an obligation to ensure that its monopoly of the legitimate use of force is not undermined by private security providers. If its inhabitants lose trust in public security forces and rely more on private security companies, we speak of fragile or failed states which are no longer able or willing to protect and ensure the human right to personal security. As the police may be assisted and supplemented to some extent by private security companies, the military may be assisted in certain support and logistical functions by private military companies. But most military and police functions, above all military combat activities, arrest and detention of individuals, interrogation of detainees and other criminal investigation functions, the use of force beyond immediate self-defense, intelligence activities, the protection of public gatherings and demonstrations against counterdemonstrators, must be considered as inherent governmental functions that may not be privatized or outsourced to PMSCs without violating the human right to personal security.

Conclusion: A Human Rights Based
Approach to Privatization

The Relationship Between Capitalism and Human Rights

The aim of the present study was to define those core governmental functions which cannot be outsourced to the corporate sector without violating human rights. This research question was addressed in relation to a selected number of economic, social, cultural, civil, and political rights by analyzing the state obligations deriving from these rights in light of the respective provisions in the two UN human rights covenants and the historical development of universal human rights law.

The international human rights framework only applies to a limited number of state activities. Most governmental functions which have been subjected to deregulation and privatization on the basis of neoliberal economic policies during the last decades have no or only a limited bearing on human rights. The privatization of state industries, banks, media, or public utilities, such as gas, electricity, roads, airports, railroads, public transport, postal and telecommunication services may have a certain impact on the human rights to work, freedom of movement, freedom of information, the right to equality, or the right to privacy, but it would be difficult in free market economies to claim that such measures would as such violate the respective human rights. On the other hand, there are certain human rights, the implementation of which requires states to take specific measures which are generally considered inherent governmental functions. The right to vote, for example, demands that states enact respective laws and organize free and fair elections which enable citizens of a certain minimum age to go to the polls and cast their votes. Similarly, states are required by the right to marry to enact respective marriage laws and to enable all human beings of marriageable age to marry a person of their choice and to have such marriage legally registered. Under the right to a fair trial, states have an obligation to establish independent and impartial courts which guarantee human beings equal access to such courts and a fair trial in criminal and civil proceedings. State courts and administrative bodies also have the public function of providing victims of human rights violations with the right to an adequate remedy and appropriate reparation for the harm suffered. Even in states adhering to far-reaching neoliberal economic policies, these inherent governmental functions are not seriously put in question and very few attempts have been made to outsource these functions to the corporate sector.

There are other human rights that explicitly protect the private sector. The right to property, although not explicitly recognized in the UN human rights covenants, is the most important human right in free market economies which ensures to private entrepreneurs the possibility to start a business subject to certain limits, such as the prohibition of slavery, servitude, or child labor. Freedom of the media guarantees to private individuals and corporations the right to establish print, broadcasting, or electronic media enterprises subject to certain requirements, such as public licensing. Whether freedom of expression and information also requires the state to operate at least a few public media channels in order to provide the public with noncommercial and objective information and to ensure media pluralism, is a highly controversial question that is, however, not a subject of the present study.[1]

Neoliberal economic policies also enabled the private sector to get involved and make profits in areas that have traditionally been considered inherent public functions and which have a direct impact on the enjoyment of certain human rights. Whether and to which extent the privatization of functions and services in the fields of education, health, social security, water management, internal and external security, and prison management violates the respective economic, social, cultural, and civil rights has been the focus of the present study.

The answer to this question is not clear-cut and depends on the formulation of the human rights concerned and the interpretation of the respective state obligations in light of the historical meaning of these rights. Traditionally, schools, hospitals, or social security measures were operated and provided in many countries by private charities or religious organizations in addition to state institutions. Many new developments in the health care services were the result of research by private pharmaceutical corporations and of drugs made available for profit by such companies. In most countries based on free market economies, health care services are provided by private doctors. The right to education even explicitly provides for the right of private individuals to establish private schools and for the freedom of parents to choose schools for their children in accordance with their religious and philosophical convictions. Social security was traditionally a function of the families rather than of states, and everybody enjoys the right to choose private insurance companies and pension funds in order to mitigate the risks emanating from accidents, sickness, unemployment, or old age. Similarly, human beings have a right to avail themselves of the services of private security companies and bodyguards.

The decisive question is, therefore, not whether corporations are allowed to provide certain services in fields that are directly related to human rights. Rather, the question is whether states are permitted to deliberately privatize these services either by selling the respective infrastructure (schools, hospitals, courts, prisons, pension funds, water facilities) or by outsourcing the management of these services to private corporations. Outsourcing the management includes delegating the respective decision making. In other words, the mere contracting out of certain support functions, such as building and maintaining hospitals, schools, courts, military barracks, police stations, or water pipelines to private business and providing the employees and clients of these services with food and other goods which are not directly related to the human rights of the clients is usually not considered as privatization. Whether these goods and services are directly related to the enjoyment of human rights depends, of course, on the human right in question. While private canteens and first medical aid services in courts and schools have nothing to do with the administration of justice, the right to fair trial, or the right to education, low quality and high prices of such services in prisons might infringe on the rights of prisoners to adequate food and health care. Where to draw the line between mere support functions and services directly related to the enjoyment of human rights seems to be particularly difficult in the health and security sectors. Does the nonaccessibility of certain drugs and vaccines to the poor caused by the desire of pharmaceutical companies to make huge profits encroach upon their right to adequate health care? Does the provision of weapons and ammunition by private military and security companies to public security forces constitute a mere support function or is it directly related to the core function related to the enjoyment of the right to personal security?

To define the limits of privatization from a human rights perspective, therefore, requires the identification of those core functions which derive from the obligation of states to respect, protect, and fulfill the respective rights. Since privatization usually relates to the provision of services, the focus of the study is less on the negative obligation of states to respect these rights and more on its positive obligation to fulfill these rights and to protect the rights-holders against interference by private parties. Article 2 CESCR requires states in this respect to take the necessary steps toward the progressive realization of economic, social, and cultural rights. In my opinion, this gradual implementation also applies to the positive obligations deriving from civil and political rights, such as the rights to life, personal security, liberty, and integrity.[2] The duty of progressive realization means, first of all, that states are, save in exceptional circumstances, legally prevented from deliberately taking retrogressive measures leading to a lower level of enjoyment of human rights as compared to the situation when these obligations were undertaken in the first place. When states are considering privatization or outsourcing human rights related services to the private sector, they are thus required to conduct a thorough human rights impact assessment in order to ensure that privatization does not lead to a lower level of enjoyment of human rights or to the exclusion of the poor and other disadvantaged or discriminated groups from the respective services. In addition to the prohibition of retrogressive measures, states have a legally binding obligation to progressively improve their services toward the full enjoyment of these rights for all people under their jurisdiction.

In order to determine whether states live up to their duty of progressive realization, we have to ascertain the level of protection and fulfillment at the time when these obligations were undertaken by states. Legally speaking, this level of protection and fulfillment is defined by the status quo at the time when the state ratified the respective treaties. But more generally, we have to understand what states envisaged when the two Covenants were adopted in 1966. This brings us to the historical evolution of universal human rights. The International Bill of Rights was drafted and adopted in the aftermath of World War II and represents a synthesis and historic compromise between the Western and the Socialist concepts of human rights. On the eastern side of the Iron Curtain, it was self-evident that all functions related to the fulfillment of human rights were inherent state functions. But also the other side of the Iron Curtain in those "Trente Glorieuses" was deeply rooted in the Keynesian consensus of the modern welfare state with extensive regulation of the economic sector. While not excluding a certain role of private charities, religious organizations, and even the corporate sector in the fulfillment of human rights, it was uncontested that the state had the principal obligation to provide for public order and security, education, health care, social security, and other services required by human rights. Based on the dramatic experiences with two world wars, the Great Depression, the rise and fall of fascism and the Holocaust, there was a broad consensus across political parties that the legitimacy and sovereignty of a state was not only based on its functions as a liberal "nightwatch" state guaranteeing freedom from fear and violence, but also on its functions as a modern welfare state ensuring freedom from want and poverty. For the first time in history, wars were outlawed and aggressors were subjected to a system of collective security under the guidance of the UN Security Council. At the same time, states committed themselves to international cooperation aimed at ensuring development and the progressive realization of human rights to all peoples in need. The interdependence of security, development, and human rights, the three main functions of the United Nations, meant that universal human rights were envisaged as a necessary precondition for sustainable international peace and security as well as international development and poverty reduction. It was beyond doubt that these noble aims and objectives could only be achieved in an international environment in which states were the principal actors and duty-bearers.

With the rise of neoliberal economic theories and policies, the Washington Consensus of 1989, and the collapse of Communism in Europe, this postwar Keynesian consensus was fundamentally put into question. Western states and global financial institutions dominated by these states pursued a vigorous policy of deregulation, privatization, and minimizing the role of the state at a time when the world economy was rapidly moving toward globalization. The privatization of formerly governmental functions in the West and, on the basis of structural adjustment policies enforced by the World Bank, the IMF, regional development banks and agencies, the European Union, and other powerful actors, upon the former Communist states and the global South also led to the sale and outsourcing of public infrastructures and services which are essential for the progressive realization of human rights. Even though the international community solemnly committed itself at the Vienna World Conference on Human Rights in 1993 to the equality, interdependence, and indivisibility of all human rights, the neoliberal economic policies of the West disregarded these commitments and regarded economic, social, and cultural rights as second-class human rights, the implementation of which could be delegated to the private sector. These neoliberal economic policies led to a rise of inequality within and between countries which in the long term undermines democracy, the rule of law, human rights, social justice, poverty reduction, development, as well as international peace and security.

Core State Functions Deriving from Selected Human Rights

In many areas governed by universal human rights obligations, the basic requirements of supply and demand, which are the cornerstones of free market economies, simply do not apply. The right to education, for example, requires that every child has a right and an obligation to primary education free of charge. Charter schools and other schools run for profit cannot effectively compete with public schools on the free market, because states have an obligation to provide school education free of charge to all children under their jurisdiction. Private schools may be attractive to parents for religious reasons or because they are so rich that they wish to provide their children with an elite education. But states are prevented from privatizing public schools if this would lead to a situation where the availability, accessibility, or quality of public school education is diminished. If states would privatize public schools and at the same time fund these schools in order to maintain the requirement of free education, they would be under an obligation, according to the principle of equality, to also fund all other private schools. Since the corporate sector aims at making profits, such a system would be much more expensive for the state than maintaining public schools. The privatization of schools would, therefore, usually constitute a retrogressive measure in violation of the right to education.

Similar arguments apply to the right to health despite the fact that states have no legal obligation to provide public health care free of charge. But states are required to ensure that everybody, including the poor, has equal access to basic health care facilities irrespective of whether they are offered by private or public health care providers. The minimum requirements of supply and demand are, however, not applicable either. Usually, people are forced by a sickness or an accident to avail themselves of the services of a hospital or other health care facility. Even if they have ample time to choose among different health care providers, they usually do not have the expertise to make an informed decision. If the choice is, however, only determined by the costs involved, this might lead to choosing the lowest quality which might undermine the "right to the highest attainable standard of health care." In other words, only the state can ensure a health care system which functions in accordance with the principles of universal availability, accessibility, and the required quality of health care without discrimination of any kind. If the state relies to a great extent on private health care providers, it must ensure, however, by means of an effective social security system, such as an obligatory health insurance scheme, that the risks of accidents and sickness are shared by the community and are not to be borne by the individual himself or herself. Since private health care providers and insurance companies aim at making profits, a health care system that relies primarily on private care management is usually more expensive for the state than a well-functioning public health system. The significantly higher health costs of the United States as compared to most European countries provide ample evidence in this respect.

The right to an adequate standard of living, including the rights to food, water, clothing, and housing, and the right to social security, including social insurance, are the two most comprehensive social rights serving the interest of social justice. The basic idea of social security, as it originated in the late nineteenth century and was further developed by the ILO after World War I, aims at protecting individuals against certain risks and vulnerabilities, such as sickness, disability, accidents, old age, unemployment, or emergencies. It implies that human beings should not have to be afraid to drift into poverty if they get sick, old, unemployed, or disabled. The term *social* illustrates that in a market economy, only the advanced social welfare state can provide the necessary safety nets by means of pooling such risks and by deliberate redistribution from the wealthy to the poor, from the healthy to the sick, from the younger and actively employed generation to the elderly. This can be achieved by contributory or insurance-based schemes, by noncontributory schemes such as universal or targeted social assistance measures paid out of the general state budget, or by a combination of both. The corporate sector by definition cannot provide such a safety net. By aiming at maximizing profits, private insurance companies and social service providers necessarily tend to exclude from their services those who are most in need of their services, namely the most vulnerable and marginalized groups. Privatizing of pension funds means in essence that the pooling of funds, where the actively employed population of a particular society pays, on the basis of a tacit "generation agreement," the pensions of the retired population, is gradually replaced or at least supplemented by a system where everybody is responsible for his or her old age pension. The same holds true for the privatization of health, accident, unemployment, and other social insurance schemes. Privatization, as experienced in Chile and many other countries, thus undermines the very essence of the pooling of social risks by means of social security measures and, therefore, usually constitutes a retrogressive measure in violation of the human right to social security.

Since water is a natural resource which has been traditionally considered a public good, the people in most societies are particularly sensitive toward the privatization of water management, as the "water wars" in Bolivia and other countries vividly illustrate. Nevertheless, the World Bank, the IMF, EU and other international organizations pursuing neoliberal economic policies have been actively pushing for the privatization of water, thereby creating huge profits for a few transnational corporations, most of which are based in Europe. Since water was not yet a scarce natural resource in the post-World War II period, the right to water is not explicitly provided in the International Bill of Rights. Thus, the international human rights community, driven primarily by the Global South, has been advocating for the explicit recognition of a right to water, to be derived from the already existing social rights to health and an adequate standard of living. Experience with water privatization in many countries shows that for-profit companies almost always tend to raise the price for water services or exclude the poor and other disadvantaged groups from their services. Despite the fact that investments of transnational water companies have also enabled many people in poor countries to gain access to water services, in the long term the privatization of water management usually turned out to be retrogressive and, therefore, a violation of the core state obligations deriving from the right to water.

The privatization of prisons and other detention facilities originated in the United States during the 1980s and spread from there primarily to other English-speaking countries, such as the United Kingdom, Australia, New Zealand, South Africa, and Canada. In a landmark judgment, the Israeli Supreme Court has held that, even if one assumes that for-profit companies are more effective and cheaper than state-run institutions and that they would reduce the number of human rights violations in detention, the very idea of delegating the custody of prisoners to for-profit companies and thereby treating prisoners as a commodity violates their human rights to personal liberty and dignity. This reasoning can be extended to the right of all detainees under Article 10 CCPR to be treated with humanity and respect for human dignity. In particular, the aim of correctional institutions to provide for the rehabilitation and social reformation of prisoners, as stipulated in Article 10(3) CCPR and the "principle of normalization" derived from it, in my opinion prevents states from privatizing prisons or outsourcing prison management to private security companies. The negative experience with private prisons and detention centers also prompted certain governments, such as in Canada, New Zealand, and Germany, to stop these neoliberal experiments and to return to the traditional public prison system.

Most controversial and alarming is the recent and rapid trend toward outsourcing police and military functions, that is, the enjoyment of the traditional liberal right to personal security from internal and external threats and violence, to mushrooming private military and security companies (PMSCs). The right to personal security and the protection of the rights to life, personal integrity, and property against criminal and other threats belongs to the core functions of the liberal state and constitutes, together with the state monopoly on the legitimate use of force, the main legitimacy of the modern sovereign nation state. While the United Nations have been active in drafting a Convention on Private Military and Security Companies, which identifies at least a core of inherent state functions that must not be outsourced to PMSCs under any circumstances, Western states, PMSCs, and their powerful lobbying groups have undermined these aims by adopting in 2008 a soft law instrument, namely the Montreux Document on Pertinent Legal Obligations and Good Practices for States Related to Operations of Private Military and Security Companies during Armed Conflict. On the basis of this "Swiss Initiative," many PMSCs voluntarily signed up to an International Code of Conduct, which provides them in return a certain legitimacy and distinguishes them from traditional mercenaries. In my opinion, the privatization of core state security functions, above all the conduct of combat operations, detention and imprisonment, interrogations, intelligence gathering, and international peacekeeping, constitutes a violation of the right to personal security.

In addition to these specific rights, the universal human rights framework also contains a general right to equality and equal protection of the law, which can be considered as a general principle that informs a human rights based approach. States are required by the right to equal protection of the law to strive toward providing substantive equality by actively combating every form of discrimination and exclusion and by providing marginalized and discriminated groups with equal access to public services, above all those related to other human rights. The ultimate goal of equality is a more just and equitable society, in which all people have equal access to the enjoyment of all human rights. Various empirical studies have shown a worrying trend toward inequality since the 1980s, which is directly related to the neoliberal economic policies vigorously pursued by Western states and international organizations dominated by them, above all the international financial institutions. While it may be difficult at this advanced stage to stop certain economic trends in a globalized capitalist system, as outlined, for example, by Thomas Piketty in his book *Capital in the Twenty-First Century*, states should at least stop taking retrogressive measures of deregulation, privatization, and minimizing the role of the state, as these measures clearly contribute to the rise in inequality of income and wealth. In addition, states and the respective international organizations, including the EU, should become more aware of their legal obligations under the right to equal protection of the law and other human rights to take positive measures aimed at returning to a more just and equal society, as envisaged during the post-World War II period.[3]

What Needs to Be Done?

In retrospect, it seems very unfortunate that the West has missed the historic window of opportunity that was opened by the collapse of communism in 1989, to create a new world order based on pluralist democracy, the rule of law, human rights, and social justice. By pursuing a radical neoliberal agenda of deregulation, privatization, and minimizing the role of the state as a guarantor of human rights, Western governments and international organizations dominated by the West contributed to a rapid development of globalization with disastrous economic, political, and social consequences, including a "clash of civilizations" with the Islamic world and growing North-South and East-West conflicts. In a recent lecture held in Oslo in honor of the Norwegian human rights pioneer Torkel Opsahl, I characterized the current status quo as follows:

> Instead of eradicating global poverty and realising the common goal of "all human rights for all," the world was driven into a global economic and financial crisis, a global food crisis, a growing gap between the rich and the poor, a global environmental crisis caused by human-made climate change, increasingly brutal armed conflicts, failed States and other global security challenges caused by organised crime, terrorism, racism, xenophobia, global migration and global surveillance. Governments seem to have lost control of global market forces and engage, at best, in crisis management rather than addressing and changing the root causes of such crises. At the same time, governments lack the will and courage to create structures of global governance which are urgently needed to deal with the global problems and challenges of the twenty-first century.[4]

My research at Stanford University strengthened my assumption that the neoliberal policies of the West heavily contributed to this unfortunate state of global affairs.

It would, of course, be far too easy and one-sided, to make only the Western policies of neoliberalism responsible for these developments. The phenomenon of globalization would also have dominated the world economic development without the deliberate policies of deregulation and privatization, but a decisive and concerted policy of Western governments and international financial institutions aimed at controlling rather than liberalizing global economic and financial markets would definitely have had a mitigating effect. Transnational terrorism and organized crime, ethnic and religious conflicts, racism, climate change, and increased migration might also have dominated the political agenda in a rapidly globalizing world without the rise of neoliberalism, but these phenomena might have been easier to combat and control had the West acted in a less arrogant and dominating manner toward other cultures and religions.

Today, it seems futile to discuss and speculate what would have happened had the West acted differently and more responsibly. But a historical perspective always helps to better understand historical trends and to learn the lessons from failures of the past for politics for the future. The global economic and political situation has developed into a status quo where politicians, whether at the national, regional, or global level, seem to have lost effective control over global market forces. But the global economic and financial crises of recent years should at least have opened our eyes to realize that global market forces are certainly not in a position to provide an answer to the global problems and challenges of the twenty-first century. We should also have learned that the realization of universal human rights for all cannot be brought about by neoliberal policies and unleashed global market forces. On the contrary, the present study has shown that deregulation and privatization have led to rising inequality and exclusion, which seriously undermines the universal post-World War II consensus for striving toward global peace, development, human rights, and social justice. Global market forces are neither able nor willing to take responsibility for the effective realization of universal human rights, but they also increasingly constitute powerful threats to human rights which often exceed the traditional violations of human rights committed by state actors. Universal human rights can only be realized if economic forces are effectively controlled by political decision makers, whether on the national, regional, or global level. We, therefore, need a fundamental change toward a system of global governance that is able and willing to effectively regulate global markets and to take the political obligations toward respecting, protecting, and fulfilling human rights seriously.

History teaches us that such fundamental reorientation toward human rights was usually brought about by revolutionary movements in reaction to social injustices, repression, exploitation, and sometimes even more dramatic events, such as world wars and barbarism. Can we learn from history and start a policy of reorientation without being forced by another world war or similar dramatic experience? Are the current problems, challenges, armed conflicts, and atrocities in all world regions not serious enough to fundamentally change our policies? After realizing that we have missed the historic opportunity to take decisive action after the fall of the Iron Curtain, the global human rights movement is searching for another window of opportunity. The new social movements were driven by the hope that the world economic and financial crisis of 2008 or the Arab Spring revolutions of 2011 might provide such a window of opportunity, but seemingly in vain.

The universal human rights movement was born during the age of Enlightenment and rationalism in Europe. As a human rights scholar, I therefore tend to believe in the rationality of human beings and political decision makers. This fundamental belief in the rationality of human beings nurtures a certain optimism which characterizes the human rights movement. It will certainly not be easy to reverse the current trend of globalization driven by neoliberal market forces, but it is possible if the political will to change is present. We know what needs to be done. The legally binding universal human rights framework provides sufficient guidance in which direction we have to move. Critical political economists have developed the tools that would be necessary to effectively regulate global market forces in order to bring about economic change. But individual nation-states lack the power to control global market forces. Governments need to cooperate by developing effective structures of global governance. There is no need to create many new institutions. The United Nations and other global organizations, including the World Bank, the International Monetary Fund, the World Trade Organization, the United Nations Development Programme, and the International Criminal Court, provide the institutional framework which is powerful enough to take the political, economic, and social measures that would be necessary to steer our planet toward a world order based upon pluralist democracy, the rule of law, human rights, and global justice. Western states might no longer be powerful enough to bring about these changes on their own. They need the cooperation of other political and economic powers, including China, India, the Russian Federation, Brazil, or South Africa. But the West has enough power to start the necessary reforms and to lead by example. In particular, Western states would have the power to fundamentally reform the economic policies of the international financial institutions and the World Trade Organization. A concerted Western approach toward reforming the UN Security Council along the lines advocated by former Secretary-General Kofi Annan would be a first step of broadening responsibility for maintaining and restoring international peace and security. A concerted Western approach toward establishing a World Court of Human Rights might be a decisive step in the direction of strengthening the implementation of universal human rights and a global rule of law.[5] A concerted Western approach aimed at fully implementing the Agenda 2030 and its seventeen "sustainable development goals" might greatly facilitate global efforts toward poverty eradication and reducing economic inequality. A concerted Western approach toward global climate change might still have a realistic chance of avoiding a global environmental disaster in the years to come. If other states and powerful non-state actors realize that the West is serious in taking genuine responsibility for tackling these and other global challenges of the twenty-first century rather than pursuing its egoistic interests and continuing its short-sighted neoliberal global agenda, they might be persuaded to join a revised and innovative global Agenda for Peace, Development, Human Rights and Social Justice. A reversal of the neoliberal policy of outsourcing state obligations to private market forces in order to ensure the effective enjoyment of the rights to education, health, social security, water, equality, personal security, liberty, and integrity, as discussed and suggested in the various chapters of this study, might be a first step to prove that the West takes its commitments to the interdependence and indivisibility of all human rights seriously.

Abbreviations preceded by an asterisk occur only once
Abbreviations naming parties to legal cases are not included

ABSA   Aguas de Buenos Aires S.A.
ACHR   American Convention on Human Rights
ACM   Australasian Correction Management
AFDC   Aid to Families with Dependent Children
AHRLR   African Human Rights Law Reports
AIMS   Australian Integrated Management Systems Corporation
AJIL   *American Journal of International Law*
AP 1   Additional Protocol 1 to the Geneva Conventions of 1977
ASEAN   Association of Southeast Asian Nations
AU   African Union
BAPSC   British Association of Private Security Companies
BIT   Bilateral Investment Treaty
BJS   U.S. Department of Justice, Bureau of Justice Statistics
CACI   Caci International
CCA   Corrections Corporation of America
CCPR   International Covenant on Civil and Political Rights
CEDAW   Convention on the Elimination of All Forms of Discrimination
    against Women
CERD   Convention on the Elimination of Racial Discrimination,
CESCR   International Covenant on Economic, Social and Cultural Rights
CIA   Central Intelligence Agency
COE   Council of Europe
*CPA   Coalition Provisional Authority
*CPT   European Committee for the Prevention of Torture
CRC   Convention on the Rights of the Child

CSCE   Conference on Security and Cooperation in Europe
*CSR   Corporate Social Responsibility
*DC, *DB   Defined Contribution (DC); Defined Benefit (DB)
DRC   Democratic Republic of Congo
ECHR   European Convention on Human Rights
ECOSOC   Economic and Social Council
ECOWAS   Economic Community of West African States
*ECPT   European Convention for the Prevention of Torture
ECtHR   European Court of Human Rights
*EHRR   European Human Rights Reports
*EIUC   European Inter-University Centre for Human Rights and
    Democratisation
EMOs   Educational Management Organizations
EO   Executive Outcomes
EU   European Union
GA   General Assembly
GDP   Gross Domestic Product
GenC   General Comment
GG   Grundgesetz
HRBA   Human Rights Based Approach
HRC   Human Rights Committee
HRQ   Human Rights Quarterly
ICC   International Criminal Court
ICESCR   International Covenant on Economic, Social and Cultural Rights
ICoC   International Code of Conduct for Private Security Service
    Providers
ICoCA   ICoC Association
ICRC   International Committee of the Red Cross
ICSID   International Centre for the Settlement of Investment Disputes
*ICWE   International Conference on Water and the Environment
*IGO   Inter-Governmental Organization
*IHRR   International Human Rights Review
ILA   International Law Association
*ILC   International Law Commission
ILO   International Labour Organization
IMF   International Monetary Fund
*INS   Immigration and Naturalization Service
*Inter-Am.Ct.H.R.   Inter-American Court of Human Rights

*INTERFET   International Force for East Timor
IPOA   International Peace Operations Association
*IPR   Intellectual Property Right
ISS   Monograph Series
*KFOR   NATO-led Kosovo Force
LICUS   Low Income Countries Under Stress
MCO   Managed Care Organization
*MoU   Memorandum of Understanding
*MPRI   Military Professional Resources Incorporated
*MTC   Management and Training Corporation
NGO   Nongovernmental Organization
NQHR   Netherlands Quarterly of Human Rights
NVwZ   Neue Zeitschrift für Verwaltungsrecht
OECD   Organisation for Economic Cooperation and Development
OMB   Office of Management and Budget
OP   Optional Protocol
OSCE   Organization for Security and Cooperation in Europe
ÖZW   Österreichische Zeitschrift für Wirtschaftsrecht
PMC   Private Military Company
PMSCs   Private Military and Security Companies
*PPIAF   Public-Private Infrastructure Advisory Facility
*PRC   People's Republic of China
R2P   Responsibility to Protect
*RUF   rebel movement in Sierra Leone
SC   Security Council, Ch. 1
SDGs   Sustainable Development Goals
*SIM   Netherlands Institute of Human Rights
TANF   Temporary Aid to Needy Families
*TNC   Trans-National Corporation
TRIPS   Trade-Related aspects of Intellectual Property rights
UCL   Human Rights Review, University College London
UDHR   Universal Declaration of Human Rights
*UNAMET   UN Mission in East Timor
UNDP   UN Development Programme
UNESCO   UN Educational, Scientific and Cultural Organization
UNGA   UN General Assembly
UNHCR   United Nations High Commissioner (or Commission) for
    Refugees

UNICEF   United Nations Children's Emergency Fund
UNITA   rebel movement in Angola
*UNMIK   UN Mission in Kosovo
*UNOSOM II   United Nations Operation in Somalia II
*UNTAET   UN Transitional Administration in East Timor
VDPA   Vienna Declaration and Programme of Action
*VVDStRL   Veröffentlichungen der Vereinigung der Deutschen
    Staatsrechtslehrer
WHO   World Health Organization
WTO   World Trade Organization

N o t e s

Chapter 1. History of Human Rights—A Dialectic View

1. John Locke, *Two Treatises of Government*, 1690, excerpted in *The Human Rights Reader: Major Political Writings, Essays, Speeches, and Documents from the Bible to the Present*, vol. 2, ed. Micheline R. Ishay (London, 1997), vol. 2, § 124. For these and other historical documents see, e.g., Ishay, *The Human Rights Reader*; Felix Ermacora, *Menschenrechte in der sich wandelnden Welt*, vol. 1, *Historische Entwicklung der Menschenrechte und Grundfreiheiten* (Vienna, 1974); Gerhard Oestreich, *Geschichte der Menschenrechte und Grundfreiheiten im Umriß*, 2nd ed. (Berlin, 1978).

2. Locke, *Two Treatises of Government*, § 123.

3. Cf. Jean-Jacques Rousseau, *Du contrat social*, 1762, ed. Bertrand de Jouvenel (Paris, 1978).

4. Cf. on these two concepts of civil and political freedom Manfred Nowak, *Politische Grundrechte* (Vienna, 1988).

5. UN *2005 World Summit Outcome* document, GA Res. 60/1 of 16 September 2005, §§ 138 and 139; cf. Manfred Nowak, "Responsibility to Protect: Is International Law Moving from Hobbes to Locke?" in *Völkerrecht und die Dynamik der Menschenrechte*, ed. Gerhard Hafner, Franz Matscher, and Kirsten Schmalenbach (Vienna, 2012), 342; Luke Glanville, *Sovereignty & the Responsibility to Protect: A New History* (Chicago, 2014).

6. See SC Resolutions 1970 and 1973 (2011).

7. Karl Marx, *On the Jewish Question*, 1843, quoted from Ishay, *Human Rights Reader*, 194–95.

8. Ibid., 195.

9. Ibid.

10. See UN Doc. A/2929, 65ff; Catarina Krause, "The Right to Property," in *Economic, Social and Cultural Rights: A Textbook*, 2nd ed., ed. Asbjørn Eide, Catarina Krause, and Allan Rosas (Dordrecht, 2001), 191 at 194; Catarina Krause and Gudmundur Alfredsson, "Article 17," in *The Universal Declaration of Human Rights: A Common Standard of Achievement*, ed. Gudmundur Alfredsson and Asbjørn Eide (The Hague, 1999), 359 at 365–66; see also Johannes Morsink, *The Universal Declaration of Human Rights: Origins, Drafting, and Intent* (Philadelphia, 1999), 139ff.

11. Friedrich Engels, *Herrn Eugen Dührings Umwälzung der Wissenschaft*, 3rd ed. (Stuttgart, 1894), 104: "Die Proletarier nehmen die Bourgeoisie beim Wort: die Gleichheit soll nicht bloß scheinbar, nicht bloß auf dem Gebiet des Staates, sie soll wirklich, auch auf dem gesellschaftlichen, ökonomischen Gebiet durchgeführt werden."

12. Cf. Micheline R. Ishay, *The History of Human Rights* (Berkeley, Calif., 2008), 135. See also Ernest Belford Bax, *The Last Episode of the French Revolution: Being a History of Gracchus Babeuf and the Conspiracy of the Equals* (London, 1911).

13. Michel Buonarroti, in Ishay, *Human Rights Reader*, 136.

14. For the text see ibid., 139.

15. See Pierre-Joseph Proudhon, *What Is Property?: An Inquiry into the Principle of Right and of Government*, 1840, excerpts in Ishay, *Human Rights Reader*, 175.

16. See Bård-Anders Andreassen, "Article 22," in *The Universal Declaration of Human Rights: A Commentary*, ed. Asbjørn Eide et al. (Oslo, 1992), 319 at 323, with reference to Peter Flora and Arnold J. Heidenheimer, eds., *The Development of Welfare States in Europe and America* (New Brunswick, N.J., 1981), at 70. In that book, Peter Flora and Jens Alber argued that "constitutional-dualistic monarchies tended to introduce social and insurance schemes earlier (in chronological and developmental time) than the parliamentary democracies."

17. Andreassen, "Article 22," at 324–25.

18. Cf. the well-known report of UN Secretary-General Kofi Annan, "In Larger Freedom," submitted to the UN Summit of 2005, UN Doc. A/59/2005 of 21 March 2005, § 17.

19. See Annan, "In Larger Freedom," who based his report aimed at reforming the UN on these two freedoms.

20. John P. Humphrey, *Human Rights and the United Nations: A Great Adventure* (New York, 1984), 12.

21. Cf., e.g., Morsink, *Universal Declaration of Human Rights*, 1ff.

22. The draft of the American Law Institute, which was in 1946 also presented by Panama to the UN General Assembly (UN Doc. A/148) and thereafter referred to the Commission on Human Rights, contained a number of economic and social rights to work, food, housing, and social security. According to Asbjørn Eide, "Article 25," in Eide et al.,*The Universal Declaration of Human Rights: A Commentary*, 385 at 390, this was "In line with predominant thinking at the time, both in the United States and elsewhere."

23. The leading role of Panama can be explained by the fact that Alfredo Alfaro, who later became foreign minister of Panama, had been a member of the committee of experts that had drafted the bill of rights within the American Law Institute: see Humphrey, *Human Rights and the United Nations*, 32; Eide, "Article 25," in Eide et al., *The Universal Declaration of Human Rights: A Commentary*, 391.

24. Humphrey, *Human Rights and the United Nations*, 13.

25. In June 1945, Sir Hersch Lauterpacht, on the initiative of the American Jewish Congress, had published his well-known book *International Bill of the Rights of Man* (New York, 1945), which contained the full text of a draft Convention, including both civil and political rights and economic, social, and cultural rights. In the following years, Lauterpacht, who was supported by the International Law Association (ILA), strongly pursued the goal of adopting a binding Convention even after it was clear that states were concentrating, as a first step, on adopting a nonbinding Declaration. This difference of opinion even led to Lauterpacht's, and the ILA's, opposition and strong criticism of the adoption of the Universal Declaration as well as to an academic conflict with John Humphrey, who even withdrew his membership from the ILA: see Eva Maria Lassen, "When Peers Are Pressing for Progress: The Clash of Hersch Lauterpacht and John Humphrey over the Universal Declaration of Human Rights," in *Europe and the Americas: Transatlantic Approaches to Human Rights*, ed. Erik Andreassen and Eva Maria Lassen (Leiden, 2015).

26. Morsink, *Universal Declaration of Human Rights*, at xiv. See also Morsink's labeling of Humphrey as a "socialist" and Cassin as a "unionist," 157.

27. Ashild Samnoy, "The Origins of the Universal Declaration of Human Rights," in Alfredsson and Eide, *Universal Declaration of Human Rights*, 3 at 11.

28. Asbjørn Eide and Wenche Barth Eide, "Article 25," in Alfredsson and Eide, *Universal Declaration of Human Rights*, 523 at 528.

29. See Humphrey, *Human Rights and the United Nations*, 1–2.

30. Ibid., 29.

31. Ibid., 2.

32. Ibid., 32. But see Andreassen, "Article 22," at 331 (note 26), who argues that Humphrey clearly overrates his contribution in this regard.

33. Humphrey, *Human Rights and the United Nations*, 40.

34. Ibid., 31–32 . Humphrey's draft ("Draft Outline") is contained in UN Doc. E/CN.4/AC.1/3 of 4 June 1947.

35. Humphrey, "Draft Outline," 42.

36. According to Morsink, *Universal Declaration of Human Rights*, 8, "Cassin clearly overstated his role." According to his own rough calculation, "three-quarters of the Cassin draft was taken from Humphrey's first draft." See also UN Doc. E/CN.4/21, Annex F.

37. Cf. Humphrey, *Human Rights and the United Nations*, 25, 44.

38. Ibid., 37.

39. Ibid., 45.

40. For the text of the fairly detailed "Geneva Draft" see UN Doc. E/600.

41. For a detailed description of the different drafting stages see Morsink, *Universal Declaration of Human Rights*, 1–2.

42. The 8 abstaining states were Byelorussia, Czechoslovakia, Poland, Saudi Arabia, South Africa, Ukraine, the USSR, and Yugoslavia. In the Third Committee, even Canada had abstained; for the reasons see Humphrey, *Human Rights and the United Nations*, 71–72.

43. See Morsink, *Universal Declaration of Human Rights*, 191–92 ; the contributions of Bård-Anders Andreassen, Kent Källström, Göran Melander, Asbjørn Eide, and Pentti Arajärvi in Eide et al., *Universal Declaration of Human Rights*, at 319–20; as well as the contributions of Bård-Anders Andreassen, Kent Källström, Asbjørn Eide, Bert Isacsson, Wenche Barth Eide, Pentti Arajärvi, Ragnar Adalsteinsson, and Páll Thórhallson in Alfredsson and Eide, *Universal Declaration of Human Rights: A Common Standard of Achievement*, at 453–53.

44. See, e.g., Humphrey, *Human Rights and the United Nations*, 49.

45. See ibid., 72–73 .

46. Morsink, *The Universal Declaration of Human Rights*, 192. After all, 21 of the 50 UN member states at that time were in the Americas.

47. Humphrey, *Human Rights and the United Nations*, 45.

48. Cf. Samnoy, "The Origins of the Universal Declaration of Human Rights," 20–21 .

49. GA Res. 421(V). On the history of the Covenants in the early 1950s see the extensive commentary of the UN Secretary-General in UN Doc. A/2929; Marc J. Bossuyt, *Guide to the "travaux préparatoires" of the International Covenant on Civil and Political Rights* (Dordrecht, 1987); Manfred Nowak, *UN Covenant on Civil and Political Rights: CCPR Commentary*, 2nd rev. ed. (Kehl, 2005), xxii–xxiii , with further references.

50. Humphrey, *Human Rights and the United Nations*, 32.

51. Ibid., 159.

52. Cf. ibid., 299, where Humphrey describes the negative reaction of Ambassador Morozov to the proposal of a UN High Commissioner for Human Rights in 1966: "The Russians were unalterably opposed to the creation of any kind of international machinery for the implementation of human rights."

53. Ibid.,, 160.

54. Ibid., 162.

55. GA Res. 543(VI): see ibid., 162.

56. UN Doc. E/2573/62.

57. The right of peoples to self-determination was not contained in the UDHR, which was one of the reasons why the Socialist states had abstained when the UDHR was adopted in 1948. It was, however, adopted in Article 1 of both Covenants on the initiative of the Soviet Union in the Commission and was drafted with the active support of various states from the South in the General Assembly. The text of Article 1 was finally adopted in the Third Committee by a majority of 33 to 12 (Western) votes, with 13 abstentions. Cf. Bossuyt, *Guide to the "travaux préparatoires,"* 841ff.; Nowak, *UN Covenant on Civil and Political Rights*, 10ff.

58. The noninclusion of minority rights in the UDHR was another reason why the Socialist states finally abstained when the UDHR was adopted in the General Assembly. The Soviet Union repeatedly proposed in the Commission and the Third Committee of the GA to adopt rights of national minorities to use their own languages and have their own schools, museums, and other cultural and educational institutions together with the right of colonial peoples to independence and self-determination: see UN Docs. E/CN.4/350, A/C.3/L.96, and E/CN.4/L.21. Already in the Commission it became clear, however, that rights of minorities were strongly supported only by Central and Eastern European countries, while the immigration countries in the "New World" were strongly against. On the initiative of the UK, United States, China, and India, the Commission decided to omit any reference to minority protection: UN Docs. E/CN.4/99 and 104. In the Third Committee of the GA, the Soviet Union, Yugoslavia, and Denmark resubmitted proposals for minority protection, which met, however, the same fate as in the Commission before: cf. Asbjørn Eide, "The Non-Inclusion of Minority Rights: Resolution 217C(III)," in Alfredsson and Eide, *Universal Declaration of Human Rights*, 701ff.

59. Article 17 of the UDHR contains the "right to own property alone as well as in association with others." The adoption of this capitalist right against the opposition of the Soviet Union and its allies was another reason the Socialist states abstained when the UDHR was adopted in 1948. But during the drafting of the two Covenants, the Socialist states made it clear from the beginning that they would not accept the right to property in any binding international human rights treaty. See UN Doc. A/2929, 65ff; Krause and Alfredsson, "Article 17," Alfredsson and Eide, *The Universal Declaration of Human Rights: A Common Standard of Achievement*, 365–66.

60. Cf. Nowak, *UN Covenant on Civil and Political Rights*, 821–822 ; Jakob Möller, "The Right of Petition: General Assembly Resolution 217B," in Alfredsson and Eide, *Universal Declaration of Human Rights*, 653.

61. GA Res. 412(V)F.

62. See the text of both Covenants adopted by the Commission in 1954 in UN Doc. E/2573/62, in particular Articles 40 to 47 CCPR.

63. Cf. Nowak, *UN Covenant on Civil and Political Rights*, 714.

64. UN Doc. A/C.3/L.1379, § 2. Cf. Bossuyt, *Guide to the "travaux préparatoires*," 652ff.; Nowak, *UN.Covenant on Civil and Political Rights*, 760–761.

65. The optional right to individual communication was adopted in Article 14 CERD on the initiative of the Philippines, Ghana, Lebanon, the Netherlands, and a number of Latin American states: see Möller, "The Right of Petition," at 680ff.

66. UN Doc. A/C.3/L.1402/Rev.2: see Bossuyt, *Guide to the "travaux préparatoires*," 797ff.; Nowak, *UN. Covenant on Civil and Political Rights*, 822ff.; Möller, "The Right of Petition," 672ff.

67. UN Doc. A/C.3/L.1411/Rev.2.

68. See Manfred Nowak, ed., *World Conference on Human Rights, Vienna, June 1993: The Contribution of NGOs, Reports and Documents* (Vienna, 1994), 65ff.

69. On the principle of due diligence in relation to the positive obligations of states to protect and fulfill human rights, see also the respective jurisprudence of the Inter-American and European Courts of Human Rights: e.g., Inter-Am.Ct.H.R., *Velázquez Rodríguez v. Honduras*, Ser. C, No. 4 (1988), 29 July 1988; *Osman v. United Kingdom* (23452, 94) [1998] ECHR 101 (28 October 1998).

70. Of the rich literature covering the development of the international protection of human rights since the end of the Cold War, see, e.g., Manfred Nowak, *Introduction to the International Human Rights Regime* (Leiden, 2003); Walter Kälin and Jörg Künzli, *The Law of International Human Rights Protection* (Oxford, 2009); Gudmundur Alfredsson, Jonas Grimheden, Bertrand G. Ramcharan, and Alfred de Zayas, eds., *International Human Rights Monitoring Mechanisms: Essays in Honour of Jakob Th. Möller*, 2nd ed. (Leiden, 2009); Olivier de Schutter, *International Human Rights Law: Cases, Materials, Commentary*, 2nd ed. (Cambridge, 2014); Rhona K. M. Smith, *International Human Rights*, 6th ed. (Oxford, 2013); Catarina Krause and Martin Scheinin, eds., *International Protection of Human Rights: A Textbook*, 2nd ed. (Turku, 2012); Manfred Nowak, Karolina M. Januszewski, and Tina Hofstätter, eds., *All Human Rights for All: Vienna Manual on Human Rights* (Vienna, 2012); Philip Alston and Ryan Goodman, *International Human Rights* (Oxford, 2012); Scott Sheeran and Nigel S. Rodley, eds., *Routledge Handbook of International Human Rights Law* (London, 2013); Andreas Føllesdal, Johan Karlsson Schaffer, and Geir Ulfstein, eds., *The Legitimacy of International Human Rights Regimes: Legal, Political and Philosophical Perspectives* (Cambridge, 2014); Yves Haeck and Eva Brems, eds., *Human Rights and Civil Liberties in the 21st Century* (Dordrecht, 2014).

71. On the concept of human security see, e.g., UNDP, *Human Development Report 1994: New Dimensions of Human Security* (New York, 1994), 24–25; Wolfgang Benedek, Matthias C. Kettemann, and Matthias Möstl, eds., *Mainstreaming Human Security in Peace Operations and Crisis Management* (Oxford, 2011); Cedric Ryngaert and Math Noortmann, eds., *Human Security and International Law: The Challenge of Non-State Actors* (Cambridge, 2014).

72. See SC Res. 660, 661 (economic sanctions), and 678 (military measures) between August and November 1990 leading to the U.S.-led Operation Desert Storm in January and February 1991 and Iraq's withdrawal from Kuwait.

73. See SC Res. 794 of December 1992 authorizing military force to create a secure environment for the delivery of humanitarian aid, which resulted in the U.S.-led Operation Restore Hope in December 1992 and later developed into a more comprehensive UN operation in Somalia (UNOSOM II established by SC Res. 814 of March 1993).

74. See SC Res. 1970 and 1973 of February and March 2011 authorizing NATO-led airstrikes that led to the fall of the repressive dictatorship of Ghadafi.

75. *2005 World Summit Outcome* document in GA Res. 60/1 of 16 September 2005, §§ 138 and 139. The R2P led to a new understanding of the concept of national sovereignty and was, for example, applied in Libya and Côte d'Ivoire in 2011.

76. SC Res. 693.

77. SC Res. 745.

78. SC Res. 867.

79. GA Res. 48, 267.

80. SC Res. 1031.

81. SC Res. 1244 establishing the UN Mission in Kosovo (UNMIK) with military security provided by the NATO-led Kosovo Force (KFOR).

82. SC Res. 1246 of June 1999 (UNAMET).

83. SC Res. 1264 of September 1999 leading to an Australian-led military intervention (INTERFET), which ended the massacres and restored security.

84. SC Res. 1272.

85. SC Res. 1410 of May 2002.

86. GA Res. 60, 251 of 3 April 2006.

87. GA Res. 48, 134.

88. SC Res. 827.

89. SC Res. 955.

90. The creation of an "international penal tribunal" was already foreseen in Article VI of the Genocide Convention of 1948 and was on the agenda of the UN and its International Law Commission (ILC) since then. But it needed the end of the Cold War and the initiative of the SC to establish two ad hoc tribunals to put it into practice.

Chapter 2. Did the West Comply with the Vienna Compromise?

1. § 5 VDPA.

2. The United States is even among a very small minority of states that failed to ratify the CRC and the CEDAW, partly because these treaties are based on the principle of the indivisibility of all human rights.

3. See, e.g., § 14(e) of Theo van Boven, Cees Flinterman, and Ingrid Westendorp, *The Maastricht Guidelines on Violations of Economic, Social and Cultural Rights*, Netherlands Institute of Human Rights, SIM Special No. 20 (Utrecht, 1997); Maastricht Centre for Human Rights, *Human Rights: Maastricht Perspectives* (Maastricht, 1999); UN Committee on Economic, Social and Cultural Rights, *General Comment No. 3: The Nature of States Parties' Obligations*, Committee on Economic, Social and Cultural Rights (CESCR), Document E/1991/23 (14 December 1990), Annex III, § 9 at 85: "Moreover, any deliberate retrogressive measures in that regard would require the most careful consideration and would need to be fully justified by reference to the totality of the rights provided for in the Covenant and in the context of the full use of the maximum available resources."

4. On the notion of the advanced welfare state see, e.g., Assar Lindbeck, "The Advanced Welfare State," Seminar Paper 395, Institute for International Economic Studies, Stockholm, 1987; Assar Lindbeck, "Consequences of the Advanced Welfare State," *World Economy* 11 (1988): 19–38; Fritz W. Scharpf, "The Viability of Advanced Welfare States in the International Economy: Vulnerabilities and Options," *Journal of European Public Policy* 7 (Cologne,

1999): 190–228; Mats Benner, "The Scandinavian Challenge: The Future of Advanced Welfare States in the Knowledge Economy," *Acta Sociologica* 46 (2003): 132–49; see the earlier book by Gunnar Myrdal, *Beyond the Welfare State* (New York, 1960).

5. See, e.g., Manfred Nowak, "The Torkel Opsahl Lecture 2013: The Right of Victims of Human Rights Violations to a Remedy: The Need for a World Court of Human Rights," *Nordic Journal of Human Rights* 32, 1 (April 2014): 3 at 14. Well-known American historian Tony Judt wrote in 2010 that the "West—Europe and the United States above all—missed a once-in-a-century opportunity to re-shape the world around agreed and improved international institutions and practices," without however clearly defining what these institutions and practices are; see Tony Judt, *Ill Fares the Land* (New York, 2010), 138.

6. In his famous book *Capitalism and Freedom* (Chicago, 1962), Milton Friedman devotes the first chapter to the relation between economic freedom and political freedom (7ff.). In his opinion, "freedom in economic arrangements is itself a component of freedom broadly understood, so economic freedom is an end in itself. In the second place, economic freedom is also an indispensable means toward the achievement of political freedom" (8).

7. See on the Keynesian Consensus, Judt, *Ill Fares the Land*, 44ff.

8. See John Maynard Keynes, *The General Theory of Employment, Interest and Money* (London, 1936, reprinted 1977).

9. See, e.g., Joseph E. Stiglitz, "Is There a Post-Washington Consensus Consensus?" in *The Washington Consensus Reconsidered: Towards a New Global Governance*, ed. Narcís Serra and Joseph E. Stiglitz (Oxford, 2008), 41: "The policies are often referred to as 'neoliberal' policies, because of the emphasis on liberalization, and because like nineteenth century liberalism, they emphasized the importance of a minimal role for the state."

10. Friedman, *Capitalism and Freedom*, 5: "Beginning in the late nineteenth century, and especially after 1930 in the United States, the term liberalism came to be associated with a very different emphasis, particularly in economic policy. It came to be associated with a readiness to rely primarily on the state rather than on private voluntary arrangements to achieve objectives regarded as desirable. The catchwords became welfare and equality rather than freedom. The nineteenth-century liberal regarded an extension of freedom as the most effective way to promote welfare and equality; the twentieth-century liberal regards welfare and equality as either prerequisites of or alternatives to freedom. In the name of welfare and equality, the twentieth-century liberal has come to favor a revival of the very policies of state intervention and paternalism against which classical liberalism fought. In the very act of turning the clock back to seventeenth-century mercantilism, he is fond of castigating true liberals as reactionary!" In the same vein, the historian Tony Judt, *Ill Fares the Land*, 4–5, argues that the term "liberal" as used today in the United States corresponds more to what Europeans call "social democracy," which however is "a hard sell in the United States." "A liberal is someone who opposes interference in the affairs of others: who is tolerant of dissenting attitudes and unconventional behavior. Liberals have historically favored keeping other people out of their lives, leaving individuals the maximum space in which to live and flourish as they choose. . . . Social democrats, on the other hand, are something of a hybrid. They share with liberals a commitment to cultural and religious tolerance. But in public policy social democrats believe in the possibility and virtue of collective action for the collective good. Like most liberals, social democrats favor progressive taxation in order to pay for public services and other social goods that individuals cannot provide themselves; but whereas many

liberals might see such taxation or public provision as a necessary evil, a social democratic vision of the good society entails from the outset a greater role for the state and the public sector."

11. Friedman, *Capitalism and Freedom*, 6: "Because of the corruption of the term liberalism, the views that formerly went under that name are now often labeled conservatism. But this is not a satisfactory alternative. The nineteenth-century liberal was a radical, both in the etymological sense of going to the root of the matter, and in the political sense of favoring major changes in social institutions. So too just be his modern heir."

12. Ibid.

13. See Friedrich von Hayek, *The Road to Serfdom* (Chicago, 1944); Friedrich von Hayek, *The Constitution of Liberty* (London, 1960). Judt, *Ill Fares the Land*, 91ff., called the strong influence of Austrian economists around Friedrich von Hayek, Ludwig von Mises, and Joseph Schumpeter on the Chicago School the "revenge of the Austrians."

14. See Milton Friedman, *A Monetary History of the United States* (Princeton, N.J., 1963).

15. See, e.g., Michel Reimon and Christian Felber, *Schwarzbuch Privatisierung: Was opfern wir dem freien Markt?* (Vienna, 2003), 138ff.

16. See, e.g. Reimon and Felber, *Schwarzbuch Privatisierung*, 11.

17. See John Williamson, "A Short History of the Washington Consensus," in Serra and Stiglitz, *The Washington Consensus Reconsidered*, 14.

18. Ibid., 16–17.

19. Ibid., 14.

20. Narcís Serra, Shari Spiegel, and Joseph E. Stiglitz, "Introduction: From the Washington Consensus Towards a New Global Governance," in Serra and Stiglitz, *The Washington Consensus Reconsidered*, 3.

21. See, e.g., Joseph E. Stiglitz, *Globalization and Its Discontents* (New York, 2002); Alice H. Amsden, "The Wild Ones: Industrial Policies in the Developing World," in Serra and Stiglitz, *The Washington Consensus Reconsidered*, 95; Alison Brysk, ed., *Gobalization and Human Rights* (Berkeley, 2002); Doris A. Oberdabernig, *The Effects of Structural Adjustment Programs on Poverty and Income Distribution*, Vienna Institute for International Economic Studies (Vienna, 2010); Reimon and Felber, *Schwarzbuch Privatisierung*.

22. See, e.g., Paul Krugman, "Inequality and Redistribution," in Serra and Stiglitz, *The Washington Consensus Reconsidered*, 31; Judt, *Ill Fares the Land*, 12ff.; Richard G. Wilkinson and Kate Pickett, *The Spirit Level: Why More Equal Societies Almost Always Do Better* (London, 2009); Thomas Piketty, *Capital in the Twenty-First Century*, trans. Arthur Goldhammer from the French original *Le capital au XXI siècle* (Paris, 2013) (Cambridge, Mass., 2014).

23. See, e.g., Cosmo Graham, "Human Rights and the Privatisation of Public Utilities and Essential Services," in *Privatisation and Human Rights in the Age of Globalisation*, ed. Koen De Feyter and Felipe Gómez Isa (Antwerp, 2005), 33.

24. See, e.g., Fons Coomans and Antenor Hallo de Wolf, "Privatisation of Education and the Right to Education," in De Feyter and Gómez, *Privatisation and Human Rights in the Age of Globalisation*, 229; Reimon and Felber, *Schwarzbuch Privatisierung*, 124ff.; see Chapter 3.

25. See, e.g., M. Gregg Bloche, "Is Privatisation of Health Care a Human Rights Problem?" in De Feyter and Gómez, *Privatisation and Human Rights in the Age of Globalisation*, 207; Reimon and Felber, *Schwarzbuch Privatisierung*, 38ff.; see below, Chapter 4.

26. See, e.g., Reimon and Felber, *Schwarzbuch Privatisierung*, 135ff.; see below, Chapter 5.

27. See, e.g., Maude Barlow, *Blue Covenant: The Global Water Crisis and the Coming Battle for the Right to Water* (New York, 2007); Karen Bakker, *Privatizing Water: Governance Failure and the World's Urban Water Crisis* (Ithaca, N.Y., 2010); Eibe Riedel and Peter Rothen, eds., *The Human Right to Water* (Berlin, 2006); Anton Kok, "Privatisation and the Right to Access to Water," in De Feyter and Gómez, *Privatisation and Human Rights in the Age of Globalisation*, 259; Reimon and Felber, *Schwarzbuch Privatisierung*, 74ff.; see below, Chapter 6.

28. See, e.g., Andrew Coyle, Allison Campbell, and Rodney Neufeld, *Capitalist Punishment: Prison Privatization and Human Rights* (Atlanta, 2003); Ira P. Robbins, "Privatisation of Corrections: A Violation of U.S. Domestic Law, International Human Rights, and Good Sense," in De Feyter and Gómez, *Privatisation and Human Rights in the Age of Globalisation*, 57; Reimon and Felber, *Schwarzbuch Privatisierung*, 191ff.; see below, Chapter 7.

29. See, e.g., Franceso Francioni and Natalino Ronzitti, eds., *War by Contract: Human Rights, Humanitarian Law and Private Contractors* (Oxford, 2011); Simon Chesterman and Chia Lehnardt, eds., *From Mercenaries to Market: The Rise and Regulation of Private Military Companies* (Oxford, 2007); Simon Chesterman and Angelina Fisher, eds., *Private Security, Public Order: The Outsourcing of Public Services and Its Limits* (Oxford, 2009); Corinna Seiberth, *Private Military and Security Companies in International Law* (Cambridge, 2014); see below, Chapter 8.

30. One of the few studies on this topic resulted from a joint research project under the auspices of the Center for Human Rights at the University of Maastricht and the Institute of Human Rights at the University of Deusto in Bilbao in the common framework of the European Inter-University Center for Human Rights (EIUC) in Venice: De Feyter and Gómez Isa, *Privatisation and Human Rights in the Age of Globalisation*. In his contribution to this research project, Felipe Gómez Isa ("Globalisation, Privatisation and Human Rights," 9 at 15 note 24) states: "It is very surprising that when one examines the existing literature on privatization, the human rights dimension is absolutely missing. There are some analyses on the effect of privatization on distribution of wealth, but not from a human rights perspective."

31. See, e.g., the jurisprudence of the European Court of Human Rights since its judgment of 25 March 1993 in *Costello-Roberts v. UK*, Series A No. 48, § 27.

32. See, e.g., Gómez, "Globalisation, Privatisation and Human Rights," 16: "In principle, International Human Rights Law is neutral on privatisation; it is neither for nor against privatisation," with a reference to a background paper of Paul Hunt for a Day of General Discussion organized by the UN Committee on the Rights of the Child on "The Private Sector as Service Provider and Its Role in Implementing Child Rights," UN Doc. CRC/C/121, 31st Session (20 September 2002), 4–5. See also Graham, "Human Rights and the Privatisation of Public Utilities and Essential Services," 37: "International human rights treaties are neutral on the systems of property ownership adopted in contracting states, assuming that these are not discriminatory, and on the means that are adopted for delivering public services." See further Sharmila L. Murthy, "The Human Right(s) to Water and Sanitation: History, Meaning, and the Controversy over Privatization," *Berkeley Journal of International Law* 31 (2013): 89 at 99: "human rights is neutral with respect to economic modes of delivery, but relevant to how such decisions are carried out."

33. For the accountability of non-state actors and IGOs under international human rights law see, e.g., Philip Alston, ed., *Non-State Actors and Human Rights* (Oxford, 2005);

Andrew Clapham, *Human Rights Obligations of Non-State Actors* (Oxford, 2006); Julia Kozma, Manfred Nowak, and Martin Scheinin, *A World Court of Human Rights, Consolidated Statute and Commentary* (Vienna, 2010); Olivier de Schutter, *International Human Rights Law*, 2nd ed .(Cambridge, 2014), 253ff.; Philip Alston and Ryan Goodman, *International Human Rights* (Oxford, 2012), 1461ff.; Manfred Nowak, Karolina Januszewski, and Tina Hofstätter, *All Human Rights for All*, 577ff.

34. See Gómez, "Globalisation, Privatisation and Human Rights," 16, quoting § 8 of GenC 3 (1990) in UN Doc. E/1991/23, Annex III.

35. Article 1(1) of the Declaration on the Right to Development adopted by the GA in 1986. While the United States had voted in 1986 against the adoption of the Declaration, it joined the Vienna Consensus in 1993 despite the fact that the World Conference on Human Rights in § 10 of the VDPA explicitly "reaffirms the right to development, as established in the Declaration on the Right to Development, as a universal and inalienable right and an integral part of fundamental human rights."

36. GenC 3 (1990) in UN Doc. E/1991/23, Annex III, § 9.

37. On the meaning and the various types of privatization see, e.g. Graham, "Human Rights and the Privatisation of Public Utilities and Essential Services," 35; William L. Megginson and Jeffry M. Netter, "From State to Market: A Survey of Empirical Studies on Privatization," *Journal of Economic Literature* 39 (2001): 321–89.

38. See Article 6(6) CCPR: "Nothing in this article shall be invoked to delay or to prevent the abolition of capital punishment by any state Party to the present Covenant." See Nowak, *UN Covenant on Civil and Political Rights*, 133ff.

39. Comm. No. 829/1998, § 10.4, *Judge v. Canada?*

40. See, e.g., Amnesty International, *Death Penalty News* (published monthly); Roger Hood, *The Death Penalty: A World-Wide Perspective* (Oxford, 1997); William A. Schabas, *The Abolition of the Death Penalty in International Law*, 3rd ed. (Cambridge, 2003); Nowak, *UN Covenant on Civil and Political Rights*, 133ff.

41. HRC, GenC 26/61 of 8 December 1997.

42. Ibid, § 3. See Nowak, *UN Covenant on Civil and Political Rights*, xxxvii.

43. HRC, GenC 26/61 of 8 December 1997, § 4.

44. See, e.g., Gómez Isa, "Globalisation, Privatisation and Human Rights," 18, again with reference to Paul Hunt.

45. See, e.g., CESCR Committee, GenC 3 (1990) in UN Doc. E/1991/23, Annex III, § 10.

46. See, e.g., Gómez, "Globalisation, Privatisation and Human Rights," 19, with further references.

47. See, e.g., Articles 13 and 41 ECHR; Articles 25 and 63 ACHR; Articles 2(3) and 9(5) CCPR. See also Koen De Feyter, Stephan Parmentier, Marc Bossuyt, and Paul Lemmens, eds., *Out of the Ashes* (Antwerp, 2005); Dinah Shelton, *Remedies in International Human Rights Law* (Oxford, 2005); The Basic Principles and Guidelines on the Right to a Remedy and Reparation for Victims of Gross Violations of International Human Rights Law and Serious Violations of International Humanitarian Law, GA Res. 60/147 of 16 December 2005.

48. See, e.g., *CostelloRoberts v. UK* (1993), ECtHR, Series A No. 48, § 27; see also *The Maastricht Guidelines*, § 2.

49. See, e.g., Gómez, "Globalisation, Privatisation and Human Rights," 21; *The Maastricht Guidelines*, § 18.

Chapter 3. Right to Education

1. On the right to education see, e.g., Ben Saul, David Kinley, and Jacqueline Mowbray, *The International Covenant on Economic, Social and Cultural Rights: Commentary, Cases and Materials* (Oxford, 2014), 1084ff.; Manisuli Ssenyonjo, *Economic, Social and Cultural Rights in International Law* (Oxford, 2009), 355ff.; Pentti Arajärvi, "Article 26," in Alfredsson and Eide, *Universal Declaration of Human Rights*, 551ff.; Beatrix Ferenci, "Right to Education," in Nowak, Januszewski, and Hofstätter, *All Human Rights for All*, 328ff.; Katarina Tomaševski, *Human Rights Obligations in Education: The 4-A Scheme* (Nijmegen, 2006); Manfred Nowak, "The Right to Education," in Eide, Krause, and Rosas, *Economic, Social and Cultural Rights* 245; Manfred Nowak, "The Right to Education: Its Meaning, Significance and Limitations," *NQHR* 9 (1991): 418.

2. Quoted from Saul, Kinley, and Mowbray, *The International Covenant on Economic, Social and Cultural Rights*, 1086.

3. CESCR Committee, GenC 13 (1999), in UN Doc. E/C.12/1999/10 of 8 December 1999, § 1.

4. On the influence of UNESCO see Saul, Kinley, and Mowbray, *The International Covenant on Economic, Social and Cultural Rights*, 1088–89; Yves Daudet and Kishore Singh, *The Right to Education: An Analysis of UNESCO's Standard-Setting Instruments* (Paris, 2001).

5. UNGA Res. 70/1: Transforming Our World: the 2030 Agenda for Sustainable Development.

6. UN Doc. E/CN.4/1999/49, § 50. See also Tomaševski, *Human Rights Obligations in Education*.

7. GenC 13 (note 3), 2–3.

8. See, e.g., the General Comments of the CESCR Committee on the rights to health, food, water, social security, etc., UN Doc. A/67/302, etc.

9. See CESCR Committee, GenC 11 (1999), UN Doc. E/2000/22, (1999).

10. See on this important principle Articles 13(3) CESCR, 18(4) CCPR, 2 1st AP ECHR.

11. GenC 13 (note 3), § 57.

12. See, e.g., GenC 13 (note 3), § 29.

13. See UN Doc. A/3764 of 5 December 1957, 10; and Saul, Kinley, and Mowbray, *The International Covenant on Economic, Social and Cultural Rights*, 1158.

14. GenC 13 (note 3), § 30.

15. Ibid.

16. Milton Friedman, *Capitalism and Freedom* (Chicago/London 1962), 89.

17. See, e.g., Gillian E. Metzger, "Privatization as Delegation," *Columbia Law Review* 103 (2003): 1367 at 1388ff.

18. See Metzger, "Privatization as Delegation," 1390 and n63, with further references.

19. See, e.g., *Zelman v. Simmons-Harris*, 536 U.S. at 639, where the U.S. Supreme Court upheld Cleveland's voucher plan against an Establishment Clause challenge; and the controversies over the Indiana and the Louisiana School Voucher Programs, the latter constituting the most sweeping voucher program in the United States so far. See, e.g., "Louisiana School Voucher Program Gets Constitutionality Hearing in Court," *Huffington Post*, 6 May 2014.

20. See, e.g., Coomans and Hallo de Wolf, "Privatisation of Education and the Right to Education," in De Feyter and Gómez, *Privatisation and Human Rights in the Age of Globalisation*, 229 at 249; Reimon and Felber, *Schwarzbuch Privatisierung*, 124ff.

21. See Reimon and Felber, *Schwarzbuch Privatisierung*, 128ff.

22. See Coomans and Hallo de Wolf, "Privatisation of Education and the Right to Education," 248.

23. See ibid., 245, with further references, in De Feyter and Gómez, *Privatisation and Human Rights in the Age of Globalisation*.

24. UN Doc. E/C.12/1/Add.70 (2001).

25. GenC 13 (note 3), § 30.

26. Ibid., § 53 and n26.

27. Ibid., § 45.

28. Coomans and Hallo de Wolf, "Privatisation of Education and the Right to Education," 256.

29. Ibid., 256–57.

30. Ibid., 257–58.

31. See, e.g., Saul, Kinley, and Mowbray, *The International Covenant on Economic, Social and Cultural Rights*, 1159 with reference to the travaux préparatoires.

32. See, e.g., the decision of the Human Rights Committee in *Waldman v. Canada* (1999), Comm. No. 694/1966, § 10.6. See Manfred Nowak, U.N. Covenant on Civil and Political Rights: CCPR Commentary, Kehl am Rhein (2005), 433; Saul, Kinley, and Mowbray, *The International Covenant on Economic, Social and Cultural* Rights, 1159–60.

33. UN Doc. A/69/402, para. 101: "The Special Rapporteur would like to emphasize that the delegation by States of their obligation to provide education to for-profit providers may be contrary to their international obligations."

34. See UN Docs. CRC/C/GHA/CO/3–5 and CRC/C/MAR/CO/3–4, 14 October 2014.

35. See United Nations Committee on the Elimination of Discrimination against Women, Half-Day General Discussion on girls'/women's right to education, Joint Statement by Lucy McKernan, Global Initiative for Economic, Social and Cultural Rights, http://www .ohchr.org/Documents/HRBodies/CEDAW/WomensRightEducation/GlobalCoalition.pdf.

36. See, e.g., Bretton Woods Project, "Going, Going, Gone? World Bank's Funding for Public Education," 9 May 2014, www.brettonwoodsproject.org.

37. Report of the Special Rapporteur on the right to education, in UN Doc. A/69/402 of 24 September 2014, para. 32.

38. Ibid., para. 31 and note 3.

39. Ibid., para. 33. See also Ian Macpherson, Susan Robertson, and Geoffrey Walford, eds., *Education, Privatisation and Social Justice: Case Studies from Africa, South Asia and South East Asia* (Oxford, 2014).

40. UN Doc A/69/402 of 24 September 2014., para. 99; Report of the Special Rapporteur,

41. Ibid., para. 100.

42. See the Statement of the UN Special Rapporteur on the right to education, Kishore Singh, of 22 March 2016: "UN rights expert urges Liberia not to hand public education over to a private company," http://ohchr.org/EN/NewsEvents/Pages/DisplayNews.aspx?News ID = 18506&LangID = E.

Chapter 4. Right to Health

1. See Andreassen, "Article 22," in Asbjørn Eide et al., *The Universal Declaration of Human Rights*.

2. See Eide and, "Article 25," in Alfredsson and Eide, *The Universal Declaration of Human Rights: A Common Standard of Achievement.*

3. Article 35 of the Humphrey draft, UN Doc. AC.1/3.

4. Morsink, *The Universal Declaration of Human Rights*, 192.

5. Ibid.

6. Ibid.

7. See Saul, Kinley, and Mowbray, *The International Covenant on Economic, Social and Cultural Rights*, 862, who note that the different rights still included in Article 11 CESCR "remain both expansive and challenging."

8. CESCR Committee, GenC 14 (2000), in UN Doc. E/C.12/2000/4, § 3.

9. Ibid., § 4.

10. See UN Doc. A/3525, 145.

11. See Saul, Kinley, and Mowbray, *The International Covenant on Economic, Social and Cultural Rights*, 980.

12. M. Gregg Bloche, "Is Privatisation of Health Care a Human Rights Problem?" in De Feyter and Gómez, *Privatisation and Human Rights in the Age of Globalisation*, 207 at 208.

13. See, e.g., Ssenyonjo, *Economic, Social and Cultural Rights in International Law*, 316, with further references.

14. Reimon and Felber, *Schwarzbuch Privatisierung*, 61–62.

15. For the privatization of Medicare and Medicaid managed care in the United States, see, e.g., Metzger, "Privatization as Delegation," 1380: "One example of the trend towards expanded privatization is Medicare and Medicaid managed care. Until recently, the basic model for both programs was fee-for-service, under which the government reimburses a doctor or other medical provider for each service provided to a beneficiary. By contrast, under managed care the beneficiary enrolls with a managed care organization (MCO), usually a for-profit enterprise, and the government pays the MCO a set amount over a given period (the 'capitated rate') regardless of the medical services actually provided. While enrollment in a MCO is optional for Medicare beneficiaries, it is mandatory for many participants in Medicaid. The number of beneficiaries enrolled in managed care in the two programs has increased dramatically since 1990, with nearly 60% of Medicaid beneficiaries and 12% of Medicare beneficiaries being treated through MCOs in 2002."

16. Bloche, "Is Privatisation of Health Care a Human Rights Problem?" in De Feyter and Gómez, *Privatisation and Human Rights in the Age of Globalisation*, 207.

17. Ibid., 220–21.

18. GenC 14 (note 8), § 12(a).

19. Ibid., § 17.

20. Ibid., § 19.

21. Ibid., §§ 39 and 64.

22. Ibid., §§ 43 and 44. On the Alma-Ata Declaration see also Saul, Kinley, and Mowbray, *The International Covenant on Economic, Social and Cultural Rights*, 989–90.

23. See, e.g., Ssenyonjo, *Economic, Social and Cultural Rights in International Law*, 331ff.

24. Judgment of the Federal Court of Administrative Appeals of Argentina of 2 June 1998 in Case No. 31.777/96 (1998). See escr-just@yahoogroups.com and www.cels.org.ar.

25. Judgment of the South African Constitutional Court of 5 July 2002: CCT 8/02, (2002) ZACC 15; 2002 (5) SA 721. See Iain Byrne, "Making the Right to Health a Reality: Legal

Strategies for Effective Implementation," paper presented at Commonwealth Law Conference, London, September 2005.

26. Judgment of the Indian Supreme Court of 6 May 1996: (1996) SCJ 25, 29; see Ssenyonjo, *Economic, Social and Cultural Rights in International Law*, 349; Saul, Kinley, and Mowbray, *The International Covenant on Economic, Social and Cultural Rights*, 1068.

27. See Sarah Joseph, "Pharmaceutical Corporations and Access to Drugs: The 'Fourth Wave' of Corporate Human Rights Scrutiny," *Human Rights Quarterly* 25 (2003): 425 at 443; Saul, Kinley, and Mowbray, *The International Covenant on Economic, Social and Cultural Rights*, 1022.

28. On the relationship between intellectual property rights of pharmaceutical companies and the human right to health see Stephen P. Marks, "Access to Essential Medicines as a Component of the Right to Health," in *Realizing the Right to Health*, ed. Andrew Clapham and Mary Robinson (Zürich, 2012), 87: "In other words, an IPR (intellectual property right) is a legally protected interest of a lower order than a human right, which implies a superior moral and legal claim." See also Saul, Kinley, and Mowbray, *The International Covenant on Economic, Social and Cultural Rights*, 1019.

29. Tribunal Superior de Justicia de Madrid, *Asociacion de Facultativos Especialistas de Madrid (AFEM) v. Comunidad de Madrid*, Recurso No. 787/2013, Decision of 11 September 2013. See in this respect also Mariela Rubio Jiménez, *Tu salud, nuestro negocio* (Your Health, Our Business), Madrid, 2014.

30. UN Doc. A/67/302 of 13 August 2012, § 3.

31. Ibid., § 9.

32. Ibid., § 11.

33. UN Doc. A/HRC/20/15/Add.2.

34. Concluding observations of the CEDAW Committee on the initial report of Armenia in 1997, UN Doc. A/52/38/Rev.1, Part II, § 60.

35. UN Doc. CEDAW/C/IND/CO/3.

36. UN Doc. CEDAW/C/PAKISTAN/CO/4.

37. UN Doc. CEDAW/C/HUN/CO/7–8.

38. UN Docs. E/C.12/1/Add. 56 and 70.

39. UN Doc. E/C.12/IND/CO/5, § 38.

40. Ibid., § 78.

41. UN Doc. E/C.12/POL/CO/5.

42. GenC 14 (note 8), §§ 39 and 64.

43. See, e.g., UN Doc. E/C.12/1/Add.70 (2001).

44. Inter-American Court of Human Rights, *Ximenes-Lopes v. Brazil*, Judgment of 4 July 2006, § 89. See also the judgment of 22 November 2007 in *Albán-Cornejo et al. v. Ecuador*, §§ 119 and 121.

45. Inter-American Court of Human Rights, *Suárez Peralta v. Ecuador*, Judgment of 21 May 2013, § 135.

46. European Court of Human Rights, *Storck v. Germany*, Judgment of 16 June 2005, § 103. See also the judgments in later cases, such as *Lazar v. Romania* of 16 May 2010, § 66, or *Z v. Poland* of 13 November 2012, § 76.

47. See, e.g., Reimon and Felber, *Schwarzbuch Privatisierung*, 38ff.

48. See, e.g., Metzger, "Privatization as Delegation," 1380ff.

49. Nate Silver, "What Is Driving Growth in Government Spending?" *New York Times*, 16 January 2013.

50. Eduardo Porter, "Health Care and Profits, a Poor Mix," *New York Times*, 8 January 2013.

51. See also Alan Singer, "What Happens if Public Education Is Privatized? Clues from the Health Care Fiasco," *Huffington Post*, 6 May 2014. Already in 2003, Reimon and Felber, *Schwarzbuch Privatisierung*, 59, had found on the basis of WHO statistics that the U.S. system spends $4,600 per inhabitant per year for its dysfunctional health care system, whereas the Swiss spend $2,500, the Germans $2,300, and the Austrians $1,700. According to WHO World Health Statistics 2014, Part III, 141 ff., per capita total expenditure on health in 2011 amounted in the United States to $8,467, surpassed only by Switzerland ($9,248), and still much higher than Canada ($5,656), Austria ($5,643), Sweden ($5,419), Germany ($4,996), France ($4,968), and Japan ($4,656). As a percentage of GDP, total U.S. expenditures ranked 17.7 percent, by far on top, compared to 11.6 percent in France, 11.3 percent in Austria and Germany, 11 percent in Switzerland, 10.9 percent in Canada, 10 percent in Japan, and 9.5 percent in Sweden.

52. See, e.g., Singer, "What Happens if Public Education Is Privatized?"

53. See Metzger, "Privatization as Delegation," 1381.

54. See Reimon and Felber, *Schwarzbuch Privatisierung*, 52ff.

55. See Singer, "What Happens if Public Education Is Privatized?"

56. Ibid.

57. Reimon and Felber, *Schwarzbuch Privatisierung*, 64.

58. Ibid., 71–72.

59. Ibid., 57ff.

60. In this respect, the right to health is closely connected to the right to social security.

61. GenC 14 (note 8), §§ 43–45.

Chapter 5. Right to Social Security

1. On the history of social security in the welfare state, see, e.g., Bård-Anders Andreassen, "Article 22," in *The Universal Declaration of Human Rights: A Common Standard of Achievement*, ed. Gudmundur Alfredsson and Asbjørn Eide (The Hague, 1999), 454ff.; Saul, Kinley, and Mowbray, *The International Covenant on Economic, Social and Cultural Rights*, 609ff.

2. Andreassen, "Article 22," 456. in Alfredsson and Eide, *The Universal Declaration of Human Rights: A Common Standard of Achievement*.

3. Saul, Kinley, and Mowbray, *The International Covenant on Economic, Social and Cultural Rights*, 609.

4. Andreassen, "Article 22," 458. See in this respect Harold Wilensky, *The Welfare State and Equality* (Berkeley, Calif., 1975); Guy Perrin, "Reflections on Fifty Years of Social Security," *International Labour Review* 99 (1969): 260. On the "Beveridge model" of social security, see also Reimon and Felber, *Schwarzbuch Privatisierung*, 61. During the drafting of Article 9 CESCR, the representative of France, for example, stated that the French system of social security had been influenced by the British "Beveridge model": UN Doc. A/C.3/SR.729, 242.

5. Andreassen, "Article 22," 455, with reference to Peter Flora and Arnold J. Heidenheimer, eds., *The Development of Welfare States in Europe and America* (New Brunswick, N.J., 1981).

6. On the so-called Keynesian Consensus, which profoundly shaped the post-World War II era, see, e.g., the historian Tony Judt, *Ill Fares the Land*, 44ff. According to Judt (192–93), "The very term 'social security'—adapted by Keynes from its new American usage—became a universal shorthand for prophylactic institutions designed to avert any return to the interwar catastrophe."

7. UN Doc. E/CN.4/21.

8. See Article 26 of the draft declaration in the report on the second session of the Commission in 1948, UN Doc. E/600; cf. Andreassen, "Article 22," 466ff.

9. See Andreassen, "Article 22," 469ff.

10. UN Doc. E/CN.4/127; and Andreassen, "Article 22," 470.

11. UN Doc. E/CN.4/SR.70, 9.

12. UN Doc. E/CN.4/SR.72, 4. According to Andreassen, "Article 22," 472, it was "largely René Cassin's merit that the reference to social security was included in the article, although no attempt was made to define the term, and uncertainty as to its definition remained."

13. UN Doc. E/CN.4/SR.72, 4; and Andreassen, "Article 22," 472.

14. See Mary Ann Glendon, *A World Made New: Eleanor Roosevelt and the Universal Declaration of Human Rights* (New York, 2001), 157.

15. Ibid.

16. See ibid., 157–58; Morsink, *The Universal Declaration of Human Rights*, 90.

17. See Andreassen, "Article 22," 475, with reference to John Rawls, *A Theory of Justice* (Cambridge, Mass., 1971).

18. See Saul, Kinley, and Mowbray, *The International Covenant on Economic, Social and Cultural Rights*, 610.

19. See Eide and Eide in Alfredsson and Eide,, 523 at 549–50 who speak in this context of a right to "livelihood security."

20. See Saul, Kinley, and Mowbray, *The International Covenant on Economic, Social and Cultural Rights*, 612ff., with further references to the discussions in the Third Committee of the General Assembly.

21. Ibid., 617–18.

22. Ibid., 618.

23. UN Doc. A/C.3/SR.726, 229.

24. See Saul, Kinley, and Mowbray, *The International Covenant on Economic, Social and Cultural Rights*, 618.

25. CESCR Committee, GenC 19 (2008) in UN Doc. E/C.12/GC/19.

26. Ibid., § 2.

27. Ibid., § 12 and and n8.

28. Ibid., § 3. See also Saul, Kinley, and Mowbray, *The International Covenant on Economic, Social and Cultural Rights*, 616: "While the right to social security does not presuppose a particular economic system, it does require some form of redistribution (whether from the state, employers or wealthier workers), demands more than mere self-insurance by employees, and requires state intervention and regulation."

29. GenC 19 (note 25), § 4. On the notion of the terms "social security," "social welfare," "social insurance," and "social assistance," see, e.g., Martin Scheinin, "The Right to Social Security," in Eide, Krause, and Rosas, *Economic, Social and Cultural Rights*, 211; Saul, Kinley, and Mowbray, *The International Covenant on Economic, Social and Cultural Rights*, 614.

30. GenC 19 (note 25), § 4(a).

31. Ibid., § 4(b).

32. Ibid., § 5.

33. Ibid., § 46.

34. Ibid., § 50.

35. Ibid., § 42.

36. In this respect, the Committee refers to the core obligations developed in GenC 14 in UN Doc E/C.12/2000/4, §§ 43 and 44, in relation to the right to health, including access to health facilities, goods, and services on a nondiscriminatory basis, provision of essential drugs, access to reproductive, maternal, and child health care, and immunization against the major infectious diseases occurring in the community.

37. GenC 19 (note 25), § 59(a). Such an emphasis on the link between Articles 9 and 11 CESCR by the CESCR Committee had been strongly advocated by Lucie Lamarche, "Social Protection Is a Matter of Human Rights: Exploring the ICESCR Right to Social Security in the Context of Globalisation," in De Feyter and Gómez, *Privatisation and Human Rights in the Age of Globalisation*, 159.

38. GenC 19 (note 25), § 59(b)–(f).

39. Ibid., §§ 83 and 58.

40. See, e.g., Christian Courtis, "Social Rights and Privatisation: Lessons from the Argentine Experience," in De Feyter and Gómez, *Privatisation and Human Rights in the Age of Globalisation*, 175 at 187ff.; Lamarche, "Social Protection Is a Matter of Human Rights," 129 at 157ff.

41. Quote translated from Reimon and Felber, *Schwarzbuch Privatisierung*, 139.

42. See World Bank, *Averting the Old Age Crisis: Policies to Protect the Old and Promote Growth* (New York, 1994); Lamarche, "Social Protection Is a Matter of Human Rights," 140; Reimon and Felber, *Schwarzbuch Privatisierung*, 140.

43. See Reimon and Felber, *Schwarzbuch Privatisierung*, 135.

44. Ibid., 140ff.

45. For the text of the British Human Rights Act, see, e.g., Sandy Ghandhi, *International Human Rights Documents*, 8th ed. (Oxford, 2012), 473 at 475.

46. *YL v. Birmingham City Council* (2007) UKHL 27; (2008) 1 AC 95. See Rodney Austin, "Human Rights, the Private Sector and New Public Management," *UCL Human Rights Review* 1 (2008): 17.

47. See Austin, "Human Rights, the Private Sector and New Public Management," 23, who also commented critically at 21: "Since the advent of the welfare state in the post-WWII era, the relief of poverty, unemployment, sickness, disability and other similar social evils arising from market failure in capitalist economies has been seen as a core function of government."

48. *Elisabeth de Blok et al. v. The Netherlands*, Comm. No. 36/2012, Views of 17 February 2014.

49. Ibid., § 2.6.

50. UN Doc. CEDAW/C/NLD/CO/4, §§ 29 and 30; *De Blok v. Netherlands.*, § 8.6.

51. *De Blok v. Netherlands*, §§ 8.8 and 8.9.

52. Metzger, "Privatization as Delegation," 1383.

53. Ibid., 1385.

54. Ibid.

55. See Lamarche, "Social Protection Is a Matter of Human Rights," 138.

56. For a fairly comprehensive analysis of the Committee's concluding observations see Saul, Kinley, and Mowbray, *The International Covenant on Economic, Social and Cultural Rights,* 630ff.

57. UN Doc. E/C.12/1994/20, § 233.

58. Saul, Kinley, and Mowbray, *The International Covenant on Economic, Social and Cultural Rights,* 631, with reference to El Salvador and Mexico.

59. UN Doc. E/C.12/1/Add.23, § 19.

60. UN Doc. E/C.12/1/Add.106, § 22.

61. UN Docs. E/C.12/AFG/CO/2–4, § 26 and E/C.12/COD/CO/4, § 24. On the DRC, see also the 2012 report of the Independent Expert of the UN Human Rights Council on Economic Reform and Foreign Debt in UN Doc. A/HRC/20/23/Add.2.

62. See, e.g., the concluding observations of 2007 to El Salvador in UN Doc. E/C.12/SLV/CO/2, §§ 15–16; and the references in Saul, Kinley, and Mowbray, *The International Covenant on Economic, Social and Cultural Rights,* 705.

63. UN Doc. E/C.12/KAZ/CO/1.

64. See Saul, Kinley, and Mowbray, *The International Covenant on Economic, Social and Cultural Rights,* 639, with further references (nn161–63).

65. UN Doc. E/C.12/1/Add.31, §§ 20–21, reproduced in full in Saul, Kinley, and Mowbray, *The International Covenant on Economic, Social and Cultural Rights,* 640.

66. UN Doc. E/C.12/1995/5, § 12. See Saul, Kinley, and Mowbray, *The International Covenant on Economic, Social and Cultural Rights,* 640.

67. UN Doc. E/C.12/1/Add.76, § 10.

68. UN Doc. E/C.12/ISR/CO/3.

69. UN Doc. E/C.12/1/Add.62, § 23.

70. Saul, Kinley, and Mowbray, *The International Covenant on Economic, Social and Cultural Rights,* 632.

71. Lamarche, "Social Protection Is a Matter of Human Rights," 163ff.

72. Ibid., 164.

73. Ibid., 168.

74. Ibid., 171.

75. Ibid., 172.

76. GenC 19 (note 25)§ 7, with reference to Michael Cichon and Krzysztof Hagemejer, "Social Security for All: Investing in Global Social and Economic Development: A Consultation," Issues in Social Protection Series, Discussion Paper 16, ILO Social Security Department, Geneva, 2006.

77. ILO, *World Social Security Report 2010/11: Providing Coverage in Times of Crisis and Beyond* (Geneva, 2010), Executive Summary, 33; Saul, Kinley, and Mowbray, *The International Covenant on Economic, Social and Cultural Rights,* 637.

78. See Wilkinson and Pickett, *The Spirit Level,* Figures I.1., I.2., pp. 7, 9.

79. Ibid., 265.

80. Ibid., 17.

81. Ibid., 235.

82. See the list of the twenty-three states in ibid., 267.

83. Ibid., 20, 174.

84. Ibid., 23.

85. Ibid., 52.

86. Ibid., 67.

87. Ibid., 71.

88. Ibid., 82.

89. Ibid., 92–93.

90. Ibid., 106.

91. Ibid., 122.

92. Ibid., 135.

93. Ibid., 139.

94. Ibid., 148.

95. Ibid., 160.

96. Ibid., 224.

97. Piketty, *Capital in the Twenty-First Century*, 323–24.

98. Ibid., 26. See also Anthony B. Atkinson, *Inequality: What Can Be Done?* (Cambridge, Mass., 2015); OECD, *Mehr Ungleichheit trotz Wachstum? Einkommensverteilung und Armut in OECD-Ländern* (Paris, 2008); OECD, *Divided We Stand: Why Inequality Keeps Rising* (Paris, 2011); OECD, *Focus on Inequality and Growth* (Paris, 2014); OECD, *In It Together: Why Less Inequality Benefits All* (Paris, 2015); Manfred Nowak, *Menschenrechte: Eine Antwort auf die wachsende ökonomische Ungleichheit* (Vienna, 2015).

99. Wilkinson and Pickett, *The Spirit Level*, 256.

100. See, e.g., Gerhard Luf, *Freiheit und Gleichheit* (Vienna, 1978).

Chapter 6. Right to Water

1. Committee on Economic, Social and Cultural Rights, *General Comment No. 15: The Right to Water (Arts. 11 and 12 of the Covenant)*, adopted 20 January 2003, UN Doc. E/C.12/2002/11.

2. See Inga Winkler, *The Human Right to Water: Significance, Legal Status and Implications for Water Allocation* (Oxford, 2012), 42; see also Sharmila L. Murthy, "The Human Right(s) to Water and Sanitation: History, Meaning, and the Controversy Over-Privatization," *Berkeley Journal of International Law* 31 (2013): 89 at 92.

3. See, e.g., §§ 15 and 20(2) of the UN Standard Minimum Rules for the Treatment of Prisoners 1955; Articles 34 and 37 of the UN Rules for the Protection of Juveniles Deprived of Their Liberty 1990.

4. See, e.g., Article 14(2) CEDAW 1979; and Article 15(a) of the 2003 Protocol to the African Charter on Human and Peoples' Rights on the Rights of Women in Africa.

5. See, e.g., Article 24(2)(c) CRC 1989 and Article 14(2)(c) of the African Charter of the Rights and Welfare of the Child 1990.

6. See, e.g., Articles 7(b) and 8(c) of ILO Recommendation No. 115 of 1961 on Workers' Housing, and Article 5 of ILO Convention No. 161 of 1985 on Occupational Health Services.

7. On the right to water see, e.g., Eibe Riedel and Peter Rothen, eds., *The Human Right to Water* (Berlin: 2006); Murthy, "The Human Right(s) to Water and Sanitation," 100ff.; Takele Soboka Bulto, *The Extraterritorial Application of the Human Right to Water in Africa* (Cambridge, 2014); Kok, "Privatisation and the Right to Access to Water," 259.

8. See UN Doc. E/CONF.70/29 (1977); for the history of the right to water discourse see Murthy, "The Human Right(s) to Water and Sanitation," 92ff., with further references.

9. GA Res. 34/191 of 19 December 1977.

10. UN Conference on Environment and Development, Rio de Janeiro, 1992, Agenda 21, UN Doc. A/CONF.151/26 (1993).

11. International Conference on Water and the Environment, *The Dublin Statement on Water and Sustainable Development* (Dublin, 1992); see Murthy, "The Human Right(s) to Water and Sanitation," 93, with further references.

12. See, e.g., Maude Barlow and Tony Clark, *Blue Gold: The Fight to Stop the Corporate Theft of the World's Water* (New York, 2002), xii; Murthy, "The Human Right(s) to Water and Sanitation," 93.

13. See Murthy, "The Human Right(s) to Water and Sanitation," 125, with further references.

14. Maude Barlow, "The Water Warriors Fight Back," in *Blue Covenant*, 62–63.

15. Murthy, "The Human Right(s) to Water and Sanitation," 126, with reference to Craig Anthony Arnold, "Water Privatization Trends in the United States: Human Rights, National Security, and Public Stewardship," *William and Mary Environmental Law and Policy Review* 33 (2009): 785 at 797. See also Reimon and Felber, *Schwarzbuch Privatisierung*, 74ff.

16. See Reimon and Felber, *Schwarzbuch Privatisierung*, 103ff.

17. Ibid., 108.

18. Barlow, *Blue Covenant*, 38. See also Adam D. Link, "The Perils of Privatization: International Developments and Reform in Water Distribution," *Global Business and Development Law Journal* 22 (2010): 379 at 381ff.

19. Murthy, "The Human Right(s) to Water and Sanitation," 124, with reference to Joseph W. Dellapenna, "Climate Disruption, the Washington Consensus, and Water Law Reform," *Temple Law Review* 81 (2008): 383 at 404.

20. See note 30 below.

21. Report of the UN Special Rapporteur on the right to water in UN Doc. A/HRC/24/44 of 11 July 2013, § 45, with reference to a Memorandum of Understanding (MoU) of 21 December 2012 between the IMF and Greece.

22. See Catarina de Albuquerque, *Report of the Independent Expert on the Issue of Human Rights Obligations Related to Access to Safe Drinking Water and Sanitation*, 29 June 2010, UN Doc. A/HRC/15/31, 6n11; Murthy, "The Human Right(s) to Water and Sanitation," 124; Karen Bakker, *An Uncooperative Commodity: Privatizing Water in England and Wales* (Oxford, 2004).

23. See also relevant case law by state courts in the United States in Kok, "Privatisation and the Right to Access to Water," 264.

24. UN Doc. A/HRC/18/33/Add.4 of 2 August 2011, § 14.

25. See World Bank, Public-Private Infrastructure Advisory Facility, *Public-Private Partnerships for Urban Water Utilities: A Review of Experiences in Developing Countries* (Washington, D.C., 2009).

26. *Pinsent Masons Water Yearbook 2011–2012*, http://wateryearbook.pinsentmasons .com.

27. UN Secretary-General, *The Millennium Development Goals Report 2014* (New York, 2014), 44.

28. For a recent table of public protests against private sector water supply in 35 countries see Bakker, *An Uncooperative Commodity*, 140–41.

29. See Barlow, *Blue Covenant*, 102ff.

30. Ibid., 103–4; Link, "The Perils of Privatization," 386ff.; Reimon and Felber, *Schwarzbuch Privatisierung*, 94ff.; Melina Williams, "Privatization and the Human Right to Water: Challenges for the New Century," *Michigan Journal of International Law* 28 (2007): 469 at 496ff.

31. See, e.g., Kenneth J. Vandevelde, *"Aguas del Tunari, S.A. v. Republic of Bolivia*, ICSID Case No. ARB/02/3," *AJIL* 101 (2007): 179; Link, "The Perils of Privatization," 386ff.

32. Link, "The Perils of Privatization," 391; Murthy, "The Human Right(s) to Water and Sanitation," 140–41.

33. Link, "The Perils of Privatization," 391–92.

34. Ibid., 394.

35. Ibid., 395.

36. UN Doc. A/HRC/21/42/Add.2 of 2 July 2012, § 16.

37. Ibid., §§ 6 and 7.

38. *Azurix Corp. v. Argentine Republic*, ICSID Case No. ARB/01/12; see Murthy, "The Human Right(s) to Water and Sanitation," 141ff., with further references.

39. See Barlow, *Blue Covenant*, 105ff.; Reimon and Felber, *Schwarzbuch Privatisierung*, 76ff.

40. See the cases of *Suez and Aguas Argentinas v. Argentine Republic* before the ICSID, Case Nos. ARB/03/17, 19; see Murthy, "The Human Right(s) to Water and Sanitation," 141ff.; Barlow, *Blue Covenant*, 105–6; Reimon and Felber, *Schwarzbuch Privatisierung*, 78ff.; Carolina Fairstein, "Legal Strategies and Right to Water in Argentina," in Riedel and Rothen, *The Human Right to Water*, 95ff.

41. See Murthy, "The Human Right(s) to Water and Sanitation," 142; Fairstein, "Legal Strategies and Right to Water in Argentina," 102.

42. See Fairstein, "Legal Strategies and Right to Water in Argentina," 110–11, with further references.

43. See Barlow, *Blue Covenant*, 107ff.

44. See Casper Human, "The Human Right to Water in Africa: The South African Example," in Riedel and Rothen, *The Human Right to Water*, 83.

45. *Biwater Gauff (Tanzania) Ltd. v. United Republic of Tanzania*, ICSID Case No. ARB/ 05/22; see Link, "The Perils of Privatization," 388ff.

46. See, e.g., Reimon and Felber, *Schwarzbuch Privatisierung*, 74ff.; Barlow, *Blue Covenant*, 117.

47. Article 27(1)(b) of the constitution provides that "Everyone has the right to access to . . . sufficient food and water." According to Article 27(2), "the state must take reasonable legislative and other measures, within its available resources, to achieve the progressive realisation of these rights." See, e.g., Human, "The Human Right to Water in Africa," 83ff.; Link, "The Perils of Privatization," 395ff.; Kok, "Privatisation and the Right to Access to Water," 268ff.

48. See Kok, "Privatisation and the Right to Access to Water," 270, with reference to Rassie Malherbe, "Privatisation and the Constitution: Some Exploratory Observations," *Journal of South African Law* 1 (2001): 12.

49. WHO cites a minimum of 20 liters per person per day for survival needs, 50 liters for personal and domestic needs such as bathing, and 100 liters as a desired level: see WHO, *Domestic Water Quantity, Service Level and Health* (Geneva, 2003); see also Bakker, *An Uncooperative Commodity*, 148; Kok, "Privatisation and the Right to Access to Water," 273.

50. Human, "The Human Right to Water in Africa," 89.

51. See Barlow, *Blue Covenant*, 117.

52. *Mazibuko v. City of Johannesburg*, 2008(4) All SA 471 (W) 40; see Link, "The Perils of Privatization," 395ff.

53. *Residents of Bon Vista Mansions v. Southern Metropolitan Local Council*, 2002 (6) BCLR 625 (W); see Kok, "Privatisation and the Right to Access to Water," 279–80.

54. See, e.g., Barlow, *Blue Covenant*, 111ff.

55. Ibid., 113–14; Reimon and Felber, *Schwarzbuch Privatisierung*, 88.

56. CESCR Committee, *General Comment No. 15: The Right to Water (Arts. 11 and 12 of the Covenant)*, adopted on 20 January 2003, contained in UN Doc. E/C.12/2002/11. On the genesis and contents of GenC 15 see, e.g., Eibe Riedel, "The Human Right to Water and General Comment No. 15 of the CESCR," in Riedel and Rothen, *The Human Right to Water*, 19 at 25ff.; see also Saul, Kinley, and Mowbray, *The International Covenant on Economic, Social and Cultural Rights*, 899ff.; Melina Williams, "Privatization and the Human Right to Water," 469 at 475ff.

57. GenC 15 (note 56), § 3.

58. Ibid., § 1.

59. Ibid., § 11.

60. Ibid., § 12(a).

61. Ibid., § 12(c).

62. Ibid., § 16.

63. Ibid., § 19.

64. Ibid., § 24.

65. Ibid., §§ 36 and 60.

66. Ibid., § 37.

67. Ibid., § 42.

68. See also Miloon Kothari, "Obstacles to Making Water a Human Right," in Riedel and Rothen, *The Human Right to Water*, 149 at 157: "While General Comment No. 15 does not explicitly mention the words privatisation and globalisation, read as a whole, it offers a carefully modulated and persistent critique of the advocates of privatisation of basic civic services." Another participant in the Berlin Conference on the right to water of October 2005, Matthew Craven ("Some Thoughts on the Emerging Right to Water," in Riedel and Rothen, *The Human Right to Water*, 37 at 46–47) is more critical on the "blanket refusal" of the Committee "to engage with the policies and politics of water distribution and management." He concludes "that the Committee may be legislating for its own absence—or excluding its own competence—in the very area in which the discussion of water rights is most acute and in which the Committee's voice is perhaps most needed."

69. UN Doc. E/CN.4/Sub.2/2005/25 of 11 July 2005 and Sub-Commission Res. 2006/10. See also Saul, Kinley, and Mowbray, *The International Covenant on Economic, Social and Cultural Rights*, 908ff.

70. UN Doc. E/CN4/Sub.2/2005/25, § 2.3.

71. HRC Dec. 2/104 of 27 November 2006.

72. UN Doc. A/HRC/6/3, § 66.

73. Ibid., § 53.

74. HRC Res. 7/22 of 28 March 2008.

75. UN Doc. A/HRC/15/31/Add.1 of 1 July 2010.

76. Ibid., § 74.

77. UN Doc. A/HRC/15/31 of 29 June 2010.

78. Ibid., § 2.

79. Ibid., § 8.

80. Ibid., § 15.

81. Ibid., §§ 43, 44.

82. Ibid., § 61.

83. Ibid., § 63.

84. GA Res. 64/292 of 28 July 2010. See Murthy, "The Human Right(s) to Water and Sanitation," 102ff.

85. HRC Res. 17/9 of 30 September 2010; see also Murthy, "The Human Right(s) to Water and Sanitation," 104.

86. HRC Res. 17/9, § 3.

87. Ibid., § 6.

88. Ibid., § 7.

89. Ibid., § 9.

90. See chapter 3 on "Water Hunters" in Barlow, *Blue Covenant*, 68ff., or chapter 4 on water as a commodity in Reimon and Felber, *Schwarzbuch Privatisierung*, 74ff.

91. HRC Res. 16/2 of 24 March 2011, § 4.

92. UN Doc. A/HRC/24/44 of 11 July 2013, § 44.

93. Ibid., § 45.

94. See also Murthy, "The Human Right(s) to Water and Sanitation," 105.

95. HRC Res. 17/9 of 30 September 2010, § 7.

96. See, e.g., the concluding observations of the CESCR Committee in relation to New Zealand in UN Doc. E/C.12/NZL/CO/3 (2012), or to Kenya in UN Doc. E/C.12/KEN/CO/1 (2008).

97. See, e.g., the recommendations in her report on her 2009 mission to Egypt in UN Doc. A/HRC/15/31/Add.3 of 5 July 2010, §§ 66–68.

98. See Saul, Kinley, and Mowbray, *The International Covenant on Economic, Social and Cultural Rights*, 915.

99. Ibid., 915–16.

100. See, e.g., Joseph Gepp, "Wasser unser," *Falter*, June 2013. See also the first popular initiative in the EU, which in 2013 led to more than 1.5 million citizens in seven EU member states demanding the EU Commission change its plans toward privatization of water, http://www.right2water.eu/.

101. See, e.g., the judgment of the High Court of Kerala in *Attakoya Thangal v. Union of India*, (1990) I KLT 580: see for this and other cases before Indian courts Saul, Kinley, and Mowbray, *The International Covenant on Economic, Social and Cultural Rights*, 918.

102. Judgment No. 36/98 of the Belgian Court of Arbitration in Commune de Memmel; see Saul, Kinley, and Mowbray, *The International Covenant on Economic, Social and Cultural Rights*, 917.

103. See Saul, Kinley, and Mowbray, *The International Covenant on Economic, Social and Cultural Rights*, 917, with further references (n144). See also Fairstein, "Legal Strategies and Right to Water in Argentina," 95 ff.

104. See the decision of the African Commission in *IHRR* 4 (1997): 89; and Saul, Kinley, and Mowbray, *The International Covenant on Economic, Social and Cultural Rights*, 919. For the approach of the African Commission to the right to water see also Bulto, *The Extraterritorial Application of the Human Right to Water in Africa*, 70ff.

105. Decision of the African Commission of 27 October 2001 in *Social and Economic Rights Action Center and the Center for Economic and Social Rights v. Nigeria*, Comm. No. 155/96, (2001) AHRLR 60; see Saul, Kinley, and Mowbray, *The International Covenant on Economic, Social and Cultural Rights*, 918; Bulto, *The Extraterritorial Application of the Human Right to Water in Africa*, 94.

106. See Saul, Kinley, and Mowbray, *The International Covenant on Economic, Social and Cultural Rights*, 919ff.

107. Decision of the Inter-American Commission on Human Rights of 5 February 2013 in *Mapuche Paynemil and Kaxipayiñ Communities v. Argentina*, Case No. 12.010; see Saul, Kinley, and Mowbray, *The International Covenant on Economic, Social and Cultural Rights*, 924.

108. Judgment of the European Court of Human Rights of 25 November 1993 in *Zander v. Sweden*, 18 EHRR (1994), 175; see Saul, Kinley, and Mowbray, *The International Covenant on Economic, Social and Cultural Rights*, 918.

109. For this trend see, e.g., Bakker, *An Uncooperative Commodity*, 92ff., 217.

110. See, in this respect also Saul, Kinley, and Mowbray, *The International Covenant on Economic, Social and Cultural Rights*, 913: "While it is true that traditionally human rights professes not to prescribe a particular economic or political philosophy, it is nevertheless neither agnostic, nor neutral, as to the outcomes that result from any particular philosophy that is adopted." Murthy, "The Human Right(s) to Water and Sanitation," although asserting in principle that "human rights law is neutral with respect to economic modes of delivery" (99), concedes that "tensions between human rights and private sector involvement in the water and sanitation sectors" exist (91, 118ff.). Kok, "Privatisation and the Right to Access to Water," 263, 264ff., 286–87, leaves this question open but seems, for pragmatic reasons, to interpret the right to water as not necessarily excluding privatization.

111. See the UN SG report (note 27), 44.

112. Miloon Kothari, "Obstacles to Making Water a Human Right," in Riedel and Rothen, *The Human Right to Water*, 149 at 151.

Chapter 7. Right to Personal Liberty and Rights of Detainees

1. See Alfred C. Aman, "Privatisation, Prisons, Democracy and Human Rights: The Need to Extend the Province of Administrative Law," in De Feyter and Gómez, *Privatisation and Human Rights in the Age of Globalisation*, 91 at 105, with reference to Martin P. Sellers, *The History and Politics of Private Prisons* (London, 1993).

2. See Aman, "Privatisation, Prisons, Democracy and Human Rights," 106: "It was not until the start of the 20th century that it became the custom of correction agencies 'to provide virtually all correctional services as governmental functions in institutions constructed and maintained at government expense,'" with reference to U.S. Department of Justice, Bureau of Justice Assistance, *Emerging Issues on Privatized Prisons* (Washington, D.C., 2001), 11.

3. Aman, "Privatisation, Prisons, Democracy and Human Rights." It seems, however, that the privately operated juvenile facilities in the United States had also other than merely for-profit interests.

4. See, for the following, e.g., Martin E. Gold, "The Privatization of Prisons," *Urban Lawyer* 28 (1996): 359 at 369ff.; Coyle, Campbell, and Neufeld, *Capitalist Punishment*; Lucas Anderson, "Kicking the National Habit: The Legal and Policy Arguments for Abolishing Private Prison Contracts," *Public Contract Law Journal* 39 (2009): 113ff.; Aman, "Privatisation, Prisons, Democracy and Human Rights," 107; Alfred C. Aman, "Private Prisons and the Democratic Deficit," in Chesterman and Fisher, *Private Security, Public Order*, 86ff.; Reimon and Felber, *Schwarzbuch Privatisierung*, 191ff.; Kim Richard Nossal and Phillip J. Wood, "The Raggedness of Prison Privatization: Australia, Britain, Canada, New Zealand and the United States Compared" (paper prepared for Prisons 2004 conference Prisons and Penal Policy: International Perspectives, City University London, 2004).

5. On the background of CCA see Christian Parenti, "Privatized Problems: For-Profit Incarceration in Trouble," in Coyle, Campbell, and Neufeld, *Capitalist Punishment*, 30 at 31.

6. By 1988, prisons in 39 states were operating under court order to remedy overcrowding and other constitutional violations; see Phillip J. Wood, "The Rise of the Prison Complex in the United States," in Coyle, Campbell, and Neufeld, *Capitalist Punishment*, 16 at 18.

7. By 1986, 25 percent of all detention facilities of the Immigration and Naturalization Service (INS) were operated by private firms. See Jeff Sinden, "The Problem of Prison Privatization: The U.S. Experience," in Coyle, Campbell, and Neufeld, *Capitalist Punishment*, 39 at 43–44.

8. On the activities of George Wackenhut, see Reimon and Felber, *Schwarzbuch Privatisierung*, 193ff.; Parenti, "Privatized Problems: For-Profit Incarceration in Trouble," 31.

9. Anderson, "Kicking the National Habit," 118.

10. Gold, "The Privatization of Prisons," 371; Nossal and Wood, "The Raggedness of Prison Privatization," 4. See also Robbins, "Privatisation of Corrections," 58, who shows how the private prison business profited from immigration detention.

11. See Wood, "The Rise of the Prison Complex in the United States," 17.

12. Ibid., 17–18.

13. Gold, "The Privatization of Prisons," 372; Wood, "The Rise of the Prison Complex in the United States," 18; The Pew Charitable Trusts, Press Release, "One in 31 U.S. Adults are Behind Bars, on Parole or Probation," http://www.pewtrusts.org/en/about/news-room/press-releases/0001/01/01/one-in-31-us-adults-are-behind-bars-on-parole-or-probation.

14. See International Centre for Prison Studies, *World Prison Brief*, http://www.prisonstudies.org/; and Roy Walmsley, *World Prison Population List*, 10th ed. (London, 2013), which lists the prison population and incarceration rates per 100,000 of the national population in a total of 223 countries and dependent territories. The United States has for many years been on top of the list with 2,217,947 prisoners and 693 prisoners per 100,000 inhabitants as of April 2016, whereas the average incarceration rate in Western Europe is about 100 (e.g., 57 in Finland, 55 in Sweden, 76 in Germany, 99 in France, and 147 in England and Wales).

15. E. Ann Carson and Daniela Golinelli, "Prisoners in 2012: Trends in Admissions and Releases, 1991–2012," U.S. Department of Justice, Bureau of Justice Statistics (BJS) *Bulletin*, December 2013.

16. Ibid., appendix Table 7.

17. See Anderson, "Kicking the National Habit," 118–19, and the appendix on "States' Statutes Regarding Contracts with Private Prison Contractors," 136ff.

18. Cited from Wikipedia, "Private Prison" (accessed 29 May 2014) with a reference to Matt Taibbi, *The Divide: American Injustice in the Age of the Wealth Gap* (New York, 2014), 214–16.

19. See the comparison between the crime and the incarceration rates in Wood, "The Rise of the Prison Complex in the United States," 21. See also Sinden, "The Problem of Prison Privatization: The U.S. Experience," 41: "How can this huge increase in the prison population be explained? Rising crime and arrests are clearly not the cause. . . . The increase is due mainly to sentencing policies."

20. See Wood, "The Rise of the Prison Complex in the United States," 18.

21. See Nossal and Wood, "The Raggedness of Prison Privatization," 13: "The problem with this perspective, which in large part reflects the public relations campaigns of the private prison companies themselves . . . , is that it confuses clusters of symptoms with causal mechanisms and their effects, and obscures the distinction between explanation and justification. As critics of this line of analysis argue, overcrowding is itself a result of a series of other factors—racial politics, correctional policy changes, the changing form and role of the state, shift in macroeconomic policy, new conceptions of social order, and so on."

22. Nossal and Wood, "The Raggedness of Prison Privatization," 17. See also Wood, "The Rise of the Prison Complex in the United States," 20ff.

23. See, e.g., Stephen Nathan, "Prison Privatization in the United Kingdom," in Coyle, Campbell, and Neufeld, *Capitalist Punishment*, 162 at 163.

24. See Nossal and Wood, "The Raggedness of Prison Privatization," 9: "In May 1995, for example, the shadow Home Secretary, Jack Straw, had promised to 'bring these prisons into proper public control'. . . . But once in power, the Blair government reversed course. . . . In May 1998, Straw, by then the Home Secretary, announced that as a matter of policy all new prisons in England and Wales would be privately built and run." On "Labour's U-turn," see also Nathan, "Prison Privatization in the United Kingdom," 168ff.

25. For a list of all private prison contracts in the UK (including year of opening, the contractor, and the prison population) by July 2002, see Nathan, "Prison Privatization in the United Kingdom," 167.

26. See, e.g., Will Tanner, "The Case for Private Prisons," *Reform Ideas* 2 (London, February 2013); The Howard League for Penal Affairs, *Weekly Prison Watch: Latest Prison Figures* (London, 2013); *Prison Reform Trust Newsletter*.

27. In the early years of the twenty-first century, Australia had the highest rate with some 20 percent (in Victoria almost 50 percent) of prisoners accommodated in private prisons: see Aman, Privatisation, Prisons, Democracy and Human Rights, 107.

28. See Nossal and Wood, "The Raggedness of Prison Privatization," 6ff.

29. See Aman, *Privatisation, Prisons, Democracy and Human Rights*, 107.

30. See Bente Molenaar and Rodney Neufeld, "The Use of Privatized Detention Centers for Asylum Seekers in Australia and the UK," in Coyle, Campbell, and Neufeld, *Capitalist Punishment*, 127 at 129.

31. See Molenaar and Neufeld, "The Use of Privatized Detention Centers for Asylum Seekers in Australia and the UK," 130–31; Reimon and Felber, *Schwarzbuch Privatisierung*, 201. See also Ira P. Robbins, "Privatisation of Corrections," 57 at 86.

32. See, e.g., Comm. Nos. 560/1993, 900/1999, 1014/2001, and 1069/2002 in Nowak, UN Covenant on Civil and Political Rights: CCPR Commentary, 226–27.

33. *Carlos Cabal and Marco Pasini Bertran v. Australia*, Comm. No. 1020/2001, views of the UN Human Rights Committee of 7 August 2003.

34. Ibid., § 7.2.

35. UN Doc. A/57/40 vol. 1 (2002) 63 at § 81(13): see Nowak, CCPR Commentary, 183.

36. See Nossal and Wood, "The Raggedness of Prison Privatization," 11–12.

37. See UN Doc. A/HRC/12/8 (2009), § 68.

38. See UN Doc. CCPR/C/NZL/CO/5 (2010), § 11.

39. See Nossal and Wood, "The Raggedness of Prison Privatization," 10–11.

40. Ibid., 11: "The 'super-jails' were designed to achieve efficiency by concentrating offenders, and to achieve savings by ensuring that the prisons were 'no frills' and austere facilities with narrow slits for windows, tiny stainless steel toilets, and concrete stools and steel beds. As the minister of correctional services, Rob Runciman, explicitly noted, 'I don't think that our goal in the correctional system . . . is to necessarily increase the quality of life for people convicted of crimes.'" See also Dawn Moore, Kellie Leclerc Burton, and Kelly Hannah-Moffat, "'Get Tough' Efficiency: Human Rights, Correctional Restructuring and Prison Privatization in Ontario, Canada," in Coyle, Campbell, and Neufeld, *Capitalist Punishment*, 152ff.

41. See Moore, Burton, and Hannah-Moffat, "'Get Tough' Efficiency," 159.

42. See the judgment of the Supreme Court of Israel in *Academic Center of Law and Business v. Minister of Finance* of 19 November 2009, HCJ 2605/05. See Daphne Barak-Erez, "The Private Prison Controversy and the Privatization Continuum," *Law and Ethics of Human Rights* 5 (2011): 138.

43. Judgment of the Supreme Court of Israel, § 23.

44. Ibid., § 25.

45. Ibid., § 36. See also § 39: "the imprisonment of a person in a privately managed prison is contrary to the basic outlook of Israeli society . . . with regard to the power of imprisonment being one of the clear sovereign powers that are unique to the state."

46. See ibid., § 53: "Naturally, in different countries there may be different outlooks with regard to the question of the scope of the state responsibility in various fields and the relationship that should exist between the fields of activity that should be managed by the public sector and the fields in which most activity will be carried out by the private sector. These outlooks are determined, *inter alia*, by political and economic ideologies, the special history of each country, the structure of the political system and the government, and various social arrangements."

47. See, e.g., Julian Zado, "Billig wegsperren? Privatisierung des Strafvollzugs," *Forum Recht* 3 (2010): 96.

48. See, e.g., Peter Badura, "Art. 33 GG," in *Grundgesetz-Kommentar* 2013, ed. Theodor Maunz and Günter Dürig; Monika Jachmann, "Art. 33 Abs. 4 GG-verbotene Differenzierungen," in *Grundgesetz-Kommentar*, {Should this title be *Kommentar zum Grundgesetz*? YES} vol. 2, 6th ed., ed. Hermann von Mangoldt, Friedrich Klein, and Christian Starck (Munich, 2010), 834ff.

49. See Jachmann, "Art. 33 Abs. 4 GG-verbotene Differenzierungen," 841.

50. Ibid., with further references.

51. See the judgment of Niedersächsischer Staatsgerichtshof of 5 December 2008, StGH 2/07. See, e.g., Alexander Thiele, "Art. 33 Abs. 4 GG als Privatisierungsschranke," *Der Staat* 49 (2010): 274.

52. Judgment of the Federal Constitutional Court of 18 January 2012, 2 BvR 133/10; NJW 2012, 1563; *NVwZ* 2012, 1033 L. See, e.g., Marcus Schladebach and Sabrina Schönrock, "Privatisierung im Maßregelvollzug," *NVwZ* 16 (2012): 1011.

53. Judgment of the Federal Constitutional Court, ibid., § 140:{More than one work is listed in the preceding note. Please specify which one is referred to here.} "Um die Ausübung hoheitsrechtlicher Befugnisse handelt es sich jedenfalls, wenn Befugnisse zum Grundrechtseingriff im engeren Sinn . . . ausgeübt werden, die öffentliche Gewalt also durch Befehl oder Zwang unmittelbar beschränkend auf grundrechtlich geschützte Freiheiten einwirkt."

54. Ibid., § 153: "Der Vollzug strafrechtlich verhängter Freiheitsentziehungen gehört zum Kernbereich hoheitlicher Tätigkeit. Der Maßregelvollzug steht darin, auch was die Intensität der möglichen Grundrechtseingriffe angeht, dem Strafvollzug in nichts nach."

55. See Zado, "Billig wegsperren? Privatisierung des Strafvollzugs," 96. On the Kötter company, see Reimon and Felber, *Schwarzbuch Privatisierung*, 199–200.

56. See *Badische Zeitung* of 1 June 2014: "JVA Offenburg: Land macht Teilprivatisierung rückgängig. Der Staat übernimmt von Juni 2014 an wieder das erste und einzige teilprivatisierte Gefängnis im Land : die JVA Offenburg. Damit beendet SPD-Justizminister Rainer Stickelberger die Politik seines FDP-Vorgängers Ulrich Goll."

57. See the Special Report of the Austrian Ombuds-Institution of May 2015: Volksanwaltschaft, *Sonderbericht Anhaltezentrum Vordernberg* (Vienna, 2015).

58. Judgment of the Austrian Constitutional Court of 14 March 1996: VfSlg 14473/1996; see Bernd-Christian Funk, "Grenzen der Ausgliederung der hoheitlichen Besorgung von Verwaltungsaufgaben (Austro-Control)- Entscheidungsbesprechung," *Österreichische Zeitschrift für Wirtschaftsrecht* (1997): 60; Michael Holoubek, "Der Staat als Wirtschaftssubjekt und Auftraggeber," *Veröffentlichungen der Vereinigung der Deutschen Staatsrechtslehrer* 60 (2001): 513; Michael Pesendorfer, "Private Militärfirmen und österreichische Rechtsordnung," in *Private Sicherheits- und Militärfirmen: Konkurrenten—Partner—Totengräber?* ed. Walter Feichtinger, Wolfgang Braumandl, and Nieves-Erzsebet Kautny (Vienna, 2008), 107 at 110.

59. Judgment of the Austrian Constitutional Court of 14 March 1996: VfSlg 14473/1996: "Was schließlich den Vorbehalt anlangt, daß der einfache Gesetzgeber nicht das System des Aufbaues der staatlichen Verwaltung verändern dürfe, so ist zwar zuzugestehen, daß etwa—um im Zusammenhang mit den der Austro Control GmbH übertragenen Aufgaben stehende Verwaltungsbereiche zu nennen—die Vorsorge für die Sicherheit im Inneren und nach außen und die Ausübung der (Verwaltungs-) Strafgewalt zu den Kernbereichen der staatlichen Verwaltung zählen, doch sind der Austro Control GmbH weder Aufgaben der allgemeinen Sicherheitspolizei noch solche des Militärwesens noch die zentralen verwaltungspolizeilichen Aufgaben des Zivilluftfahrtwesens, sondern nur ganz bestimmte, oben näher genannte (vgl. Pkt. III.1.b)) Teilbereiche dieser Verwaltungsmaterie—und damit keine nicht ausgliederbaren Aufgaben im genannten Sinn—übertragen."

60. Judgment of the Austrian Constitutional Court of 14 March 1996: VfSlg 14473/1996: "Der Verfassungsgerichtshof hat auch nicht das Bedenken, daß jene Bestimmungen der Bundesverfassung ausgeschaltet wären, die eine Einbindung in den Weisungszusammenhang, die Organisationsverantwortung und die Verantwortlichkeit der obersten Organe verlangen."

61. See, e.g., the judgments of the Constitutional Court in VfSlg 16.400/2001 (BWA), 16.995/2003 (E-Control GmbH), and 17.421/2004 (GIS).

62. Judgment of the Austrian Constitutional Court of 15 October 2004, VfSlg 17.341/ 2004. See Chapter 8, this volume, on the right to personal security.

63. See, e.g., the comparative analysis carried out by the Supreme Court of Israel (note 42), §§ 48ff.

64. See Nathan, "Prison Privatization in the United Kingdom"; see also Rob Allen, "Prisons: State Duty or Market Opportunity?" Penal Reform International, London, 2014, www .penalreform.org/blog/prisons-state-duty-market-opportunity.

65. Supreme Court of Israel (note 42), § 58, with reference to David E. Pozen, "Managing a Correctional Marketplace: Prison Privatization in the United States and the United Kingdom," *Journal of Law and Politics* 19 (2003): 253 at 277–78. See also Anderson, "Kicking the National Habit"; Gold, "The Privatization of Prisons"; Reimon and Felber, *Schwarzbuch Privatisierung*; Nossal and Wood, "The Raggedness of Prison Privatization."

66. See, e.g., Aman, "Privatisation, Prisons, Democracy and Human Rights," 119–20.

67. See Allen, "Prisons: State Duty or Market Opportunity?"

68. See, e.g., the discussion of the Israeli policy, which first considered the "French model," but later opted for an "improved English model," in Supreme Court of Israel (note 42), §§ 48ff.

69. See, e.g., Gold, "The Privatization of Prisons," 365.

70. Ibid., 366.

71. See Robbins, "Privatisation of Corrections," 59.

72. Gold, "The Privatization of Prisons," 366ff.

73. Although the well-known book, *Capitalist Punishment: Prison Privatization and Human Rights*, edited by Andrew Coyle, Allison Campbell, and Rodney Neufeld, refers to "Prison Privatization and Human Rights," there are, surprisingly, no legal discussions about the limits of prison privatization under Article 10 CCPR or other provisions of international human rights law. Although Coyle concludes this book by clearly stating that the responsibility of the nation to treat its prisoners "should not be delegated to commercial companies" (Andrew Coyle, "Conclusion," in Coyle, Campbell, and Neufeld, *Capitalist Punishment*, 211 at 217), this is based not on a legal analysis, but on moral and political arguments.

74. See Robbins, "Privatisation of Corrections," 75, 83.

75. Ibid., 63ff.

76. Ibid., 71.

77. Ibid., 71n68.

78. Ibid., 75ff.

79. SeeSupreme Court of Israel (note 42).

80. Robbins, "Privatisation of Corrections," 88.

81. See Aman, 91 at 105ff.

82. Ibid., 95.

83. See, e.g., the trend toward "exporting inmates" (e.g., from Hawaii to Minnesota and from Alaska to Arizona) driven by economic considerations; see ibid., 120ff.

84. See Manfred Nowak, *Folter: Die Alltäglichkeit des Unfassbaren* (Vienna, 2012).

85. See Manfred Nowak, *Study on the Phenomena of Torture, Cruel, Inhuman or Degrading Treatment or Punishment in the World, Including an Assessment of Conditions of Detention*, in UN Doc. A/HRC/13/39/Add. 5 of 5 February 2010, §§ 9, 229–37, 256, 259(e).

86. See International Centre for Prison Studies (note 14).

87. On the "principle of normalization," see the report on my mission to Denmark in UN Doc.A/HRC/10/44/Add. 2 of 18 February 2009.

88. See Nowak, *CCPR Commentary*, 253–54.

Chapter 8. Right to Personal Security

1. John Locke, *Two Treatises of Government*, 1690, excerpted in Ishay, *Human Rights Reader*, vol. 2, § 124.

2. Ibid., §§ 6, 87, 94, 124. See also Nowak, *Politische Grundrechte*, 27ff.

3. Locke, *Two Treatises of Government*, vol. 2, § 123.

4. See also Chapter 1.

5. See Nowak, *Politische Grundrechte*, 28, with further references to the Dutch Constitution 1798 and the Austrian draft bill of rights of Kremsier 1848.

6. Locke, *Two Treatises of Government*, vol. 2, §§ 8, 11, 13, 87, 128.

7. See Max Weber, *Staatssoziologie: Soziologie der rationalen Staatsanstalt und der modernen politischen Parteien und Parlamente*, 2nd. ed., ed. Johannes Winckelmann (Berlin, 1966), 27: "In der Vergangenheit haben die verschiedensten Verbände—von der Sippe angefangen—physische Gewaltsamkeit als ganz normales Mittel gekannt. Heute dagegen werden wir sagen müssen: Staat ist diejenige menschliche Gemeinschaft, welche innerhalb eines bestimmten Gebietes—dies: das 'Gebiet' gehört zum Merkmal—das Monopol legitimer physischer Gewaltsamkeit für sich (mit Erfolg) beansprucht. Denn das der Gegenwart Spezifische ist, daß man allen anderen Verbänden oder Einzelpersonen das Recht zur physischen Gewaltsamkeit nur soweit zuschreibt, als der Staat sie von ihrer Seite zuläßt: er gilt als alleinige Quelle des 'Rechts' auf Gewaltsamkeit." See also Anne Peters, "Privatisierung, Globalisierung und die Resistenz des Verfassungsstaates," in *Staats- und Verfassungstheorie im Spannungsfeld der Disziplinen*, ed. Philippe Mastronardi and Denis Taubert, Archiv für Rechts- und Sozialphilosophie Beiheft 105 (Stuttgart, 2006), 100 at 117ff., who speaks of an erosion of the state monopoly of force (Erosion des Gewaltmonopols) through globalization and privatization; Corinna Seiberth, *Private Military and Security Companies in International Law* (Cambridge, 2014), 69.

8. See, e.g., Lars Adam Rehof, "Article 3," in Eide et al., *Universal Declaration of Human Rights: A Commentary*, 73; similarly Lars Adam Rehof, "Article 3," in Alfredsson and Eide, *Universal Declaration of Human Rights: A Common Standard of Achievement*, 89; Morsink, *Universal Declaration of Human Rights*, 39ff.

9. See Manfred Nowak, "The Three Pillars of the United Nations: Security, Development and Human Rights," in *Casting the Net Wider: Human Rights, Development and New Duty-Bearers*, ed. Margot E. Salomon, Arne Tostensen, and Wouter Vandenhole (Antwerp, 2007), 25–41. On the concept of human security see UN Development Programme (UNDP), *Human Development Report: New Dimensions of Human Security* (New York, 1994), 24–25; Commission on Human Security, *Human Security Now* (New York, 2003); *2005 World Summit Outcome* document, UNGA Res. 60/1 of 16 September 2005, § 143; Report of the UN Secretary-General in UN Doc. A/66/763 (2011); UNGA Res. 66/290 (2012); Benedek, Kettemann, and Möstl, *Mainstreaming Human Security in Peace Operations and Crisis Management*; Ryngaert and Noortmann, *Human Security and International Law: The Challenge of Non-State Actors*.

10. UNGA Res. 66/290 (2012), § 3(d).

11. Ibid., § 3(f).

12. On the concept of R2P see *2005 World Summit Outcome* document, UNGA Res. 60/
1 of 16 September 2005, §§ 137 and 138; Gareth Evans, *The Responsibility to Protect: Ending
Mass Atrocity Crimes Once and for All* (Washington, D.C., 2008); Alex J. Bellamy, *Global
Politics and the Responsibility to Protect: From Words to Deeds* (New York, 2011); Manfred
Nowak, "Responsibility to Protect: Is International Law Moving from Hobbes to Locke?", in
Völkerrecht und die Dynamik der Menschenrechte, ed. Gerhard Hafner/Franz Matscher/Kirsten
Schmalenbach (Vienna: Liber Amicorum Wolfram Karl, 2012) 342; Peter Hilpold, ed., *Die
Schutzverantwortung (R2P): Ein Paradigmenwechsel in der Entwicklung des internationalen
Rechts?* (Leiden, 2013); Charles Sampford and Ramesh Thakur, eds., *Responsibility to Protect
and Sovereignty* (Surrey, 2013); Luke Glanville, *Sovereignty & the Responsibility to Protect: A
New History* (Chicago, 2014).

13. Math Noortmann and Cedric Ryngaert, "Towards a (New) Human Security-Based
Agenda for International Law and Non-State Actors?" in Ryngaert and Noortmann, *Human
Security and International Law: The Challenge of Non-State Actors*, 195 at 199.

14. See, e.g., the judgment of the ECtHR in *Bozano v. France* of 18 December 1986,
Series A 111 at 23. See also Christoph Grabenwarter, *European Convention on Human Rights:
Commentary* (Munich, 2014), 64.

15. See, e.g., Bossuyt, *Guide to the "travaux préparatoires,"* 196.

16. See UN Doc. A/C.3/SR.863, § 8; and Nowak, *UN Covenant on Civil and Political
Rights*, 214.

17. Human Rights Committee, Final Views of 12 July 1990 in *Delgado Páez v. Colombia*,
No. 195/1985, §§ 5.5, 5.6, 6. See Nowak, *UN Covenant on Civil and Political Rights*, 215.

18. See Nowak, *UN Covenant on Civil and Political Rights*, 215, with further references;
Sarah Joseph and Melissa Castan, *The International Covenant on Civil and Political Rights:
Cases, Materials, and Commentary*, 3rd ed. (Oxford, 2013), 341ff.

19. See Grabenwarter, *European Convention on Human Rights*, 21ff., 40–41.

20. For the rich literature on this subject, see, e.g., Chesterman and Lehnardt, eds., *From
Mercenaries to Market*; Sabelo Gumedze, ed., *Private Security in Africa: Manifestations, Chal-
lenges and Regulation*, ISS Monograph Series 139 (Pretoria, 2007); Walter Feichtinger, Wolfgang Braumandl, and Nieves-Erzsebet Kautny, *Private Sicherheits- und Militärfirmen:
Konkurrenten - Partner - Totengräber?*(Wien, 2008); Simon Chesterman and Angelina Fisher,
Private Security, Public Order: The Outsourcing of Public Services and Its Limits (Oxford, 2009);
Franceso Francioni and Natalino Ronzitti, eds., *War by Contract: Human Rights, Humanitar-
ian Law and Private Contractors* (Oxford: 2011); Corinna Seiberth, *Private Military and Secur-
ity Companies in International Law* (Cambridge, 2014); José L. Gómez del Prado, "Impact on
Human Rights of a New Non-State Actor: Private Military and Security Companies," *Brown
Journal of World Affairs* 18 (2011): 151.

21. Judgment of the Federal Constitutional Court of 18 January 2012, 2 BvR 133/10;
NJW 2012, 1563; NVwZ 2012, 1033 L.

22. Judgment of the Austrian Constitutional Court of 15 October 2004, VfSlg 17.341/
2004.

23. See the judgment of the Supreme Court of Israel in *Academic Center of Law and
Business v Minister of Finance* of 19 November 2009, HCJ 2605/05.

24. See the judgment of the Supreme Court of Israel of 12 December 2006 in *Majority
Camp et al. v. Israel Police et al.*, HCJ 2557/05, § 15 (opinion delivered by President Emeritus
A. Barak).

25. See below, notes 125 and 126.

26. See the 7–2 judgment of the U.S. Supreme Court of 27 June 2005 in *Town of Castle Rock v. Gonzales*, 545 U.S. 748 (2005), 125 S.Ct. 2796, at 2805ff. The majority opinion, which was heavily criticized by human rights groups, was written by Justice Antonin Scalia. But see the dissenting opinion by Justice John Paul Stevens, who emphasized that a protected "property interest" under the Fourteenth Amendment does not require a monetary value.

27. See the Report No. 80/11 of the Inter-American Commission on Human Rights of 21 July 2011 in *Jessica Lenahan (Gonzales) et al. v. United States*, Case 12.626, §§ 5 and 199.

28. See, e.g., UN Doc. E/CN.4/2006/11, 5 and 11.

29. See UN Doc. CCPR/C/GTM/CO/3, § 16.

30. See, e.g., Reimon and Felber, *Schwarzbuch Privatisierung*, 193ff.; Kevin A. O'Brien, "What Should and What Should Not Be Regulated?" in Chesterman and Lehnardt, *From Mercenaries to Market*, 29 at 37.

31. See Gumedze, *Private Security in Africa.*

32. See Gómez del Prado, "Impact on Human Rights of a New Non-State Actor," 159.

33. See below, note 77.

34. See Marc von Boemcken, "Das private Militärgewerbe: Ursachen, Typen und Probleme," in Feichtinger, Braumandl, and Kautny, *Private Sicherheits- und Militärfirmen*, 47 at 51.

35. According to O'Brien, "What Should and What Should Not Be Regulated?" 31 and 38, there were more than 6,000 private "security" companies operating in Russia alone in 1994 and well over 12,000 registered with the Russian government in 1999.

36. See, e.g., O'Brien, "What Should and What Should Not Be Regulated?" 30; Angela McIntyre and Taya Weiss, "Weak Governments in Search of Strength: Africa's Experience of Mercenaries and Private Military Companies," in Chesterman and Lehnardt, *From Mercenaries to Market*, 67 at 75ff. Gómez del Prado, "Impact on Human Rights of a New Non-State Actor," 157; see also my report as UN Special Rapporteur on Torture on a fact-finding mission to Equatorial Guinea, where we interviewed some of the British and South African mercenaries, including Simon Mann and Nick du Toit, who had been detained at the infamous Black Beach Prison in Malabo, UN Doc. A/HRC/13/39/Add. 4 of 7 January 2010, Appendix 1, 26ff.

37. See, e.g., O'Brien, "What Should and What Should Not Be Regulated?" 29ff.; Boemcken, "Das private Militärgewerbe," 56; McIntyre and Weiss, "Weak Governments in Search of Strength," 70ff.; David J. Francis, "Mercenary Intervention in Sierra Leone: Providing National Security or International Exploitation?" *Third World Quarterly* 20 (1999): 319; Herbert Howe, "Private Security Forces and African Stability: The Case of Executive Outcomes," *Journal of Modern African Studies* 36 (1998): 307; Sabelo J. Ndlovu-Gatsheni, "Weak States and the Growth of the Private Security Sector in Africa: Whither the African State?" in Gumedze, *Private Security in Africa*, 17; Mpako H. Foaleng, "Private Military and Security Companies and the Nexus Between Natural Resources and Civil Wars in Africa," in Gumedze, *Private Security in Africa*, 39; Surabhi Ranganathan, "Constructive Constraints? Conceptual and Practical Challenges to Regulating Private Military and Security Companies," in Ryngaert and Noortmann, *Human Security and International Law*, 175 at 180ff.

38. See, e.g., O'Brien, "What Should and What Should Not Be Regulated?" 34; Francis, "Mercenary Intervention in Sierra Leone," 329. See also Elke Krahmann, "Transitional States in Search of Support," in Chesterman and Lehnardt, *From Mercenaries to Market*, 94 at 100ff.

39. On the complexity and interdependence of the major root causes for the rise of the PMSCs during the 1990s and 2000s see, e.g., Boemcken, "Das private Militärgewerbe," 51ff.

40. In 2006, the World Bank had included a total of 35 states in its Low Income Countries Under Stress (LICUS) initiative. These states are defined as sharing a common fragility, in two particular respects, namely weak state policies and institutions, and risk of conflict and political instability: see World Bank Operations Policy and Country Services, *Low-Income Countries Under Stress: Update* (Washington, D.C., 19 December 2005), § 2; see also Walter Feichtinger, "Private Militärfirmen im Vormarsch: Ungeliebt, aber unverzichtbar?" in Feichtinger, Braumandl, and Kautny, *Private Sicherheits- und Militärfirmen*, 13 at 18, who puts the figure of "states under stress" with reference to reports of the World Bank and the International Crisis Group even as high as between 40 and 70.

41. See, e.g., Gómez del Prado, "Impact on Human Rights of a New Non-State Actor," 151ff.; Boemcken, "Das private Militärgewerbe," 49.

42. Seiberth, *Private Military and Security Companies in International Law*, 6.

43. See Feichtinger, "Private Militärfirmen im Vormarsch," 32.

44. See, e.g., Sabrina Schulz, "Private Sicherheit als Exportschlager? Die private Sicherheitsindustrie in Großbritannien im Spannungsfeld freier Marktkräfte und internationaler Rechtsgüter," in Feichtinger, Braumandl, and Kautny, *Private Sicherheits- und Militärfirmen*, 147 at 152: "Die britische private Sicherheitsbranche verdankt ihren Aufstieg allerdings nicht der Nähe zum britischen Staat, sondern—im Gegenteil—der Erschließung privatwirtschaftlicher Marktpotenziale."

45. See Alan Travis and Zoe Williams, "Revealed: Government Plans for Police Privatisation," *The Guardian*, 2 March 2012.

46. See Matthew Taylor and Alan Travis, "G4S Chief Predicts Mass Police Privatisation," *The Guardian*, 20 June 2012.

47. See www.g4s.com.

48. See Paul Peachey, "Police Forces Put £1.5bn Privatisation Plan on Hold: The Proposal Was Being Discussed at a Time When Forces Face 20 Per Cent Spending Cuts," *Independent*, 18 May 2012.

49. See, e.g., Seiberth, *Private Military and Security Companies in International Law*, 6–7: "More than half of the security personnel for the Olympic Games in the United Kingdom in summer 2012 were to be provided by G4S based on a contract with the government. The initial number of about 9,000 police and 10,000 security guards estimated to secure the event had been corrected by the Olympic Committee prior to the event to 21,000 security guards. The additional guards were to consist of army personnel, volunteers and newly trained G4S personnel as part of a 'Bridging the Gap' plan. However, after G4S failed to fulfil its contract the UK army had to step in and the recruitment process of G4S was criticised."

50. But see Ian Drury, "Police Use Staff from Olympic Disaster Firm G4S to Help Solve Murders in Latest Privatisation of Frontline Jobs," *Mail Online News*, 14 April 2013.

51. On the eroding concept of inherent governmental functions in the United States, see below, notes 125 to 128.

52. U.S. Department of Defense, *Quadrennial Defense Review 2001* (Washington, D.C., 30 September 2001). See also Rolf Uesseler, "Entstaatlichung von Gewalt: Herausforderung für die Demokratie," in Feichtinger, Braumandl, and Kautny, *Private Sicherheits- und Militärfirmen*, 67 at 75.

53. See Nick Mathiason, "The First Privatised War: Private Contractors Are Carving Up Defence Procurement," *Observer*, 1 March 2002, cited in Boemcken, "Das private Militärgewerbe," 47 note 2. Austrian brigadier Walter Feichtinger estimated in 2008 that the war in Iraq by U.S. forces would have probably collapsed quickly without the support of PMSCs. By the end of 2007, 160,000 regular U.S. forces were supported by roughly 100,000 private support and 25,000 private military staff, of which only 3,000 were U.S. citizens: Feichtinger, "Private Militärfirmen im Vormarsch," 13, 27, 28. Rolf Uesseler, "Entstaatlichung von Gewalt," at 79, cites a report by the *New York Times*, according to which the United States could no longer be governed without or against the interests of Lockheed-Martin, the world's largest military armaments corporation, based in Maryland close to Washington, D.C., which controls many PMSCs. It is interesting to note that despite this obvious trend toward privatizing war and violence, there are still military experts who believe fears are overstated and that it would be "absurd" to see in private military companies a competition with the armed forces of states. See Erwin A. Schmidl, "Soldaten - Söldner - Freiwillige," in Feichtinger, Braumandl, and Kautny, *Private Sicherheits- und Militärfirmen*, 35 at 42: "Angesichts der herrschenden Zahlenverhältnisse . . . wäre es absurd, in PMCs eine Konkurrenz zu staatlichem Militär zu sehen"; ibid., 46: "Die Befürchtung einer ‚Privatisierung des Krieges' greift als Überbegriff wohl deutlich zu weit, waren doch stets nur Teilbereiche ausgegliedert bzw. an ‚contractors' ‚out-gesourced', wie das auf Neudeutsch heißt."

54. See Chia Lehnardt, "Peacekeeping," in Chesterman and Fisher, *Private Security, Public Order*, 205ff.

55. See UN Doc. A/HRC/10/14/Add. 2.

56. See Gómez del Prado, "Impact on Human Rights of a New Non-State Actor," 152.

57. See Rita Abrahamsen and Michael C. Williams, "The Globalisation of Private Security: Country Report Kenya" (University of Aberystwyth, 2005), cited in Boemcken, "Das private Militärgewerbe," 55n28.

58. See UN Doc. A/HRC/16/52/Add. 5 of 7 February 2011, § 35.

59. See also Sabelo Gumedze, "To Embrace or Not Embrace: Addressing the Private Security Industry Phenomenon in Africa," in Gumedze, *Private Security in Africa*, 3; Foaleng, "Private Military and Security Companies," 50ff.; Ndlovu-Gatsheni, "Weak States and the Growth of the Private Security Sector"; Ranganathan, "Constructive Constraints?" 180.

60. Chesterman and Fisher, *Private Security, Public Order*, 226.

61. See, e.g., Gómez del Prado, "Impact on Human Rights of a New Non-State Actor," 152ff.; Boemcken, "Das private Militärgewerbe," 59ff.; Uesseler, "Entstaatlichung von Gewalt," 74ff.; Ranganathan, "Constructive Constraints?" 182; David Eisenberg, "A Government in Search of Cover: Private Military Companies in Iraq," in Chesterman and Lehnardt, *From Mercenaries to Market*, 82.

62. See Boemcken, "Das private Militärgewerbe," 48.

63. See Gómez del Prado, "Impact on Human Rights of a New Non-State Actor," 161 and n51. According to Schulz, "Private Sicherheit als Exportschlager?" 15ff., who is director of policy of BAPSC, this association was founded in 2006 with the aim of regulating and controlling the private military and security industry.

64. See Boemcken, "Das private Militärgewerbe," 50 with further references; Feichtinger, "Private Militärfirmen im Vormarsch," 23.

65. See Uesseler, "Entstaatlichung von Gewalt," 83.

66. See Gómez del Prado, "Impact on Human Rights of a New Non-State Actor," 153, 155.

67. See, e.g., Boemcken, "Das private Militärgewerbe," 62ff.

68. As Uesseler, "Entstaatlichung von Gewalt," 77–78, emphasizes correctly, the "out-sourcing" of the "dirty work" to nonstate actors is not a new phenomenon related to PMSCs. See, e.g., the activities of state-sponsored death squads in Central and South America since the 1970s, of Serbian and Croatian paramilitary groups in the Balkans in 1992 to 1995, or of Indonesian militias in East Timor in 1999.

69. See Boemcken, "Das private Militärgewerbe," 64, with reference to Jeremy Bigwood, *DynCorp in Colombia: Outsourcing the Drug War* (CorpWatch online document, 2001); Gómez del Prado, "Impact on Human Rights of a New Non-State Actor," 157.

70. See Francis, "Mercenary Intervention in Sierra Leone," 328, 334; Boemcken, "Das private Militärgewerbe," 64n62.

71. See, e.g., Gómez del Prado, "Impact on Human Rights of a New Non-State Actor," 156–57; see also the reports of Dick Marty on secret detention in Council of Europe member states to the Parliamentary Assembly of the Council of Europe: CoE Docs. AS/Jur (2006) 03 rev. of 22 January 2006 and CoE Doc. 11302 rev. of 11 June 2007; see further the Joint Study by four special procedures of the UN Human Rights Council on global practices in relation to secret detention in the context of countering terrorism, in UN Doc. A/HRC/13/42 of 19 February 2010.

72. According to the infamous Order No. 17 issued by the Coalition Provisional Authority (CPA) on 27 June 2004 (revised version), "Contractors shall be immune from Iraqi legal process with respect to acts performed by them pursuant to the terms and conditions of a Contract or any subcontract thereto." See, e.g., Schulz, "Private Sicherheit als Exportsch-lager?" 155; Boemcken, "Das private Militärgewerbe," 65; Gómez del Prado, "Impact on Human Rights of a New Non-State Actor," 155.

73. Protocol Additional to the Geneva Conventions of 12 August 1949, and relating to the Protection of Victims of International Armed Conflicts (Protocol 1), adopted 8 June 1977. See, e.g., Marina Mancini, Faustin Z. Ntoubandi, and Thilo Marauhn, "Old Concepts and New Challenges: Are Private Contractors the Mercenaries of the Twenty-First Century?" in Francioni and Ronzitti, *War by Contract*, 321 at 322–23.

74. See, e.g., Seiberth, *Private Military and Security Companies in International Law*, 60, with further references.

75. See Jean de Preux, "Mercenaries," in International Committee of the Red Cross, *Commentary on the Additional Protocols of 8 June 1977 to the Geneva Conventions of 12 August 1949*, ed. Yves Sandoz, Christophe Swinarski, and Bruno Zimmermann (Dordrecht , 1987), 571 at 579. See also Seiberth, *Private Military and Security Companies in International Law*, 60n301.

76. See, e.g., Antonio Cassese, "Mercenaries: Lawful Combatants or War Criminals?" *Zeitschrift für ausländisches öffentliches Recht und Völkerrecht* 40 (1980): 1; Mancini, Ntou-bandi, and Marauhn, "Old Concepts and New Challenges," 323.

77. International Convention against the Recruitment, Use, Financing and Training of Mercenaries, adopted on 4 December 1989, entry into force on 20 October 2001; see Seiberth, *Private Military and Security Companies in International Law*, 60ff.; Gómez del Prado, "Impact on Human Rights of a New Non-State Actor," 158ff.

78. See, e.g., Mancini, Ntoubandi, and Marauhn, "Old Concepts and New Challenges," 324ff.

79. See, e.g., ibid., 339–40, with further references; Gómez del Prado, "Impact on Human Rights of a New Non-State Actor," 159ff.; Seiberth, *Private Military and Security Companies in International Law*, 58ff.

80. See UN GA Res. 31/34 of 1976 and annual resolutions thereafter. See, e.g., Sarah Percy, "Morality and Regulation," in Chesterman and Lehnardt, *From Mercenaries to Market*, 11 at 24ff.

81. See Comm. Res. 1987/16, which decided to appoint a "Special Rapporteur on the use of mercenaries as a means of violating human rights and impeding the exercise of the right of peoples to self-determination."

82. See, e.g., his various reports to the Commission and the General Assembly, including those in UN Docs. A/49/362 (1994) and E/CN.4/2004/15, §§ 10–11. See critically to the fairly rigid approach of Ballesteros, e.g., Ranganathan, "Constructive Constraints?" 178.

83. See Comm. Res. 2004/5.

84. See her 2005 report in UN Doc. A/60/263, 17; see also Percy, "Morality and Regulation," 25.

85. See Comm. Res. 2005/2 of 7 April 2005 which replaced the Special Rapporteur by a "Working Group on the use of mercenaries as a means of violating human rights and impeding the exercise of the right of peoples to self-determination." See also the extension of the mandate by Human Rights Council Resolutions 7/21 of 28 March 2008 and 15/12 of 6 October 2010.

86. On the activities of the Working Group, see, e.g., Seiberth, *Private Military and Security Companies in International Law*, 1ff., 58–59, 68ff., 140–41, 240ff., 253–54.

87. See UN Doc. A/HRC/18/32/Add. 4.

88. See UN Doc. A/HRC/7/7/Add. 2.

89. See UN Doc. A/HRC/4/42/Add. 2.

90. See UN Doc. A/HRC/7/7/Add. 4.

91. See UN Doc. A/HRC/10/14/Add. 2.

92. Council Res. 7/21 of 28 March 2008, § 2. See Seiberth, *Private Military and Security Companies in International Law*, 59.

93. See, e.g., Gómez del Prado, "Impact on Human Rights of a New Non-State Actor," 162ff.

94. Ibid., 163.

95. See UN Docs. A/HRC/15/25 of 5 July 2010, Annex, 21ff., and A/65/325 of 25 August 2010. See Gómez del Prado, "Impact on Human Rights of a New Non-State Actor," 162ff.; Seiberth, *Private Military and Security Companies in International Law*, 68ff., 129–30; Nigel White, "The Privatisation of Military and Security Functions and Human Rights: Comments on the UN Working Group's Draft Convention," *Human Rights Law Review* 11 (2011): 133; Laurence Juma, "Privatisation, Human Rights and Security: Reflections on the Draft International Convention on Regulation, Oversight and Monitoring of Private Military and Security Companies," *Law, Democracy & Development* 15 (2011): 182.

96. A "Private Military and/or Security Company (PMSC)" is defined in Article 2(a) of the draft Convention as "a corporate entity which provides on a compensatory basis military and/or security services by physical persons and/or legal entities." According to Article 2(b),

the term "military services" refers to "specialized services related to military actions including strategic planning, intelligence, investigation, land, sea or air reconnaissance, flight operations of any type, manned or unmanned, satellite surveillance, any kind of knowledge transfer with military applications, material and technical support to armed forces and other related activities." The term "security services" is defined in Article 2(c) as "armed guarding or protection of buildings, installations, property and people, any kind of knowledge transfer with security and policing applications, development and implementation of informational security measures and other related activities."

97. See the explicit purpose in Article 1 of the draft Convention. See White, "The Privatisation of Military and Security Functions and Human Rights"; Juma, "Privatisation, Human Rights and Security," 188ff.

98. Articles 12 to 18 of the draft Convention.

99. According to Article 3(1), the draft Convention applies to "States and intergovernmental organizations within the limits of their competence with respect to PMSCs, their activities and personnel." See, e.g., Juma, "Privatisation, Human Rights and Security," 196, who welcomes the proposed extension of legal responsibility to intergovernmental organizations.

100. Gómez del Prado, "Impact on Human Rights of a New Non-State Actor," 163.

101. Article 18(1) on the regulation of use of force and firearms of the draft Convention reads as follows: "Each State party shall take such legislative, judicial, administrative and other measures as may be necessary to establish rules on the use of force and firearms by the personnel of PMSCs, taking into account that employees may carry firearms in providing military and security services, including such principles described in this Convention and any other relevant principles of international law." See also White, "The Privatisation of Military and Security Functions and Human Rights," 136ff.

102. HRC Res. 15/26, adopted by 32 votes (African, Asian, and Latin American states as well as the Russian Federation) against 12 (Western states, including Belgium, France, Japan, Moldova, Ukraine, UK, and US) and 3 abstentions (Maldives, Norway, Switzerland).

103. UN Doc. A/HRC/22/41 of 24 December 2012.

104. Ibid., §§ 63 and 69.

105. For the text of the Montreux Document see, e.g., the website of the International Committee of the Red Cross. For a thorough analysis see Seiberth, *Private Military and Security Companies in International Law*, 123ff; Ranganathan, "Constructive Constraints?" 188ff.

106. See Gómez del Prado, "Impact on Human Rights of a New Non-State Actor," 161n52.

107. See the website of the Swiss Department of Foreign Affairs, Participating States of the Montreux Document. See www.eda.admin.ch/psc and www.icrc.org.

108. See White, "The Privatisation of Military and Security Functions and Human Rights," 133–34; Seiberth, *Private Military and Security Companies in International Law*, 125.

109. See, e.g., Gómez del Prado, "Impact on Human Rights of a New Non-State Actor," 161; see also James Cockayne, "Regulating Private Military and Security Companies: The Content, Negotiations, Weaknesses and Promise of the Montreux Document," *Journal of Conflict and Security Law* 13 (2008): 401. See also Seiberth, *Private Military and Security Companies in International Law*, 127: "Additionally, the fact that industry associations were included in the negotiations has a legitimising effect for the PMSC industry. The institutional setting of a Swiss/ICRC initiative gives the industry a 'clean vest.'"

110. See Cockayne, "Regulating Private Military and Security Companies," 422–23; Seiberth, *Private Military and Security Companies in International Law*, 128.

111. See the website of the ICoC in www.icoc-psp.org. See also Ranganathan, "Constructive Constraints?" 186. On the role of voluntary codes of conduct in relation to PMSCs see Carsten Hoppe and Ottavio Quirico, "Codes of Conduct for Private Military and Security Companies: The State of Self-Regulation in the Industry," in Francioni and Ronzitti, *War by Contract*, 363.

112. See www.icoca.ch. See also Ranganathan, "Constructive Constraints?" 186–87.

113. See www.icoca.ch/assets/icoca-member-companies.

114. See the final report of UN Special Representative John Ruggie to the UN Human Rights Council in UN Doc. A/HRC/17/31 of 21 March 2011, and the HRC Res. 17/4 of 16 June 2011. For the applicability of the Ruggie framework to PMSCs see Sorcha MacLeod, "The Role of International Regulatory Initiatives on Business and Human Rights for Holding Private Military and Security Contractors to Account," in Francioni and Ronzitti, *War by Contract*, 343.

115. See UN Doc. E/CN.4/Sub.2/2003/12.

116. See White, "The Privatisation of Military and Security Functions and Human Rights," 142ff.

117. See, e.g., Uesseler, "Entstaatlichung von Gewalt," 79–80.

118. See, e.g., the examples of Israel, Germany, and Austria in Chapter 7. Anne Peters, "Privatisierung, Globalisierung und die Resistenz des Verfassungsstaates," 122, concludes that historically, these core functions have developed in a fairly similar manner in most modern constitutional states, and include the protection of internal and external security, guarantees of a sphere of freedom, creation of conditions for achieving prosperity and a minimum of social cohesion, provision of facilities for elementary education, and protection of the environment.

119. But see Peters, "Privatisierung, Globalisierung und die Resistenz des Verfassungsstaates," 123–24, who, after a thorough analysis of public functions, seems to argue that core functions of the state, which cannot be outsourced to private actors, cannot be derived from present international law and state theory: "Weil diese drei Bedingungen praktisch nie kumulativ erfüllt sind, ist ein privatisierungsfester Kern von Staatsaufgaben (über eine grundsätzliche Einstandspflicht für die Bereitstellung öffentlicher Güter, insbesondere die öffentliche Sicherheit, hinaus) nicht normativ begründbar."

120. Ranganathan, "Constructive Constraints?" 179.

121. See Chapter 7 above.

122. On the outsourcing of the "inherent government function" of intelligence services, see Simon Chesterman, "Intelligence Services," in Chesterman and Fisher, *Private Security, Public Order*, 184ff. But see Juma, "Privatisation, Human Rights and Security," 198, who questions that "functions such as intelligence-gathering or knowledge transfer within the military should be inherently governmental."

123. See, e.g., Simon Chesterman and Angelina Fisher, "Conclusion: Private Security, Public Order," in Chesterman and Fisher, *Private Security, Public Order*, 222 at 225–26.

124. See notes 96ff.

125. See, e.g., Simon Chesterman, "Intelligence Services," in Chesterman and Fisher, *Private Security, Public Order*, 184 at 199ff.

126. OMB Circular No. A-76: Performance of Commercial Activities, White House Office of Management and Budget, 1983, para (b), quoted in Chesterman, 200.

127. U.S. Congress, Federal Activities Inventory Reform Act of 1998, 31 USC § 501 (1998), Section 5.

128. See Chesterman, "Intelligence Services," 201.

129. See, e.g. Uesseler, "Entstaatlichung von Gewalt," 74.

130. Articles 2(4), 42, and 51 of the UN Charter.

131. See the "Operation Desert Storm," authorized by UNSC Res. 678 of 29 November 1990; and the "International Force for East Timor" authorized by UNSC Res. 1264 of 15 September 1999; see, e.g., Manfred Nowak, *Introduction to the International Human Rights Regime* (Leiden, 2003), 307 ff.

132. See the "Operation Restore Hope" authorized by UNSC Res. 794 of 3 December 1992.

133. See, e.g., Francis, "Mercenary Intervention in Sierra Leone," 329: "In the case of Angola, the series of military defeats suffered by UNITA thanks to EO's direct military assistance forced the rebel movement to the negotiation table and brought about the subsequent Lusaka Accord. In effect, EO's immediate strategic impact created the conditions for negotiations and a peace settlement, something which the UN and the AU had not been able to achieve throughout the conflict. . . . As far as the beleaguered government of Sierra Leone was concerned EO was a positive security provider." However, David Francis also proves that both Executive Outcomes and Sandline International intervened primarily in order to secure the control of diamonds and other minerals; ibid., 335: "The case of Sierra Leone illustrates the fact that, despite the huge mineral concessions and cash payments, mercenary intervention did not provide security. Mercenary activities in Sierra Leone only accentuated the international exploitation of the country. This free market response of the privatisation of security is not in the best interest of unstable, but mineral rich countries." See also O'Brien, "What Should and What Should Not Be Regulated?" 29–30; Ranganathan, "Constructive Constraints?" 175; Simon Chesterman and Chia Lehnardt, "Introduction," in Chesterman and Lehnardt, *From Mercenaries to Market*, 1ff.

134. See Kofi Annan, "Secretary-General Reflects on 'Intervention' in Thirty-Fifth Annual Ditchley Foundation Lecture," UN Press Release SG/SM/6613/Rev.1 (26 June 1998). This event has been described repeatedly by academics: see, e.g., Lehnardt, "Peacekeeping," 221; Ranganathan, "Constructive Constraints?" 175.

135. See, e.g., Juma, "Privatisation, Human Rights and Security," 186, with further references.

136. On the extent to which PMSCs are already involved in international peace operations by the UN, the African Union, or the Economic Community of West African States, see Lehnardt, "Peacekeeping," 205ff., with further references. This development was strongly supported by PMSCs and their lobbying associations, such as IPOA and BAPSC. In this context, the expression that PMSCs would mutate from "dogs of war" to "pussycats of peace" was coined by the General Director of BAPSC in the *Economist* of 19 November 2006; see Lehnardt, "Peacekeeping," 206; Ranganathan, "Constructive Constraints?" 177, with reference to Simon Chesterman, "Leashing the Dogs of War: The Rise of Private Military and Security Companies," *Carnegie Reporter* 5 (2008): 36.

137. Lehnardt, "Peacekeeping," 221.

138. See also ibid., 219.

139. Kofi Annan, "In Larger Freedom: Towards Development, Security and Human Rights for All," UN Doc. A/59/2005 of 21 March 2005. See § 14: " I have named the present report 'In Larger Freedom' to stress the enduring relevance of the Charter of the United Nations and to emphasize that its purposes must be advanced in the lives of individual men and women. The notion of larger freedom also encapsulates the idea that development, security and human rights go hand in hand."

140. Ibid., § 17: "Accordingly, we will not enjoy development without security, we will not enjoy security without development, and we will not enjoy either without respect for human rights. Unless all these causes are advanced, none will succeed. In this new millennium, the work of the United Nations must move our world closer to the day when all people have the freedom to choose the kind of lives they would like to live, the access to the resources that would make those choices meaningful and the security to ensure that they can be enjoyed in peace."

141. Ibid., §§ 167ff.

142. UNGA Res. 60/1 of 16 September 2005, §§ 138 and 139 (Responsibility to protect populations from genocide, war crimes, ethnic cleansing and crimes against humanity).

143. See, e.g., Nowak, "Responsibility to Protect: Is International Law Moving from Hobbes to Locke?"

144. See, e.g., Uesseler, "Entstaatlichung von Gewalt," 75; Lehnardt, "Peacekeeping," 218ff.

145. See, e.g., Uesseler, "Entstaatlichung von Gewalt," 80: "Um der unzähligen Krisen und gewaltsamen Auseinandersetzungen Herr werden und sie einer zivilen Konfliktlösung zuführen zu können, muss die Entstaatlichung von Gewalt schrittweise aufgehoben und das staatliche Gewaltmonopol wiederhergestellt werden." See also ibid., 87.

Conclusion: A Human Rights Based Approach to Privatization

1. See in this respect, e.g., Walter Berka and Hannes Tretter, *Public Service Media Under Article 10 of the European Convention on Human Rights: Study on Behalf of the European Broadcasting Union* (Geneva, 2013).

2. See Manfred Nowak, *Introduction to the International Human Rights Regime* (Leiden, 2003), 48ff.

3. See Manfred Nowak, *Menschenrechte: Eine Antwort auf die wachsende ökonomische Ungleichheit* (Vienna, 2015), with references to Thomas Piketty, *Capital in the Twenty-First Century*; Anthony B. Atkinson, *Inequality: What Can Be Done?*; and recent OECD reports and similar economic studies.

4. See Manfred Nowak, "Torkel Opsahl Lecture—The Right of Victims of Human Rights Violations to a Remedy: The Need for World Court of Human Rights," *Nordic Journal of Human Rights* 32, 1 (3 April 2014), 14.

5. Ibid. The legal framework for a World Court of Human Rights can be found in Kozma, Nowak, and Scheinin, *A World Court of Human Rights*.

Bibliography

Books

Alfredsson, Gudmundur, and Asbjørn Eide, eds. *The Universal Declaration of Human Rights: A Common Standard of Achievement.* The Hague, 1999.

Alfredsson, Gudmundur, Jonas Grimheden, Bertrand G. Ramcharan, and Alfred de Zayas, eds. *International Human Rights Monitoring Mechanisms: Essays in Honour of Jakob Th. Möller.* 2nd ed. Leiden, 2009.Alston, Philip, ed. *Non-State Actors and Human Rights.* Oxford, 2005.

Alston, Philip, and Ryan Goodman. *International Human Rights.* Oxford, 2012.

Atkinson, Anthony B. *Inequality: What Can Be Done?* Cambridge, Mass., 2015.

Bakker, Karen. *Privatizing Water: Governance Failure and the World's Urban Water Crisis.* Ithaca, N.Y., 2010.

———. *An Uncooperative Commodity: Privatizing Water in England and Wales.* Oxford, 2004.

Barlow, Maude. *Blue Covenant: The Global Water Crisis and the Coming Battle for the Right to Water.* New York, 2007.

Barlow, Maude, and Tony Clark. *Blue Gold: The Fight to Stop the Corporate Theft of the World's Water.* New York, 2002.

Bax, Ernest Belford. *The Last Episode of the French Revolution: Being a History of Gracchus Babeuf and the Conspiracy of the Equals.* London, 1911.

Bellamy, Alex J. *Global Politics and the Responsibility to Protect: From Words to Deeds.* New York, 2011.

Benedek, Wolfgang, Matthias C. Kettemann, and Markus Möstl, eds. *Mainstreaming Human Security in Peace Operations and Crisis Management.* New York, 2011.

Berka, Walter, and Hannes Tretter. *Public Service Media Under Article 10 of the European Convention on Human Rights: Study on Behalf of the European Broadcasting Union.* Geneva, 2013.

Bossuyt, Marc J. *Guide to the "Travaux Préparatoires" of the International Covenant on Civil and Political Rights.* Dordrecht, 1987.

Brysk, Alison, ed. *Globalization and Human Rights.* Berkeley, 2002.

Bulto, Takele Soboka. *The Extraterritorial Application of the Human Right to Water in Africa.* Cambridge, 2014.

Chesterman, Simon, and Angelina Fisher, eds. *Private Security, Public Order: The Outsourcing of Public Services and Its Limits.* Oxford, 2009.

Chesterman, Simon, and Chia Lehnardt, eds. *From Mercenaries to Market: The Rise and Regulation of Private Military Companies.* Oxford, 2007.

Cicero, Marcus Tullius. *De Re Publica*. In *Cicero: De Re Publica: Selections*, ed. James Zetzel. Cambridge, 1995.

Clapham, Andrew. *Human Rights Obligations of Non-State Actors*. Oxford, 2006.

Coyle, Andrew, Allison Campbell, and Rodney Neufeld. *Capitalist Punishment: Prison Privatization and Human Rights*. Atlanta, 2003.

Dahrendorf, Ralph. *Life Chances: Approaches to Social and Political Theory: The End of the Social Democratic Consensus*. Chicago, 1979.

Daudet, Yves, and Kishore Singh. *The Right to Education: An Analysis of UNESCO's Standard-Setting Instruments*. Paris, 2001.

De Feyter, Koen, and Felipe Gómez Isa, eds. *Privatisation and Human Rights in the Age of Globalisation*. Antwerp, 2005.

De Feyter, Koen, Stephan Parmentier, Marc Bossuyt, and Paul Lemmens, eds. *Out of the Ashes: Reparation for Victims of Gross and Systematic Human Rights Violations*. Antwerp, 2005.

De Schutter, Olivier. *International Human Rights Law: Cases, Materials, Commentary*. 2nd ed. Cambridge, 2014.

Eide, Asbjørn, Gudmundur Alfredsson, Göran Melander, Lars Adam Rehof, and Allan Rosas, eds. *Universal Declaration of Human Rights: A Commentary*. Oslo, 1992.

Engels, Friedrich. *Herrn Eugen Dührings Umwälzung der Wissenschaft*. 3rd ed. Stuttgart, 1894.

Ermacora, Felix. *Menschenrechte in der sich wandelnden Welt*. Vol. 1, *Historische Entwicklung der Menschenrechte und Grundfreiheiten*. Vienna, 1974.

Evans, Gareth. *The Responsibility to Protect: Ending Mass Atrocity Crimes Once and for All*. Washington, D.C., 2008.

Feichtinger, Walter, Wolfgang Braumandl, and Nieves-Erzsebet Kautny, eds. *Private Sicherheits- und Militärfirmen: Konkurrenten—Partner—Totengräber?* Vienna, 2008.

Flora, Peter, and Arnold J. Heidenheimer, eds. *The Development of Welfare States in Europe and America*. New Brunswick, N.J., 1981.

Føllesdal, Andreas, Johan Karlsson Schaffer, and Geir Ulfstein, eds. *The Legitimacy of International Human Rights Regimes: Legal, Political and Philosophical Perspectives*. Cambridge, 2014.

Francioni, Francesco, and Natalino Ronzitti, eds. *War by Contract: Human Rights, Humanitarian Law and Private Contractors*. Oxford, 2011.

Friedman, Milton. *Capitalism and Freedom*. Chicago, 1962.

———. *A Monetary History of the United States*. Princeton, N.J., 1963.

Ghandhi, Sandy. *International Human Rights Documents*. 8th ed. Oxford, 2012.

Gini, Corrado. *Variabilità e mutabilità*. Bologna, 1912.

Glanville, Luke. *Sovereignty and the Responsibility to Protect: A New History*. Chicago, 2014.

Glendon, Mary Ann. *A World Made New: Eleanor Roosevelt and the Universal Declaration of Human Rights*. New York, 2001.

Grabenwarter, Christoph. *The European Convention on Human Rights: Commentary*. Munich, 2014.

Greenwald, Glenn. *With Liberty and Justice for Some: How the Law Is Used to Destroy Equality and Protect the Powerful*. New York, 2011.

Gumedze, Sabelo, ed. *Private Security in Africa: Manifestations, Challenges and Regulation*. ISS Monograph Series 139. Pretoria, 2007.

Haeck, Yves, and Eva Brems, eds. *Human Rights and Civil Liberties in the 21st Century*. Dordrecht, 2014.

Hilpold, Peter, ed. *Die Schutzverantwortung (R2P): Ein Paradigmenwechsel in der Entwicklung des internationalen Rechts?* Leiden, 2013.

Hood, Roger. *The Death Penalty: A Worldwide Perspective*. Oxford, 1997.

Humphrey, John P. *Human Rights and the United Nations: A Great Adventure*. New York, 1984.

Ishay, Micheline R. *The History of Human Rights*. Berkeley, 2008.

Jiménez, Mariela Rubio. *Tu salud, nuestro negocio*. Madrid, 2014.

Joseph, Sarah, and Melissa Castan. *The International Covenant on Civil and Political Rights: Cases, Materials, and Commentary*. 3rd ed. Oxford, 2013.

Judt, Tony. *Ill Fares the Land*. New York, 2010.

Kälin, Walter, Künzli, Jörg. *The Law of International Human Rights Protection*. Cambridge, 2009.

Kant, Immanuel. *Die Metaphysik der Sitten, Einleitung in die Rechtslehre*. Vol. 8 of *Immanuel Kant: Werke in zwölf Bänden*, ed. Wilhelm Weischedel. Frankfurt, 1977.

Keynes, John Maynard. *The General Theory of Employment, Interest and Money*. London, 1936; reprinted 1977.

Kozma, Julia, Manfred Nowak, and Martin Scheinin. *A World Court of Human Rights: Consolidated Statute and Commentary*. Vienna, 2010.

Krause, Catarina, and Martin Scheinin, eds. *International Protection of Human Rights: A Textbook*. 2nd ed. Turku, 2012.

Lauterpacht, Hersch. *International Bill of the Rights of Man*. New York, 1945.

Locke, John. *Two Treatises of Government*. 1690. Excerpted in *The Human Rights Reader: Major Political Writings, Essays, Speeches, and Documents from the Bible to the Present*, vol. 2, ed. Micheline R. Ishay. London, 1997.

Luf, Gerhard. *Freiheit und Gleichheit*. Vienna, 1978.

Macpherson, Ian, Susan Robertson, and Geoffrey Walford, eds. *Education, Privatisation and Social Justice: Case Studies from Africa, South Asia and South East Asia*. Oxford, 2014.

Marx, Karl. *On the Jewish Question*. 1843. Excerpted in *The Human Rights Reader: Major Political Writings, Essays, Speeches, and Documents from the Bible to the Present*, ed. Micheline R. Ishay. London, 1997.

Morsink, Johannes. *The Universal Declaration of Human Rights: Origins, Drafting, and Intent*. Philadelphia, 1999.

Myrdal, Gunnar. *Beyond the Welfare State*. New York, 1960.

Nowak, Manfred. *Folter: Die Alltäglichkeit des Unfassbaren*. Vienna, 2012.

———. *Introduction to the International Human Rights Regime*. Leiden, 2003.

———. *Menschenrechte: Eine Antwort auf die wachsende ökonomische Ungleichheit*. Vienna, 2015.

———. *Politische Grundrechte*. Vienna, 1988.

———. *UN Covenant on Civil and Political Rights: CCPR Commentary*. 2nd rev. ed. Kehl, 2005.

———, ed. *World Conference on Human Rights, Vienna, June 1993: The Contribution of NGOs*. Reports and Documents. Vienna, 1994.

Nowak, Manfred, Karolina M. Januszewski, and Tina Hofstätter, eds. *All Human Rights for All: Vienna Manual on Human Rights*. Vienna, 2012.

Oberdabernig, Doris A. *The Effects of Structural Adjustment Programs on Poverty and Income Distribution*, Vienna Institute for International Economic Studies. Vienna, 2010.

Oestreich, Gerhard. *Geschichte der Menschenrechte und Grundfreiheiten im Umriss*. 2nd ed. Berlin, 1978.

Pickett, Kate, and Richard Wilkinson. *The Spirit Level: Why More Equal Societies Almost Always Do Better*. London, 2009.

Piketty, Thomas. *Capital in the Twenty-First Century*. Cambridge, Mass., 2014.

Proudhon, Pierre-Joseph. *What Is Property? An Inquiry into the Principle of Right and of Government*. 1840. Excerpted in *The Human Rights Reader: Major Political Writings, Essays, Speeches, and Documents from the Bible to the Present*, ed. Micheline R. Ishay, 175. London, 1997.

Rawls, John. *A Theory of Justice*. Cambridge, Mass., 1971.

Reimon, Michel, and Christian Felber. *Schwarzbuch Privatisierung*. Vienna, 2003.

Riedel, Eibe, and Peter Rothen, eds. *The Human Right to Water*. Berlin, 2006.

Rousseau, Jean-Jacques. *Du contrat social*. 1762. Ed. Bertrand de Jouvenel. Paris, 1978.

Ryngaert, Cedric, and Math Noortmann, eds. *Human Security and International Law: The Challenge of Non-State Actors*. Cambridge, 2014.

Salomon, Margot E., Arne Tostensen, and Wouter Vandenhole, eds. *Casting the Net Wider: Human Rights, Development and New Duty-Bearers*. Antwerp, 2007.

Sampford, Charles, and Ramesh Thakur, eds. *Responsibility to Protect and Sovereignty*. Surrey, 2013.

Saul, Ben, David Kinley, and Jacqueline Mowbray. *The International Covenant on Economic, Social and Cultural Rights: Commentary, Cases, and Materials*. Oxford, 2014.

Schabas, William A. *The Abolition of the Death Penalty in International Law*. 3rd ed. Cambridge, 2003.

Seiberth, Corinna. *Private Military and Security Companies in International Law*. Cambridge, 2014.

Sellers, Martin P. *The History and Politics of Private Prisons: A Comparative Analysis*. Teaneck, N.J., 1993.

Serra, Narcís, and Joseph E. Stiglitz. *The Washington Consensus Reconsidered: Towards a New Global Governance*. Oxford, 2008.

Sheeran, Scott, and Nigel S. Rodley, eds. *Routledge Handbook of International Human Rights Law*. London, 2013.

Shelton, Dinah. *Remedies in International Human Rights Law*. Oxford, 2005.

Smith, Rhona K. M. *International Human Rights*. Oxford, 2013.

Ssenyonjo, Manisuli. *Economic, Social and Cultural Rights in International Law*. Oxford, 2009.

Stiglitz, Joseph E. *Globalization and Its Discontents*. New York, 2012.

Taibbi, Matt. *The Divide: American Injustice in the Age of the Wealth Gap*. New York, 2014.

Tomaševski, Katarina. *Human Rights Obligations in Education: The 4-A Scheme*. Nijmegen, 2006.

van Boven, Theo, Cees Flinterman, and Ingrid Westendorp, *The Maastricht Guidelines on Violations of Economic, Social and Cultural Rights*. Netherlands Institute of Human Rights, SIM Special No. 20 (Utrecht, 1997).

Von Hayek, Friedrich A. *The Constitution of Liberty*. London, 1960.

———. *The Road to Serfdom*. Chicago, 1944.

Walmsley, Roy. *World Prison Population List*. 10th ed. Colchester, 2013

Weber, Max. *Staatssoziologie: Soziologie der rationalen Staatsanstalt und der modernen politischen Parteien und Parlamente*. 2nd ed. Berlin, 1956.

Wilensky, Harold. *The Welfare State and Equality*. Berkeley, Calif., 1975.

Winkler, Inga. *The Human Right to Water: Significance, Legal Status and Implications for Water Allocation*. Oxford, 2012.

Articles

Abrahamsen, Rita, and Michael C. Williams. "The Globalisation of Private Security: Country Report Kenya." University of Aberystwyth, Wales, 2005.

Allen, Rob. "Prisons: State Duty or Market Opportunity?" *Penal Reform International*, 23 May 2014.

Aman, Alfred C. "Private Prisons and the Democratic Deficit." In *Private Security, Public Order: The Outsourcing of Public Services and Its Limits*, ed. Simon Chesterman and Angelina Fisher, 86. Oxford, 2009.

————. "Privatisation, Prisons, Democracy and Human Rights: The Need to Extend the Province of Administrative Law." In *Privatisation and Human Rights in the Age of Globalisation*, ed. Koen De Feyter and Felipe Gómez Isa, 91–105. Oxford, 2005.

Amsden, Alice H. "The Wild Ones: Industrial Policies in the Developing World." In *The Washington Consensus Reconsidered: Towards a New Global Governance*, ed. Narcís Serra and Joseph E. Stiglitz, 95. Oxford, 2008.

Anderson, Lucas. "Kicking the National Habit: The Legal and Policy Arguments for Abolishing Private Prison Contracts." *Public Contract Law Journal* 39 (2009): 113.

Andreassen, Bård-Anders. "Article 22." In *The Universal Declaration of Human Rights: A Commentary*, ed. Asbjørn Eide et al., 319. Oslo, 1992.

Arajärvi, Pentti. "Article 26." In *The Universal Declaration of Human Rights: A Common Standard of Achievement*, ed. Gudmundur Alfredsson and Asbjørn Eide, 551. The Hague, 1999.

Arnold, Craig Anthony. "Water Privatization Trends in the United States: Human Rights, National Security, and Public Stewardship." *William and Mary Environmental Law and Policy Review* 33 (2009): 785.

Austin, Rodney. "Human Rights, the Private Sector and New Public Management." *University College London Human Rights Review* 1 (2008): 17.

Badura, Peter. "Art. 33." In *Grundgesetz-Kommentar* 2013, ed. Theodor Maunz and Günter Dürig. Tübingen, 2013.

Barak-Erez, Daphne. "The Private Prison Controversy and the Privatization Continuum." *Law and Ethics of Human Rights* 5 (2011): 138.

Benner, Mats. "The Scandinavian Challenge: The Future of Advanced Welfare States in the Knowledge Economy." *Acta Sociologica* 46 (2003): 132–49.

Bloche, M. Gregg. "Is Privatisation of Health Care a Human Rights Problem?" In *Privatisation and Human Rights in the Age of Globalisation*, ed. Koen De Feyter and Felipe Gómez Isa, 207. Antwerp, 2005.

Bigwood, Jeremy. "DynCorp in Colombia: Outsourcing the Drug War." *CorpWatch online*, May 23, 2001.

Boemcken, Marc von. "Das private Militärgewerbe: Ursachen, Typen und Probleme." In *Private Sicherheits- und Militärfirmen: Konkurrenten—Partner—Totengräber?* ed. Walter Feichtinger, Wolfgang Braumandl, and Nieves-Erzsebet Kautny, 47–51. Vienna, 2008.

Byrne, Iain. "Making the Right to Health a Reality: Legal Strategies for Effective Implementation." Paper presented at Commonwealth Law Conference, London, September 2005.

Carson, E. Ann, and Daniela Golinelli. "Prisoners in 2012: Trends in Admissions and Releases,
1991–2012." U.S. Department of Justice, Bureau of Justice Statistics (BJS) *Bulletin*,
December 2013.

Cassese, Antonio. "Mercenaries: Lawful Combatants or War Criminals?" *Zeitschrift für ausländisches öffentliches Recht und Völkerrecht* 40 (1980): 1.

Chesterman, Simon, "Intelligence Services." In *Private Security, Public Order: The Outsourcing
of Public Services and Its Limits*, ed. Simon Chesterman and Angelina Fisher, 184. Oxford,
2009.

———. "Leashing the Dogs of War: The Rise of Private Military and Security Companies."
Carnegie Reporter 5 (2008): 36.

Chesterman, Simon, and Angelina Fisher. "Conclusion: Private Security, Public Order." In
Private Security, Public Order: The Outsourcing of Public Services and Its Limits, ed. Simon
Chesterman and Angelina Fisher, 222. Oxford, 2009.

Chesterman, Simon, and Chia Lehnardt. "Introduction." In *From Mercenaries to Market: The
Rise and Regulation of Private Military Companies*, ed. Simon Chesterman and Chia Lehnardt, 1. Oxford, 2007.

Cichon, Michael, and Krzysztof Hagemejer. "Social Security for All: Investing in Global Social
and Economic Development: A Consultation." Issues in Social Protection Series, Discussion Paper 16. ILO Social Security Department. Geneva, 2006.

Cockayne, James. "Regulating Private Military and Security Companies: The Content, Negotiations, Weaknesses and Promise of the Montreux Document." *Journal of Conflict and
Security Law* 13 (2008): 401.

Coomans, Fons, and Antenor Hallo de Wolf. "Privatisation of Education and the Right to
Education." In *Privatisation and Human Rights in the Age of Globalisation*, ed. Koen De
Feyter and Felipe Gómez Isa, 229. Antwerp, 2005.

Courtis, Christian. "Social Rights and Privatisation: Lessons from the Argentine Experience."
In *Privatisation and Human Rights in the Age of Globalisation*, ed. Koen De Feyter and
Felipe Gómez Isa, 175. Antwerp, 2005.

Coyle, Andrew. "Conclusion." In *Capitalist Punishment: Prison Privatization and Human
Rights*, ed. Andrew Coyle, Allison Campbell, and Rodney Neufeld, 211. Atlanta, 2003.

Craven, Matthew. "Some Thoughts on the Emerging Right to Water." In *The Human Right
to Water*, ed. Eibe Riedel and Peter Rothen, 37. Berlin, 2006.

Dellapenna, Joseph W. "Climate Disruption, the Washington Consensus, and Water Law
Reform." *Temple Law Review* 81 (2008): 383–404.

De Preux, Jean. "Mercenaries." In International Committee of the Red Cross. *Commentary
on the Additional Protocols of 8 June 1977 to the Geneva Conventions of 12 August 1949*,
ed. Yves Sandoz, Christophe Swinarski, and Bruno Zimmermann, 571. Dordrecht, 1987.

Drury, Ian. "Police Use Staff from Olympic Disaster Firm G4S to Help Solve Murders in
Latest Privatisation of Frontline Jobs." *Mail Online News*, 14 April 2013.

Eide, Asbjørn. "Article 25." In *The Universal Declaration of Human Rights: A Commentary*,
ed. Asbjørn Eide et al., 385. Oslo, 1992.

———. "The Non-Inclusion of Minority Rights: Resolution 217 C (III)." In *The Universal
Declaration of Human Rights: A Common Standard of Achievement*, ed. Gudmundur
Alfredsson and Asbjørn Eide, 523. The Hague, 1999.

Eide, Asbjørn, and Wenche Barth Eide. "Article 25." In *The Universal Declaration of Human Rights: A Common Standard of Achievement*, ed. Gudmundur Alfredsson and Asbjørn Eide, The Hague, 1999

Eisenberg, David. "A Government in Search of Cover: Private Military Companies in Iraq." In *From Mercenaries to Market: The Rise and Regulation of Private Military Companies*, ed. Simon Chesterman and Chia Lehnardt, 82. Oxford, 2007.

Fairstein, Carolina. "Legal Strategies and Right to Water in Argentina." In *The Human Right to Water*, ed. Eibe Riedel and Peter Rothen, 95. Berlin, 2006.

Feichtinger, Walter. "Private Militärfirmen im Vormarsch: Ungeliebt, aber unverzichtbar?" In *Private Sicherheits- und Militärfirmen:—Konkurrenten—Partner—Totengräber?* ed. Walter Feichtinger, Wolfgang Braumandl, and Nieves-Erzsebet Kautny, 13. Vienna, 2008.

Ferenci, Beatrix. "Right to Education." In *All Human Rights for All: Vienna Manual on Human Rights*, ed. Manfred Nowak, Karolina M. Januszewski, and Tina Hofstätter, 328. Vienna, 2012.

Fisher, Max. "Map: U.S. Ranks Near Bottom on Income Inequality." *Atlantic*, 19 September 2011.

Foaleng, Mpako H. "Private Military and Security Companies and the Nexus Between Natural Resources and Civil Wars in Africa." In *Private Security in Africa: Manifestations, Challenges and Regulation*. ISS Monograph Series 139, ed. Sabelo Gumedze, 39. Pretoria, 2007.

Francis, David J. "Mercenary Intervention in Sierra Leone: Providing National Security or International Exploitation?" *Third World Quarterly* 20 (1999): 319.

Funk, Bernd-Christian. "Grenzen der Ausgliederung der hoheitlichen Besorgung von Verwaltungsaufgaben (Austro-Control)-Entscheidungsbesprechung." *Österreichische Zeitschrift für Wirtschaftsrecht (ÖZW)* (1997): 60.

Gepp, Joseph. "Wasser unser." *Falter*, June 2013.

Gini, Corrado. "On the Measure of Concentration with Special Reference to Income and Statistics." *Colorado College Publication. General Series* 208 (1936): 73.

Gold, Martin E. "The Privatization of Prisons." *Urban Lawyer* 28 (1996): 359.

Gómez del Prado, José L. "Impact on Human Rights of a New Non-State Actor: Private Military and Security Companies." *Brown Journal of World Affairs* 18 (2011): 151.

Gómez Isa, Felipe. "Globalisation, Privatisation and Human Rights." In *Privatisation and Human Rights in the Age of Globalisation*, ed. Koen De Feyter and Felipe Gómez Isa. Antwerp, 2005

Graham, Cosmo. "Human Rights and the Privatisation of Public Utilities and Essential Services." In *Privatisation and Human Rights in the Age of Globalisation*, ed. Koen De Feyter and Felipe Gómez Isa, 33. Antwerp, 2005.

Gumedze, Sabelo. "To Embrace or Not Embrace: Addressing the Private Security Industry Phenomenon in Africa." In *Private Security in Africa: Manifestations, Challenges and Regulation*, ed. Sabelo Gumedze. ISS Monograph Series 139. Pretoria, 2007.

Holoubek, Michael. "Der Staat als Wirtschaftssubjekt und Auftraggeber." *Veröffentlichungen der Vereinigung der Deutschen Staatsrechtslehrer (VVDStRL)* 60 (2001): 513.

Hoppe, Carsten, and Ottavio Quirico. "Codes of Conduct for Private Military and Security Companies: The State of Self-Regulation in the Industry." In *War by Contract: Human Rights, Humanitarian Law and Private Contractors*, ed. Francesco Francioni and Natalino Ronzitti, 363. Oxford, 2011.

Howe, Herbert. "Private Security Forces and African Stability: The Case of Executive Out-comes." *Journal of Modern African Studies* 36 (1998): 307.

Human, Casper. "The Human Right to Water in Africa: The South African Example." In *The Human Right to Water*, ed. Eibe Riedel and Peter Rothen, 83. Berlin, 2006.

Jachmann, Monika. "Art. 33 Abs. 4 GG-verbotene Differenzierungen." In *Grundgesetz-Kommentar*, vol. 2., 6th ed., ed. Hermann von Mangoldt, Friedrich Klein, and Christian Starck, 834. Munich, 2010.

Joseph, Sarah. "Pharmaceutical Corporations and Access to Drugs: The 'Fourth Wave' of Corporate Human Rights Scrutiny." *Human Rights Quarterly* 25 (2003): 425–43.

Juma, Laurence. "Privatisation, Human Rights and Security: Reflections on the Draft International Convention on Regulation, Oversight and Monitoring of Private Military and Security Companies." *Law, Democracy & Development* 15 (2011): 182.

Kok, Anton. "Privatisation and the Right to Access to Water." In *Privatisation and Human Rights in the Age of Globalisation*, ed. Koen De Feyter and Felipe Gómez Isa, 259. Oxford, 2005.

Kothari, Miloon. "Obstacles to Making Water a Human Right." In *The Human Right to Water*, ed. Eibe Riedel and Peter Rothen, 149. Berlin, 2006.

Krahmann, Elke. "Transitional States in Search of Support." In *From Mercenaries to Market: The Rise and Regulation of Private Military Companies*, ed. Simon Chesterman and Chia Lehnardt, 94. Oxford, 2007.

Krause, Catarina. "The Right to Property." In *Economic, Social and Cultural Rights: A Textbook*. 2nd ed., ed. Asbjørn Eide, Catarina Krause, and Allan Rosas, 191. Dordrecht, 2001.

Krause, Catarina, and Gudmundur Alfredsson. "Article 17." In *The Universal Declaration of Human Rights: A Common Standard of Achievement*, ed. Gudmundur Alfredsson and Asbjørn Eide, 359. The Hague, 1999.

Krugman, Paul. "Inequality and Redistribution." In *The Washington Consensus Reconsidered: Towards a New Global Governance*, ed. Narcís Serra and Joseph E. Stiglitz, 12. Oxford, 2008.

Lamarche, Lucie. "Social Protection Is a Matter of Human Rights: Exploring the ICESCR Right to Social Security in the Context of Globalisation." In *Privatisation and Human Rights in the Age of Globalisation*, ed. Koen De Feyter and Felipe Gómez Isa, 129. Antwerp, 2005.

Lassen, Eva Maria. "When Peers Are Pressing for Progress: The Clash of Hersch Lauterpacht and John Humphrey over the Universal Declaration of Human Rights." In *Europe and the Americas: Transatlantic Approaches to Human Rights*, ed. Erik Andreassen and Eva Maria Lassen. Leiden, 2015.

Lehnardt, Chia. "Peacekeeping." In *Private Security, Public Order: The Outsourcing of Public Services and Its Limits*, ed. Simon Chesterman and Angelina Fisher, 205. Oxford, 2009.

Lindbeck, Assar. "The Advanced Welfare State." Seminar Paper 395. Institute for International Economic Studies, Stockholm, 1987.

———. "Consequences of the Advanced Welfare State." *World Economy* 11 (1988): 19–38.

Link, Adam D. "The Perils of Privatization: International Developments and Reform in Water Distribution." *Global Business and Development Law Journal* 22 (2010): 379.MacLeod, Sorcha. "The Role of International Regulatory Initiatives on Business and Human Rights for Holding Private Military and Security Contractors to Account." In *War by Contract:*

Human Rights, Humanitarian Law and Private Contractors, ed. Francesco Francioni and Natalino Ronzitti, 343. Oxford, 2011.

Malherbe, Rassie. "Privatisation and the Constitution: Some Exploratory Observations." *Journal of South African Law* 1 (2001): 1–12.

Mancini, Marina, Faustin Z. Ntoubandi, and Thilo Marauhn. "Old Concepts and New Challenges: Are Private Contractors the Mercenaries of the Twenty-First Century?" In *War by Contract: Human Rights, Humanitarian Law and Private Contractors*, ed. Francesco Francioni and Natalino Ronzitti, 312. Oxford, 2011.

Marks, Stephen P. "Access to Essential Medicines as a Component of the Right to Health." In *Realizing the Right to Health*, ed. Andrew Clapham and Mary Robinson, 87. Zürich, 2012.

Mathiason, Nick. "The First Privatised War: Private Contractors Are Carving Up Defence Procurement." *Observer*, 1 March 2003.

McIntyre, Angela, and Taya Weiss. "Weak Governments in Search of Strength: Africa's Experience of Mercenaries and Private Military Companies." In *From Mercenaries to Market: The Rise and Regulation of Private Military Companies*, ed. Simon Chesterman and Chia Lehnardt, 67. Oxford, 2007.

Megginson, William L., and Jeffry M. Netter. "From State to Market: A Survey of Empirical Studies on Privatization." *Journal of Economic Literature* 39 (2001): 321–89.

Metzger, Gillian E. "Privatization as Delegation." *Columbia Law Review* 103 (2003): 1367.

Molenaar, Bente, and Rodney Neufeld. "The Use of Privatized Detention Centers for Asylum Seekers in Australia and the UK." In *Capitalist Punishment: Prison Privatization and Human Rights*, ed. Andrew Coyle, Allison Campbell, and Rodney Neufeld, 127. Atlanta, 2003.

Möller, Jakob. "The Right of Petition: General Assembly Resolution 217B." In *The Universal Declaration of Human Rights: A Common Standard of Achievement*, ed. Gudmundur Alfredsson and Asbjørn Eide, 653. The Hague, 1999.

Moore, Dawn, Kellie Leclerc Burton, and Kelly Hannah-Moffat. "'Get Tough' Efficiency: Human Rights, Correctional Restructuring and Prison Privatization in Ontario, Canada." In *Capitalist Punishment: Prison Privatization and Human Rights*, ed. Andrew Coyle, Allison Campbell, and Rodney Neufeld, 152. Atlanta, 2003.

Murthy, Sharmila L. "The Human Right(s) to Water and Sanitation: History, Meaning, and the Controversy over Privatization." *Berkeley Journal of International Law* 31 (2013): 89–99.

Nathan, Stephen. "Prison Privatization in the United Kingdom." In *Capitalist Punishment: Prison Privatization and Human Rights*, ed. Andrew Coyle, Allison Campbell, and Rodney Neufeld, 162. Atlanta, 2003

Ndlovu-Gatsheni, Sabelo J. "Weak States and the Growth of the Private Security Sector in Africa: Whither the African State?" In *Private Security in Africa: Manifestations, Challenges and Regulation*, ed. Sabelo Gumedze. ISS Monograph 139, 17. Pretoria, 2007.

Noortmann, Math, and Cedric Ryngaert. "Towards a (New) Human Security-Based Agenda for International Law and Non-State Actors?" In *Human Security and International Law: The Challenge of Non-State Actors*, ed. Cedric Ryngaert and Math Noortmann. Cambridge, 2014.

Nossal, Kim Richard, and Phillip J. Wood. "The Raggedness of Prison Privatization: Australia, Britain, Canada, New Zealand and the United States Compared." Paper prepared for

Prisons 2004 conference Prisons and Penal Policy: International Perspectives, City University London, 2004.

———. "Responsibility to Protect: Is International Law Moving from Hobbes to Locke?" In *Völkerrecht und die Dynamik der Menschenrechte: Liber Amicorum Wolfram Karl*, ed. Gerhard Hafner, Franz Matscher, and Kirsten Schmalenbach, 342. Vienna, 2012.

———. "The Right to Education." In *Economic, Social and Cultural Rights: A Textbook*. 2nd ed. Ed. Asbjørn Eide, Catarina Krause, and Allan Rosas, 245. Dordrecht, 2001.

———. "The Right to Education: Its Meaning, Significance and Limitations." *NQHR* (1991): 418–25.

———."The Three Pillars of the United Nations: Security, Development and Human Rights." In *Casting the Net Wider: Human Rights, Development and New Duty-Bearers*, ed. Margot E. Salomon, Arne Tostensen, and Wouter Vandenhole, 25–41. Antwerp, 2007.

———. "The Torkel Opsahl Lecture 2013: The Right of Victims of Human Rights Violations to a Remedy: The Need for a World Court of Human Rights." *Nordic Journal of Human Rights* 32, 1 (April 2014): 3–14.O'Brien, Kevin A. "What Should and What Should Not Be Regulated?" In *From Mercenaries to Market: The Rise and Regulation of Private Military Companies*, ed. Simon Chesterman and Chia Lehnardt, 29–48. Oxford, 2007.

Parenti, Christian. "Privatized Problems: For-Profit Incarceration in Trouble." In *Capitalist Punishment: Prison Privatization and Human Rights*, ed. Andrew Coyle, Allison Campbell, and Rodney Neufeld, 30. Atlanta, 2003.

Peachey, Paul. "Police Forces Put £1.5bn Privatisation Plan on Hold: The Proposal Was Being Discussed at a Time When Forces Face 20 Per Cent Spending Cuts." *Independent*, 18 May 2012.

Percy, Sarah. "Morality and Regulation." In *From Mercenaries to Market: The Rise and Regulation of Private Military Companies*, ed. Simon Chesterman and Chia Lehnardt. Oxford, 2007.

Perrin, Guy. "Reflections on Fifty Years of Social Security." *International Labour Review* 99 (1969): 260.

Pesendorfer, Michael. "Private Militärfirmen und österreichische Rechtsordnung." In *Private Sicherheits- und Militärfirmen: Konkurrenten—Partner—Totengräber?*, ed. Walter Feichtinger, Wolfgang Braumandl, and Nieves-Erzsebet Kautny, 107. Vienna, 2008.

Peters, Anne. "Privatisierung, Globalisierung und die Resistenz des Verfassungsstaates." In *Staats- und Verfassungstheorie im Spannungsfeld der Disziplinen*, ed. Philippe Mastronardi and Denis Taubert, 100. Archiv für Rechts- und Sozialphilosophie 105. Stuttgart, 2006.

Porter, Eduardo. "Health Care and Profits, a Poor Mix." *New York Times*, 8 January 2013.

Pozen, David E. "Managing a Correctional Marketplace: Prison Privatization in the United States and the United Kingdom." *Journal of Law and Politics* 19 (2003): 253–84.

Ranganathan, Surabhi. "Constructive Constraints? Conceptual and Practical Challenges to Regulating Private Military and Security Companies." In *Human Security and International Law: The Challenge of Non-State Actors*, ed. Cedric Ryngaert and Math Noortmann, 175. Cambridge, 2014.

Rehof, Lars Adam. "Article 3." In *Universal Declaration of Human Rights: A Commentary*, ed. Asbjørn Eide et al. (Oslo, 1992);

Rehof, Lars Adam. "Article 3." In *The Universal Declaration of Human Rights: A Common Standard of Achievement*, ed. Gudmundur Alfredsson and Asbjørn Eide. The Hague, 1999.

Riedel, Eibe. "The Human Right to Water and General Comment No. 15 of the CESCR." In *The Human Right to Water*, ed. Eibe Riedel and Peter Rothen, 19. Berlin, 2006.

Robbins, Ira P. "Privatisation of Corrections: A Violation of U.S. Domestic Law, International Human Rights, and Good Sense." In *Privatisation and Human Rights in the Age of Globalisation*, ed. Koen De Feyter and Felipe Gómez Isa, 57–86. Antwerp, 2005.

Samnoy, Ashild. "The Origins of the Universal Declaration of Human Rights." In *The Universal Declaration of Human Rights: A Common Standard of Achievement*, ed. Gudmundur Alfredsson and Asbjørn Eide, 3–11. The Hague, 1999.

Scharpf, Fritz W. "The Viability of Advanced Welfare States in the International Economy: Vulnerabilities and Options." *Journal of European Public Policy* 7 (1999): 190–228.

Scheinin, Martin. "The Right to Social Security." In *Economic, Social and Cultural Rights: A Textbook*. 2nd ed, ed. Asbjørn Eide, Catarina Krause, and Allan Rosas. Dordrecht, 2001.

Schladebach, Marcus, and Sabrina Schönrock. "Privatisierung im Massregelvollzug." *NVwZ* 16 (2012): 1011.

Schmidl, Erwin A. "Soldaten: Söldner: Freiwillige." in *Private Sicherheits- und Militärfirmen: Konkurrenten—Partner—Totengräber?*, ed. Walter Feichtinger, Wolfgang Braumandl, and Nieves-Erzsebet Kautny, 35–42. Vienna, 2008.

Schulz, Sabrina. "Private Sicherheit als Exportschlager? Die private Sicherheitsindustrie in Grossbritannien im Spannungsfeld freier Marktkräfte und internationaler Rechtsgüter." In *Private Sicherheits- und Militärfirmen: Konkurrenten—Partner—Totengräber?*, ed. Walter Feichtinger, Wolfgang Braumandl, and Nieves-Erzsebet Kautny, 147–52. Vienna, 2008.

Serra, Narcís, Shari Spiegel, and Joseph E. Stiglitz. "Introduction: From the Washington Consensus Towards a New Global Governance." In *The Washington Consensus Reconsidered: Towards a New Global Governance*, ed. Narcís Serra and Joseph E. Stiglitz, 3. Oxford, 2008.

Silver, Nate. "What Is Driving Growth in Government Spending?" *New York Times*, 16 January 2013.

Sinden, Jeff. "The Problem of Prison Privatization: The U.S. Experience." In *Capitalist Punishment: Prison Privatization and Human Rights*, ed. Andrew Coyle, Allison Campbell, and Rodney Neufeld, 39. Atlanta, 2003

Singer, Alan. "What Happens if Public Education Is Privatized? Clues from the Health Care Fiasco." *Huffington Post*, 6 May 2014.

Stiglitz, Joseph E. "Is There a Post-Washington Consensus Consensus?" In *The Washington Consensus Reconsidered: Towards a New Global Governance*, ed. Narcís Serra and Joseph E. Stiglitz, 41. Oxford, 2008.

Tanner, Will. "The Case for Private Prisons." *Reform Ideas* 2. London, February 2013.

Taylor, Matthew, and Alan Travis. "G4S Chief Predicts Mass Police Privatisation." *Guardian*, 20 June 2012.

Thiele, Alexander. "Art. 33 Abs. 4 GG als Privatisierungsschranke." *Der Staat* 49 (2010): 274.

Travis, Alan, and Zoe Williams. "Revealed: Government Plans for Police Privatisation." *Guardian*, 2 March 2012.

Uesseler, Rolf. "Entstaatlichung von Gewalt: Herausforderung für die Demokratie." In *Private Sicherheits- und Militärfirmen—Konkurrenten—Partner—Totengräber?*, ed. Walter Feichtinger, Wolfgang Braumandl, and Nieves-Erzsebet Kautny, 67–75. Vienna, 2008.

- Marty, Dick. *Alleged Secret Detentions in Council of Europe Member States.* COE Doc. AS/Jur (2006) 03 Rev (22 January 2006).
- ———. *Secret Detentions and Illegal Transfers of Detainees Involving Council of Europe Member States: Second Report.* COE Doc. 11302 Rev. (11 June 2007).
- ———. *Study on the Phenomena of Torture, Cruel, Inhuman or Degrading Treatment or Punishment in the World, Including an Assessment of Conditions of Detention.* Doc. A/HRC/13/39/Add. 5 (5 February 2010).

———. *Focus on Inequality and Growth*. Paris, 2014.

———. "Income Inequality." In Organisation for Economic Co-Operation and Development (OECD). *OECD Factbook 2013: Economic, Environmental and Social Statistics*. Paris, 2013.

———. *In It Together: Why Less Inequality Benefits All*. Paris, 2015.

———. *Mehr Ungleichheit Trotz Wachstum? Einkommensverteilung und Armut in OECD-Ländern*. Paris, 2008. *Pinsent Masons Water Yearbook 2011–2012*. http://wateryear book.pinsentmasons.com.

Ruggie, John. *Report of the Special Representative of the Secretary-General on the Issue of Human Rights and Transnational Corporations and Other Business Enterprises*. UN Doc. A/HRC/17/31 (21 March 2011).

United Nations. *Annotations on the Text of the Draft International Covenants on Human Rights*. Doc. A/2929 (New York, 1 July 1955).

———. *Annual Report of the United Nations High Commissioner for Human Rights on the Scope and Content of the Relevant Human Rights Obligations Related to Equitable Access to Safe Drinking Water and Sanitation Under International Human Rights Instruments and Reports of the Office of the UN High Commissioner for Human Rights and the Secretary-General*. Doc. A/HRC/6/3 (16 August 2007).

———. Committee on Economic, Social and Cultural Rights (CESCR), *General Comment No. 3: The Nature of States Parties' Obligations (Art. 2, Para. 1, of the Covenant)*. Doc. E/1991/23 (14 December 1990).

———. Committee on Economic, Social and Cultural Rights (CESCR)*General Comment No. 13: The Right to Education (Art. 13 of the Covenant).*, Doc. E/C.12/1999/10 (8 December 1999).

———. Committee on Economic, Social and Cultural Rights (CESCR), *General Comment No. 14: The Right to the Highest Attainable Standard of Health (Art. 12 of the Covenant)*. Doc. E/C.12/2000/4 (11 August 2000).

———. Committee on Economic, Social and Cultural Rights (CESCR), *General Comment No. 15: The Right to Water (Arts. 11 and 12 of the Covenant)*. Doc. E/C.12/2002/11 (20 January 2003).

———. Committee on Economic, Social and Cultural Rights (CESCR), *General Comment No. 19: The Right to Social Security (Art. 9 of the Covenant)*. Doc. E/C.12/GC/19 (4 February 2008). *Conference on Environment and Development*. Rio de Janeiro, 1992.Doc.A/Conf.151/26 (1993).

———. Human Rights Committee, *Report of the Human Rights Committee*. Doc. A/57/40. Vol. 1. New York, 2002.

———. *The Right to Education (Art. 13)*. Doc. E/C.12/1999/10 (8 December 1991).

———. *2005 World Summit Outcome* document. Resolution Adopted by the General Assembly 60/1. Doc. A/RES/60/1 (16 September 2005).

UN Development Programme (UNDP). *Human Development Report 1994: New Dimensions of Human Security*. New York, 1994.

UN Human Rights Council. *Joint Study by Four Special Procedures on Global Practices in Relation to Secret Detention in the Context of Countering Terrorism*. UN Doc. A/HRC/13/42 (19 February 2010).

UN Secretary-General. *The Millennium Development Goals Report 2014*. New York, 2014.

U.S. Department of Defense. *Quadrennial Defense Review 2001*. Washington, D.C., 30 September 2001.

U.S. Department of Justice, Bureau of Justice Assistance. "Emerging Issues on Privatized Prisons." Washington, D.C., February 2001.

World Bank. *Averting the Old Age Crisis: Policies to Protect the Old and Promote Growth.* New York, 1994.

———. Public-Private Infrastructure Advisory Facility (PPIAF). *Public-Private Partnerships for Urban Water Utilities: A Review of Experiences in Developing Countries.* Washington, D.C., 2009.

———. *2014 World Development Indicators: Distribution of Income or Consumption.* Washington, D.C., 2014.

World Bank Operations Policy and Country Services. *Low-Income Countries Under Stress: Update.* Washington, D.C., 2005.

World Health Organization (WHO). *Domestic Water Quantity, Service Level and Health.* Geneva, 2003.

Index

Acknowledgments

I spent the first seven months of 2014, together with my family, as Austrian Chair Visiting Professor at Stanford University in California. This was a remarkable experience. I taught one course on international human rights law with fewer than 20 students, delivered a few lectures at the Stanford Human Rights Center, and for the rest I was free to pursue my own research. The academic environment for delving into new fields of research could not have been more inspiring and innovative than at Stanford. Although I had been fascinated already for many years by the relationship between neoliberal economic policies in times of globalization and the development of universal human rights, I had never found the time to study the relevant economic literature. Now I was suddenly sitting in the heart of the Silicon Valley with all its famous IT companies that had influenced the dynamics of globalization in a more profound way than any other region of the world! There was simply no better and more inspiring place to try to understand the difficult relationship between the economy and human rights. Some fifteen years ago, Mary Robinson, UN High Commissioner for Human Rights, had asked me, together with Paul Hunt and Siddiq Osmani, to advise her on a human rights based approach to poverty reduction strategies. After many discussions with policy makers in bilateral and multilateral development agencies, UN specialized agencies, and international financial institutions, I started to understand why it is so difficult to integrate human rights thinking into the economic and political decision making structures of the World Bank and the International Monetary Fund. Despite all efforts by Kofi Annan, Mary Robinson, and others about mainstreaming human rights into all policy areas of the United Nations, it turned out to be impossible to bridge the gap between the universal human rights discourse and the neoliberal economic thinking prevailing at the Bretton Woods Institutions. Our guidelines and principles and other innovative documents about a human rights based approach to poverty reduction strategies might have had some influence on the policies of development cooperation, but certainly not on the politics of international trade, investment and financial institutions.

At Stanford, I decided to put the focus of my research on two very specific aspects of the relationship between global economic policies and universal human rights: the phenomenon of rising economic inequality and the limits of privatization from a human rights perspective. The results of my inequality studies have recently been published in German in a book on "Human Rights: A Response to Growing Economic Inequality," Manfred Nowak, *Menschenrechte: Eine Antwort auf die wachsende ökonomische Ungleichheit*. The findings on my research on privatization are covered by the present book, and I am grateful to the University of Pennsylvania Press, above all to Bert Lockwood, Peter Agree, and Alison Anderson, for publishing it in Penn's Human Rights Series. At Stanford, I was employed at the Freeman Spogli Institute for International Studies; I wish to most warmly thank Helen Stacy, Karen Haley, and Ken Scheve for their support and for enabling me to teach at Stanford. Since my office was at the beautiful Neukom Building of the Law School, I am equally grateful to Dean Liz Magill, Amy Applebaum, and all the professors, including Allan Weiner and Jenny Martinez, with whom I had the pleasure to exchange views about the relationship between the global economy and universal human rights. At the Stanford Human Rights Center, I cooperated most closely with Jim Cavallaro, Claret Vargas, and Stephan Sonnenberg. In particular, Claret was always available for coffee or lunch to discuss difficult issues with me. But the person to whom I am most indebted for making my research work at Stanford as easy as possible is librarian Sergio Stone. There was no book in the world and no scientific article Sergio would not find and deliver to my office within a few hours or at a maximum a few days. The efficiency of all the different libraries at Stanford seems like a miracle to European scholars! Toward the end of my studies at Stanford, a young German student, Anastasia Schuster, assisted me with some of my research questions.

During my visiting professorship at Stanford, I had the pleasure to live in the lovely Mexican style house of my beloved friends Rich and Rhoda Simmons at 44 Alvarado Avenue in Los Altos, less than half an hour by bike away from the Stanford campus. Most of the book was written while sitting in their beautiful garden, which I shared with my wife Suada, who followed courses on comparative literature at Stanford, my kids Una and Dino, who enjoyed their respective American primary and high schools in

Los Altos, and three lovely bunnies we were taking care of, Benjamin, Missy, and Midnight. I spent many hours with Rich and Rhoda discussing the current global economic and political situation. Intellectually, Rich was my most important source of inspiration. He critically read the entire manuscript and provided me with his most thoughtful feedback.

Back in Vienna, I first concentrated on the chapter on the human right to equality and growing economic inequality, but then I decided to publish this aspect in a separate book in German. On the limits of privatization, I had very intensive discussions with my colleague Karolina Januszewski, who is specializing on private military and security companies herself. During an internship at my institute at Vienna University, Anastasia Schuster, Hanna Patalong, and Katharina Siegl assisted me with the bibliography and footnotes. Last but not least, I am extremely grateful to my colleague Antonia Walter, who critically read the entire manuscript and enriched it with her thoughts.

Lightning Source UK Ltd.
Milton Keynes UK
UKOW08n2334140517

301131UK00007B/146/P